# Sniffy™
## THE VIRTUAL RAT
### Pro Version 2.0

**Tom Alloway**
University of Toronto at Mississauga

**Greg Wilson**
DID Software

**Jeff Graham**
University of Toronto at Mississauga

THOMSON
WADSWORTH

Australia • Canada • Mexico • Singapore • Spain • United Kingdom • United States

**THOMSON**

™

**WADSWORTH**

---

## In memory of Edward Thorndike, Ivan Pavlov, and B. F. Skinner

---

Psychology Editor: *Marianne Taflinger*
Assistant Editor: *Jennifer Keever*
Editorial Assistant: *Justin Courts*
Technology Project Manager: *Darin Derstine*
Marketing Manager: *Chris Caldeira*
Marketing Assistant: *Laurel Anderson*
Advertising Project Manager: *Brian Chaffee*
Art Director: *Vernon Boes*
Print/Media Buyer: *Lisa Claudeanos*

Permissions Editor: *Audrey Pettengill*
Production Service/Compositor: *Scratchgravel Publishing Services*
Copy Editor: *Margaret C. Tropp*
Cover Designer: *Katherine Minerva*
Cover Image: *Integrated Circuits © Lester Lefkowitz/ CORBIS White Mouse, Getty Images, Inc.*
Cover Printer: *Webcom*
Printer: *Webcom*

For more information about our products,
contact us at:
**Thomson Learning Academic Resource Center**
**1-800-423-0563**

For permission to use material from this text or product, submit a request online at
**http://www.thomsonrights.com.**
Any additional questions about permissions can be submitted by email to **thomsonrights@thomson.com.**

**Thomson West**
**10 Davis Drive**
**Belmont, CA 94002-3098**
**USA**

**Asia**
Thomson Learning
5 Shenton Way #01-01
UIC Building
Singapore 068808

**Australia**
Nelson Thomson Learning
102 Dodds Street
South Melbourne, Victoria 3205
Australia

**Canada**
Nelson Thomson Learning
1120 Birchmount Road
Toronto, Ontario M1K 5G4
Canada

**Europe/Middle East/Africa**
Thomson Learning
High Holborn House
50/51 Bedford Row
London WC1R 4LR
United Kingdom

Library of Congress Control Number: 2004111595

ISBN 0-534-63360-9

# Contents

# Preface: Installing and Running Sniffy Pro

## System Requirements

### Windows

You need an IBM-compatible computer with a Pentium II, or later, processor, running Windows 98 or later, with at least 32 MB of RAM (64 MB recommended), an 8X CD-ROM, a 16 bit sound card with speakers or headphones, and a 600 X 800 color display.

On some computers, the Sniffy Pro program may appear to pause repeatedly while the hard-disk light flashes on and off. This problem occurs when there is not enough RAM available to run the Sniffy Pro program and the computer is attempting to use virtual memory. If this happens, you need to optimize your computer's memory usage by reducing the number of colors displayed. In such cases, we recommend that you set your computer to display 16 bit color. To set your computer's color depth:

- Use your (left) mouse button to open the My Computer window either by selecting on the icon with that name on your Windows desktop or by selecting it from the Start menu.
- Open Control Panel.
- Open Display.
- The details of the appearance of the dialog box vary considerably in different versions of Windows, but somewhere you will find an icon labeled Display. Click on it.
- In the dialog box that opens, look for Settings.
- Choose the setting for 16 Bit Color.

- Click the OK command button in the dialog box.
- Follow any additional instructions that the Windows operating system gives you at this point. It may suggest or require that you restart your computer.

## Macintosh

You need an Apple Macintosh computer with a Power PC or later processor, running Mac OS 8.6 or later. The computer must have at least 64 MB of RAM (128 MB recommended), an 8X CD-ROM, an 800 X 600 color display capable of displaying "thousands of colors," a sound card, and speakers or headphones.

## Installation

*The Sniffy Pro program is designed to be installed on the hard drive of the user's computer. It is not designed to be run from the CD or from a server. Attempting to run the program from the CD or from a server is likely to produce erratic and unpredictable results.*

## FAQ and Read Me Files

Before installing the program, read the FAQ and Read Me files that are included on your CD. It would also be a very good idea to check the Sniffy Web site to find out whether a revised FAQ file or an update to the Sniffy Pro program is available there. We will post a new FAQ file on the Web site whenever new information becomes available.

## Windows

- Use your (left) mouse button to double-click the installer program called Install Sniffy Pro on your Sniffy Pro CD, and follow the instructions as you progress. The first screen that you will see is shown below.

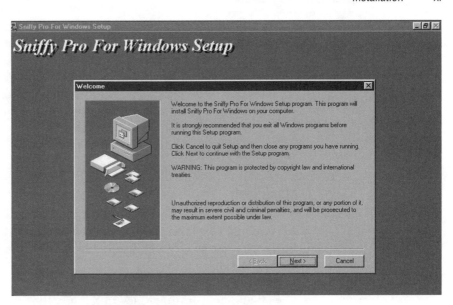

- Click on the Next button.
- In the second screen, you will be asked to enter your name and the name of your organization. For most users, the name of your school would be an appropriate entry for organization.
- In the third screen, you will be asked where on your hard drive you want the installer to place the program. Unless you have a very good reason for selecting another location, accept the installer's suggested destination.
- In the fourth screen, you will be asked whether you want a Typical, Compact, or Custom installation. Almost all users will want a Typical installation.
- The fifth screen asks you to confirm that you want to proceed with the installation.
- Finally, you will see a screen with a progress bar indicating that the installation is in progress. When the installer has completed its work, it will tell you so. You should then Exit the installer application.
- The installer will place
  □ The Sniffy Pro program and Sample Files folder inside a folder titled Sniffy Pro for Windows that is in the Program Files folder at the root of your C drive.
  □ A shortcut to launch the program easily in your Start menu.

- *You should save all your Sniffy files in your Sniffy Pro for Windows folder so that they are all together in the same place where you can find them easily. When performing the exercises, there will be many occasions when you can save yourself time and effort if you have the file from a previous exercise available to use as the basis for a new exercise.*

## Macintosh

All you need to do to install the program on a Macintosh is to copy the Sniffy Pro for Macintosh application from the CD onto your Macintosh's hard drive.

- If you are running Mac OS X, copy the application from the CD into the Applications folder on your hard drive.
- If you are running Mac OS 9, copy the application from the CD into the Applications (Mac OS 9) folder on your hard drive.
- If you are running Mac OS 8, copy the application from the CD into any location on your hard drive except the System Folder.[1]
- *We also strongly recommend that you create a folder called Sniffy Files on your hard drive and save all your Sniffy files in your Sniffy Files folder. When performing the exercises, there will be many occasions when you can save yourself time and effort if you have the file from a previous exercise available to use as the basis for a new exercise.*
- If you are running Mac OS X, Apple recommends that you keep all your files in the Documents folder associated with your user name. Thus, the best place for you to create your Sniffy Files folder is inside your own Documents folder. To find your Documents folder:
  - Double-click on the hard drive icon, which is probably located in the upper right-hand corner of your screen.
  - Double-click on the Users folder.
  - Double-click on your own User identity.
  - Your Documents folder should now be visible.

[1]If you do not know which version of the Mac OS you are running, go to the Apple menu in the upper left-hand corner of your screen and choose About This Mac or About This Computer. The resulting information screen will tell you which version of the operating system you are running.

- If you are running Mac OS 8 or Mac OS 9, you may create your Sniffy Files folder in any convenient location on your hard drive.
- Once you have created your Sniffy Files folder, copy the Sample Files folder from the CD into your Sniffy Files folder. The Sample Files folder contains a number of Sniffy files that you may find useful when you are doing Sniffy exercises.

**If you are running Mac OS 8 or Mac OS 9, you must have CarbonLib 1.6 or later installed on your computer. Without it, the Sniffy program will not run.** To determine whether you have CarbonLib, go to the Apple menu, control panel, open the Extensions Manager, scroll down to the Extensions section, and look for an entry called CarbonLib. If it's there, the Extensions Manager will tell you what version you have. If you do not have CarbonLib or if the version you have is less than 1.6, the needed file can be downloaded from the support section of the Apple Computer Web site (www.apple.com).

## Contacts, Support, and Information

*In the United States:*

Wadsworth Publishing Company
10 Davis Drive
Belmont, CA 94002
E-mail: sniffy@wadsworth.com

For order inquiries, call (800) 423-0563, or fax your order form to (800) 487-8488.

For technical support, call (800) 423-0563
or e-mail tl.support@thomson.com

*In Canada:*

Contact Nelson Canada/Thomson, College Division at (800) 668-0671.

*International:*
Call Melissa Camp at +1-650-637-7596 or e-mail
melissa.camp@thomsonlearning.com

*For the latest information and updates, check out Sniffy on the Web at*

http://psychology.wadsworth.com/sniffy

*To contact the authors via e-mail:*

| | |
|---|---|
| Dr. Tom Alloway | antguy@abspruce.org |
| Dr. Jeff Graham | jgraham@utm.utoronto.ca |
| Greg Wilson | didsoft@rogers.com |

# Acknowledgments

We thank the many students, friends, and colleagues who have helped since the inception of this project in 1991. This is the third edition of the software, as we implemented more realistic animations in 2000 and new animations and exercises in 2004. We appreciate the help and support of Professor Doug Chute of Drexel University, who was the first "outsider" to see Sniffy's potential and who helped bring the project to fruition. We thank the CNN, Télée Quebec, and CBC news teams, who helped promote Sniffy as an ethical alternative to the use of live animals in teaching.

Many thanks go to our art director, Allan Sura, for designing and creating the Sniffy movements based on real video of a live rat (although he did have to push the creative envelope for some of the new tricks Sniffy can now perform!). The research assistants in the Psychology Computer Laboratory were our tireless testers. Special thanks go to our testing team, which included Andrew Tomkins, Marie Wong, Nadine Esho, Tiffany Mah, Tracy Lennertz, Luke Kim, Kimberly Chang Alloy, Rafeena Haniff, Edona Caku, Suzana Grozavescu, Vikram Tangri, Roc Scalera, Hubert Marczuk, Mike Hynes, Chris England, Anne Dmitrovic, B. J. Balanquit, Kirk Broadhead, and Keith Seim.

We are grateful to the thousands of introductory psychology students at the University of Toronto at Mississauga who have, over the past 10 years, used early prototypes of the software in class and to the students in Tom Alloway's Introduction to Learning class, who pilot-tested 40 of the exercises used in this edition of Sniffy Pro.

We acknowledge the support of the principal and deans of the University of Toronto at Mississauga, who backed us in the early days before Sniffy attracted the interest of a publisher. We thank the many reviewers who helped refine and polish operational features and pedagogical issues: Jay Allen, University of Georgia; Tim Bockes,

Nazareth College; Victoria Kazmerski, Penn State Erie, The Behrend College; Gail Knapp, Mott Community College; Hal Miller, Brigham Young University; and Nina Tarner, Gettysburg College. Hal Miller's students at BYU did class tests, for which we thank them as well: Jason Allen, Amber Bentzien, Tami Blake, Levi Boren, Matthew Brown, Scott Chamberlain, Danielle Cheesman, Delbert Farley, Jacqueline Gardner, Christopher Gravett, Michael Haderlie, Scott Harrison, Brandon Henscheid, Michelle Hogan, Sarah Johnson, Ben Jones, Elisha Kamalu, Dustin Logan, Kristyn McQuarrie, Amanda Morphy, April Murdock, Jonathan Naylor, Sara Ofahengaue, Amber Orosco, Jessica Pratt, Benjamin Salazar, Jeffrey Skousen, Clinton Snow, Kristen Turley, Michael Turner, and Sonia Yaksich.

Tom Alloway and Jeff Graham congratulate our co-author, Greg Wilson, on his achievement in programming Sniffy Pro for the Macintosh and Windows operating systems. Greg tirelessly tackled the complex assignment of converting psychological principles into demonstrable artificial intelligence and did so while dealing with the complex technical problems of cross-platform development.

Finally, we thank all our Wadsworth editorial team, especially Marianne Taflinger.

# Quick Guide to Menus and Commands

This section provides a quick overview of the menu commands available in Sniffy Pro. The Sniffy Tutor also contains a brief discussion of the program's principal commands. The Sniffy Tutor illustrates the most common procedures required to save and open Sniffy data files, as well as the menu commands required to set up elementary training and testing scenarios.

## The File Menu

The File menu contains the standard operating system commands for saving and opening files: **New**, **Open**, **Save**, **Save As**, **Revert**, **Print**, and **Exit (Quit)**. See the appendix to this book if you need detailed information about how to save and open files.

- **New** provides a new rat ready to be trained.
- **Open** brings up the dialog box for opening files.
- **Save** saves the current file under its current name. If the file has not been saved previously, a dialog box appears so that you can give the file an appropriate name and choose an appropriate location on your computer to save it.
- **Save As** brings up a dialog box that enables you to give the file a new name and choose an appropriate location on your computer to save the file.
- **Revert** restores the file to the state it was in the last time you saved it.
- **Export Data** produces a tab-delimited text file containing the data in the currently active window. These data files can be opened in

most spreadsheet and statistical analysis programs. You can use this command with the Cumulative Record, Movement Ratio, Suppression Ratio, DS Response Strength, and CS Response Strength windows.

- **Print Window** prints the currently active window. You can use this command with any window except the Operant Chamber.
- **Preferences** brings up the following dialog box. In Mac OS X, the Preferences command is located under the Sniffy menu.

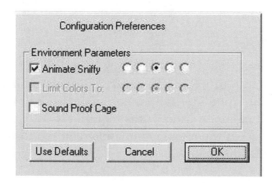

In the dialog box:

- The **Animate Sniffy** settings control Sniffy's animation when he is visible in his operant chamber.
  - □ The Slow–Fast settings determine the speed of Sniffy's movements when he is visible in the operant chamber.
  - □ Placing a check mark next to Animate Sniffy causes Sniffy to be visible.
  - □ Clicking on the box next to Animate Sniffy to remove the check mark is equivalent to executing the Isolate Sniffy (Accelerate Time) command, which is explained below under the description of commands available under the Experiment menu.
- **Limit Colors To:** enables Macintosh users to control the number of colors displayed in the Sniffy Pro program. The number of colors displayed in other programs is unaffected. This setting is unavailable to Windows users. In Windows, the number of colors displayed is determined by a setting in the Display section of the Control Panel; this setting affects the display of colors in all programs.
- **Sound Proof Cage,** when selected, turns off the program's sound effects. (Selecting this option will make you more popular with your roommates or family!)

## The Edit Menu

- The **Undo**, **Copy, Cut**, **Paste**, and **Clear** commands are not implemented in Sniffy Pro.
- **Copy Window Image** copies a bitmap image of the contents of the currently active window to the clipboard. This command provides a convenient way to insert images from Sniffy Pro windows into a word processor document. To insert an image from a Sniffy Pro window into a word processor document:
  - □ Select the window whose image you want to copy by clicking on the window once with your (left) mouse button.
  - □ Execute the Copy Window Image command.
  - □ Go to the place in your word processor document where you want to insert the image. (If your computer has enough RAM, you can run your word processor and Sniffy Pro at the same time.)
  - □ Select the Paste (or Paste Special) command from the File menu of the word processor program to insert your Sniffy Pro image into the word processor document.

## The Experiment Menu

| | |
|---|---|
| Design Classical Conditioning Experiment... | |
| Run Classical Conditioning Experiment | Ctrl+R |
| Change Nature of Association... | |
| Design Operant Conditioning Experiment... | |
| Remove Sniffy for Time-Out | |
| Isolate Sniffy (Accelerated Time) | |
| Pause | Ctrl+G |
| Mark | Ctrl+M |

The commands in this menu determine the experimental conditions that are in effect during operant and classical conditioning experiments and control certain other functions.

### Design Classical Conditioning Experiment

Executing the Design Classical Conditioning Experiment command brings up the following dialog box. Settings in this dialog box determine the experimental conditions in effect during classical conditioning experiments.

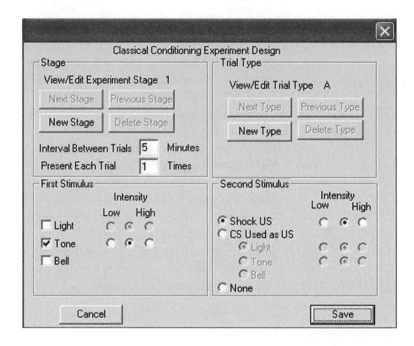

Detailed instructions for using this dialog box are given in Chapter 2.

## Run Classical Conditioning Experiment

Executing the Run Classical Conditioning Experiment command causes the Sniffy Pro program to execute a classical conditioning experiment that has been saved in the Design Classical Conditioning Experiment dialog box. The command is dimmed (unavailable) if no classical conditioning experimental design has been specified or if a classical conditioning experiment is in progress.

## Change Nature of Association

Executing the Change Nature of Association command brings up the following dialog box.

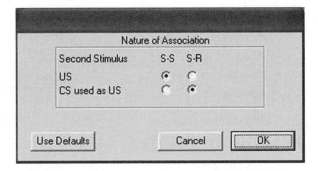

Settings in this dialog box determine whether Sniffy learns S–S or S–R associations during classical conditioning experiments. Chapter 7 contains a detailed discussion of the circumstances under which changes in these settings are appropriate.

- By clicking on the S–S or S–R alternatives, you determine whether Sniffy learns a stimulus–stimulus (S–S) or a stimulus–response (S–R) association to CSs that have been paired either with the shock US or with another CS used as a US.
- Click the Use Defaults command button to set the association model to the program's default values:
  - □ S–S for CSs paired with the shock US.
  - □ S–R for CSs paired with another CS used as a US.
- Click the Cancel command button to dismiss the dialog box without making any changes in the association model.
- Click the OK command button to dismiss the dialog box and put the current settings into effect.
- Nature of Association settings cannot be changed after the Run Classical Conditioning Experiment command has been executed for the first time in any Sniffy Pro file.

## Design Operant Conditioning Experiment

Selecting Design Operant Conditioning Experiment brings up the dialog box shown below, which is used to control operant conditioning experiments.

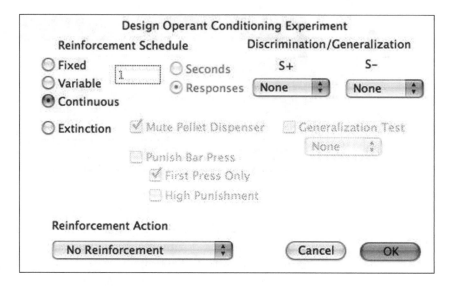

The left-hand side of the dialog box under **Reinforcement Schedule** determines the conditions of reinforcement.

- Selecting **Continuous** causes each instance of the response selected under the Reinforcement Action pull-down menu to be reinforced.
- To set up a schedule of reinforcement:
  - □ Select **Fixed** for fixed-interval (FI) or fixed-ratio (FR) schedules.
  - □ Select **Variable** for variable-interval (VI) or variable-ratio (VR) schedules.
  - □ Select **Responses** for ratio (FR or VR) schedules.
  - □ Select **Seconds** for interval (FI or VI) schedules.
  - □ The number you type in the text box in this section determines the value of the schedule, in responses for ratio schedules or seconds for interval schedules.
- Selecting **Extinction** causes reinforcement to be turned off. None of Sniffy's bar presses produce food pellets.
  - □ Selecting **Mute Pellet Dispenser** eliminates the sound of the pellet dispenser as a consequence of bar pressing.
  - □ To produce **standard extinction** conditions, Mute Pellet Dispenser should be selected.
  - □ If Mute Pellet Dispenser is not selected, Sniffy will continue to hear the sound of the pellet dispenser whenever he presses the bar. Extinction with Mute Pellet Dispenser turned off is used to study the effect of **secondary reinforcement.**
- The selection made in the drop-down menu under **Reinforcement Action** determines which operant response the program automatically reinforces.

Conditions in effect during **discrimination-learning** experiments and **stimulus generalization** tests are controlled by the right-hand side of the dialog box under **Discrimination/Generalization.** When a discrimination or generalization experiment is *not* being conducted, the None alternative should be selected for both S+ and S–.

- During discrimination-learning experiments, Sniffy is exposed to alternating 1-minute intervals during which the stimulus conditions selected under S+ and S– are presented.
  - During S+ periods, Sniffy's bar presses are reinforced according to the reinforcement schedule established in the left-hand side of the dialog box.
  - During S– periods, Sniffy's bar presses are never reinforced.
  - Chapter 13 contains a detailed description of the kinds of discrimination-learning experiments that Sniffy Pro simulates.
- To set up a stimulus generalization test:
  - Select Extinction.
  - Make sure Mute Pellet Dispenser is selected.
  - Place a check mark in the box next to Generalization Test.
  - Select the stimulus condition that will be in effect during the test from the pull-down menu under Generalization Test.

### Remove Sniffy for Time-Out

The Remove Sniffy for Time-Out command brings up the following dialog box.

This command is used in experiments on **spontaneous recovery.** See Chapters 3 and 10 for detailed descriptions of experiments in which the command is employed. In the dialog box:

- Click the OK command button to simulate giving Sniffy a 24-hour rest period in his home cage.
- Click the Cancel command button to dismiss the dialog box without giving Sniffy a rest period.

## Isolate Sniffy (Accelerate Time)

The Isolate Sniffy (Accelerate Time) command is available whenever Sniffy is visible. Executing the command replaces the view of Sniffy moving around in his operant chamber with the following graphic.

The graphic depicts the outside of a soundproof, air-conditioned chamber of the type that many psychologists who study operant conditioning use to isolate their easily distracted live animals from extraneous stimuli in the laboratory. Whenever this graphic is visible, your computer will run the current experiment much faster than when Sniffy is visible, because the computer does not have to display Sniffy's movements.

### Show Sniffy

The Show Sniffy command is available whenever Sniffy's isolation chamber is being displayed. Executing the command causes the Sniffy animation to reappear.

### Pause and Resume

The Pause command is available whenever the program is running. Executing it causes program operation to halt until the Resume command is executed. The Pause command is helpful when something interrupts you while an experiment is running.

### Mark (Record)

This command causes a small vertical mark to be placed just below the top of the Cumulative Record window to mark the fact that some event you want to record has occurred. For example, when training Sniffy to bar-press, you might want to mark the record to indicate the time when the Lab Assistant said that Sniffy's training was complete.

## The Windows Menu

| Operant Chamber |
| --- |
| Cumulative Records ▸ |
| Suppression Ratio |
| Movement Ratio |
| Mind Windows ▸ |
| Lab Assistant |
| Arrange Icons |

The commands in the Windows menu make specific Sniffy Pro windows visible. Selecting a window will reopen a window that has been closed or bring to the front any window that is currently obscured by another window. Note that the Cumulative Records and Mind Windows are grouped in separate submenus.

# 1

## Introduction to Sniffy

### Why We Created Sniffy

Sniffy Pro is an affordable and humane way to give students hands-on access to the main phenomena of classical and operant conditioning that courses on the psychology of learning typically discuss. Although psychologists believe that the phenomena that the Sniffy Pro program simulates play a prominent role in both human and animal behavior, courses that discuss these topics are usually taught in a lecture format that gives students no chance to obtain laboratory experience. There are two main reasons for this omission.

The first reason is cost. The most common apparatus that psychologists use to study classical and operant conditioning is the **operant chamber,** a special cage that contains a lever that a rat can be trained to press and devices for dispensing food and water and presenting other stimuli. A computer connected to the chamber automatically records the rat's responses and controls stimulus presentation. A basic setup consisting of an operant chamber, a computer to control it, and an appropriate interface between the two costs about $3,500 in U.S. money. Few schools can afford to purchase this equipment in the quantity required to offer a laboratory component for a course in the psychology of learning. In addition, modern animal-care regulations specify rigorous standards for maintaining animals used for teaching and research. Typically, these regulations not only require that the animals be housed in clean cages and receive adequate food and water; they also specify that animal rooms must receive more fresh air and have better temperature and humidity control than rooms that people occupy. Facilities that comply with these standards are expensive to build and maintain. To cover these costs, animal facilities usually charge daily maintenance fees for each animal kept; these fees would add up to a large sum if each student enrolled in a learning course had his or her own rat to study.

A second reason why students in learning courses rarely have access to animals is that some people think that the use of live animals for teaching purposes, where the outcome of each experiment can be confidently predicted on the basis of previous findings, violates the ethical principles of humane animal treatment. Some people hold this view even when the animals used for teaching are never exposed to any discomfort. Opposition is much more widespread if the animals are subjected to noxious stimuli.

Nevertheless, studying animal learning without being able to see how experiments are set up and data are collected isolates students from an important and fascinating set of behavioral phenomena. The Sniffy Pro program is designed to end that isolation.

## How We Created Sniffy, the Animated Creature

We created the animated Sniffy character that you see on your computer screen by videotaping a live laboratory rat as it moved around spontaneously in a glass cage with a blue background. The taping sessions occurred in a comfortable, reasonably quiet room, and we just let the rat perform whatever behaviors it happened to produce. From the several hours of videotape that we accumulated, we selected 40 short behavior sequences that show the rat walking around the cage, rearing up against the walls, grooming itself, and performing other typical rat behaviors. Finally, we removed the blue background from each frame of these video clips and adjusted the brightness and contrast in the resulting images to produce almost 600 animation frames that depict the rat in different postures and orientations. The Sniffy Pro program plays these frames in various sequences and positions to produce the virtual animal that you see.

## Sniffy, the Program

The Sniffy Pro program lets you set up and perform a wide variety of classical and operant conditioning experiments and enables you to collect and display data in ways that simulate the ways in which psy-

chologists do these things in their laboratories. In addition, because the program both simulates and displays some of the psychological processes that psychologists believe animals (and people) employ, Sniffy Pro shows you some things about learning that you could not observe if you were working with a live animal.

In a real rat, learning is the result of biochemical interactions among billions of neurons in the brain. As a consequence of these physiological processes, animals acquire information about events in the outside world and about how their behavior affects those events. One aspect of learning involves acquiring information about sequences of events in the world. When one stimulus regularly precedes and thus predicts another, animals modify their behavior in certain ways; psychologists call this kind of learning **classical** (or **respondent**) **conditioning.** A second aspect of learning involves acquiring associations between behaviors (responses) and external events (stimuli); psychologists call this kind of learning **operant** (or **instrumental**) **conditioning.**

Although we believe that neurophysiological processes in the brain are ultimately responsible for the learned changes in behavior that we observe, psychologists generally discuss classical and operant conditioning in terms of the acquisition and modification of associations. To some extent, we describe learning in associative terms because we do not understand the physiological processes well enough to explain our findings fully in physiological terms. However, psychological and physiological processes also constitute different levels of explanation (Keller & Schoenfeld, 1950; Skinner, 1938). Thus, we do not need to understand the physiological processes in detail in order to explain learning in psychological terms.

To a degree, the relationship between neurophysiological processes and psychological explanations of learning is analogous to the relationship between the electrical activity in your computer's electronic circuitry and the simulated psychological processes that form the basis for Sniffy's behavior. Your computer contains the equivalent of several million transistors that are in some ways analogous to neurons in a rat's brain. The Sniffy Pro program uses the electronic circuitry of your computer to simulate the psychological mechanisms that many psychologists use to explain learning in real animals and people. One advantage of computer simulation is that we can program a computer not only to simulate certain psychological processes but also to display the simulated processes. This possibility has enabled us to develop a set of displays that we call **mind windows.** The mind windows show how Sniffy's behavior interacts with the events in the operant chamber to create, strengthen, and weaken the associations that produce changes in Sniffy's behavior. Thus the Sniffy Pro program not only allows you to set up experiments and record and display behavioral data in a fashion similar to the ways psychologists do these things, it also lets you observe how Sniffy's psychological processes operate. We think that being able to observe Sniffy's psychological processes will make it easier to understand how learning works.

Another difference between Sniffy and a real rat is that you can determine the nature of Sniffy's learning process in some situations. Because the psychological processes of real animals are unobservable, psychologists often perform experiments designed to enable them to infer which of two or more plausible psychological processes is actually involved in a particular learning situation. In a few cases, we have endowed Sniffy with the capacity to learn in two different ways. In these instances, you can determine which kind of psychological process Sniffy will employ in a particular experiment, observe the psychological process in operation, and see how your choice affects the results. In many cases, two different mechanisms will produce identical results. However, we will also show you some experiments in which the results will be different when Sniffy employs different learning processes. We hope that being able to see how the choice of a psychological process sometimes will, but often will not, affect the outcome of an experiment will help you understand how challenging a task it is for psychologists to design experiments that enable them to infer what psychological processes real organisms actually employ.

## Sniffy Is a Learning Tool, Not a Research Tool

The Sniffy Pro program is the result of developments in computer technology that permit the simulation and display of complex processes on relatively inexpensive computers. However, the psychological processes and behavioral phenomena that the program simulates are characteristics of living organisms. Discovering those processes and phenomena required more than a century of research with animal and human subjects. Future advances in the scientific understanding of learning will also require research on living organisms. Sniffy Pro and other computer simulations are fascinating tools for demonstrating what we already know, but they cannot substitute for the real thing when it comes to acquiring new scientific insights.

Sniffy is not a real rat. In fact, Sniffy isn't even the most realistic simulation of a real rat that we could have produced. The Sniffy Pro

program uses a rat as a kind of metaphor to help you understand the psychology of learning. In designing Sniffy as a learning aid, we deliberately sacrificed realism whenever we thought that it got in the way of creating a useful tool for students. In addition to immediately obvious things like the mind windows and the capacity to choose which learning process Sniffy will employ in certain situations, here are some of the deliberately unrealistic things about Sniffy:

- You will be using food as a reinforcer (reward) to train Sniffy to press the bar or do other things in the operant chamber. Sniffy is always ready to work for food no matter how much he has recently eaten. In contrast, real rats satiate for food and stop working to obtain it when they have had enough. We could have simulated satiation but decided not to because satiation is mainly a motivational, not a learning, phenomenon. If you ever do research using food reinforcement with real animals, you will have to learn how psychologists control for this motivational factor when they design learning experiments. However, textbooks on the psychology of learning rarely discuss satiation, psychological explanations of learning phenomena make little reference to it, and we thought that simulating satiation would introduce a needless inconvenience for students of the psychology of learning.

- Real rats learn some things quite slowly. In an experiment in which an animal is taught to discriminate between the presence and absence of a stimulus by reinforcing bar presses when the stimulus is turned on and not reinforcing bar presses when the stimulus is turned off, a real rat requires many training sessions before the maximum difference in bar-pressing rate in the presence and absence of the stimulus is obtained (Keller & Schoenfeld, 1950). In contrast, Sniffy will learn the discrimination in less than an hour. Sniffy also adapts to changes in reinforcement schedules much faster than a real rat. Making Sniffy learn unrealistically fast in these situations gives you time to study more learning phenomena, and we thought that providing the opportunity to study additional phenomena was more important than realistically simulating the speed at which rats learn.

## Applying What You Learn From Sniffy

The principles of learning that Sniffy illustrates have many real-world applications in such diverse areas as the therapeutic modification of human behavior and animal training for utility, fun, sport, or profit. In

addition to a thorough understanding of learning principles, effectively applying the principles of operant and classical conditioning to real-life situations nearly always involves large measures of creative ingenuity and finesse. To become a practitioner of therapeutic human behavior modification, you need to obtain a bachelor's degree in psychology, attend graduate school, study behavior modification under the direction of a professional, and fulfill the professional licensing requirements of the jurisdiction in which you plan to work. These educational and professional requirements have been established in an effort to ensure the effective and ethical application of the learning principles that Sniffy simulates.

Standards for would-be animal trainers are much less stringent. Anybody can purchase a puppy and attempt to train it. However, if you obtain a puppy and subsequently want to transform the unruly little beast that you actually possess into the obedient, well-behaved member of the household that you had envisioned, you would be well advised to enroll yourself and your puppy in classes at a reputable dog training school. As with human behavior modification, effective, ethical animal training involves combining a thorough understanding of scientific principles with ingenuity and finesse. The best animal trainers understand both the science and the art. Sniffy will help you learn the science, but you must acquire the art elsewhere. Failure to acquire the art before you try to apply the science can produce unexpected and sometimes even dangerous results.

# 2

## Introduction to Classical Conditioning

## A First Look at Sniffy Pro

The time has come to have a look at the Sniffy Pro program and to begin Sniffy's training.[1]

- Locate the folder where you installed the Sniffy Pro program and sample files on your computer's hard disk.
  - □ In Windows, the installer placed Sniffy Pro program and sample files in a folder called Sniffy Pro for Windows, which is in the Program Files folder on your C drive.
  - □ On a Macintosh, you should have placed the Sniffy Pro application and sample files in the locations specified in the installation instructions.
- Start the program.
  - □ In Windows, the most basic way is to select the Sniffy Pro program from the Programs section of the Start menu. Another way is to left double-click a Sniffy file icon inside your Sniffy Pro for Windows folder. The appendix to this manual provides information on how to simplify the process of getting to your Sniffy Pro for Windows folder by placing a shortcut to the folder on your Windows desktop.
  - □ On a Macintosh, the simplest way to start the program is to open your Applications folder and double-click the program icon. If you're running Mac OS X, you may want to place an icon for Sniffy Pro and Sniffy Files folder in the dock. The appendix to this manual provides instructions for placing aliases in the dock.

[1]In this manual, specific detailed instructions for performing particular exercises are presented with a gray background.

7

Depending on whether you're running Sniffy Pro under Windows XP or the Mac OS X, when the program opens, your computer screen should resemble one of the following pictures. (If you are running older versions of Windows or the Mac OS, the appearance of the program and its associated windows will be slightly different.)

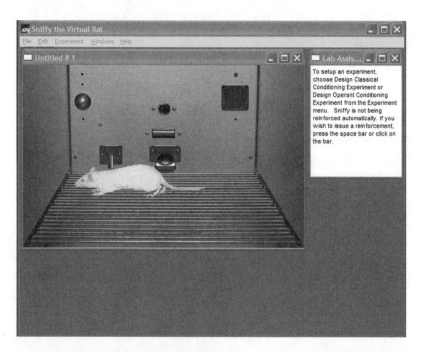

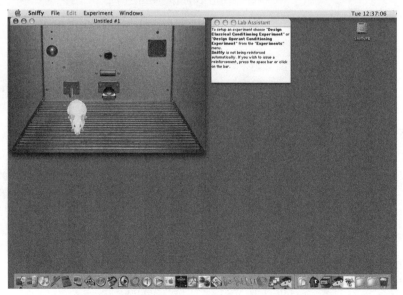

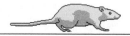

When you first start Sniffy Pro, two windows will be visible:

- The Operant Chamber window is the window where you see Sniffy moving about. The title bar at the top of the window contains the name of the Sniffy file that is currently being run. Because you have not yet saved a Sniffy file, the file is called Untitled.
- The Lab Assistant window provides you with useful suggestions about what to do next or about the status of your current Sniffy experiment. In this instance, it is suggesting that to set up a classical conditioning experiment, you should select the Design Classical Conditioning Experiment from the Experiment menu, or to set up an operant conditioning experiment, you should select the Design Operant Conditioning Experiment command.

Throughout the rest of this manual, we will sometimes show illustrations of the way the program looks in Windows XP and sometimes show how things look in Mac OS X. Because the program operates identically in both operating systems, always showing illustrations from both operating systems would be redundant.

## Classical Conditioning Background

Classical conditioning is the form of learning that results when two stimuli reliably occur in a sequence so that the first stimulus predicts the occurrence of the second. Usually, the stimuli have differing degrees of biological importance to the organism, with the less important stimulus coming before the more important stimulus. Many of the phenomena of classical conditioning were first described by the Russian physiologist Ivan Pavlov and his associates, who were the first to explore this form of learning systematically (Pavlov, 1927). Two other names for the same kind of learning are **Pavlovian conditioning** and **respondent conditioning.**

In classical conditioning, the stimulus that comes first in the temporal sequence is called the **conditioned stimulus (CS),** and the stimulus that comes second is called the **unconditioned stimulus (US).** The US initially possesses the capacity to elicit an obvious, easy-to-measure response called the **unconditioned response (UR).** The initial response to the CS is called the **orienting response (OR),** but the OR is often so inconspicuous that psychologists treat the CS as if it were a neutral stimulus that initially elicits no response at all. In other words, the OR to the CS is rarely measured.

The **classical conditioning acquisition procedure** consists of re-peatedly presenting the CS shortly before the US. As a consequence of this repeated, sequential pairing of the two stimuli, the CS gradually acquires the capacity to elicit a new learned response, which is called the **conditioned response (CR).** Usually, but not always, the CR re-sembles the UR in the sense that the CR consists of certain compo-nents of the UR.

In their early experiments, Pavlov and his associates used food placed in the mouths of food-deprived dogs as the US. Food in a hun-gry dog's mouth elicits chewing, swallowing, and salivation as a UR. As CSs, Pavlov's group used various medium-intensity sounds, lights, and tactile stimuli, none of which had any initial tendency to elicit a response resembling the UR to food. When repeatedly paired with food presentation, all these CSs gradually acquired the capacity to elicit salivation. During the almost century since Pavlov first reported his findings, thousands of classical conditioning experiments have been performed, employing dozens of different species and a wide variety of different stimuli as US and CS.

## The Conditioned Emotional Response (CER)

Sniffy Pro simulates a form of classical conditioning called the **condi-tioned emotional response (CER)** or **conditioned suppression,** the ex-perimental paradigm for the measurement of which was first described by Estes and Skinner (1941). Sudden, intense sounds and electric shocks delivered to a rat's feet are stimuli that intrinsically possess the capacity to interrupt a rat's ongoing train of behavior. The rat jumps when the loud sound or shock occurs and then freezes; that is, it re-mains motionless for a period of time. Thus, very loud noises and foot shock can be used as USs to produce freezing as a UR. In contrast, less intense sounds and moderately bright lights initially have little or no effect on a rat's ongoing behavior. For this reason, these stimuli can be used as CSs. The conditioning procedure consists of turning on the stimulus that is serving as the CS for a period of time before very briefly presenting the US. Usually, the CS and US terminate simulta-neously. In different experiments, the period of time during each trial when the CS is presented by itself typically ranges between 30 and 120 seconds (Mazur, 1998; Domjan, 1998, 2003). The duration of the US is usually 1 second or less. As a consequence of pairing the CS with the

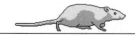

US, the CS gradually acquires the capacity to interrupt the rat's chain of behavior and induce freezing.

Over the past 30 years or so, the CER has become the form of classical conditioning that North American psychologists most commonly study. There are probably two main reasons for this popularity. First, the CER provides an experimental preparation for studying the acquisition of a very important and interesting response—fear. Second, because the entire process of presenting stimuli and collecting data can be automated, the CER is a very convenient form of classical conditioning to study.

As originally described (Estes & Skinner, 1941) and in most present-day laboratories, studies involving the CER typically start by employing operant conditioning procedures to train a rat to bar-press for food or water reinforcement on a schedule of reinforcement that produces steady, rapid responding.[2] The rat's steady bar-pressing rate is then used as a baseline against which to measure the effects of presenting stimuli. However, because almost all textbooks on the psychology of learning discuss classical conditioning before operant conditioning, we thought that it was important to provide users of Sniffy Pro with a means of studying the CER before they learn about operant conditioning. Accordingly, Sniffy Pro enables you to measure fear-related freezing in two ways.

To measure freezing behavior in experiments where Sniffy has not been trained to press the bar, we employ a measurement called the **movement ratio.** This measure is the proportion of time during each presentation of the CS that Sniffy is manifesting freezing and other fear-related behaviors. As the number of times the US has followed occurrences of the CS increases, the proportion of time during the CS when Sniffy will manifest fear behaviors increases. As implemented in Sniffy Pro, the movement ratio provides a robust behavioral measure of classical conditioning *whether or not* Sniffy has previously been trained to press the bar in the operant chamber.

The other way of measuring Sniffy's conditioned fear responses requires that Sniffy first be trained to press the bar in his operant chamber to obtain food reinforcement. This second measure, which is called the **suppression ratio,** is the response measure most commonly used by researchers who study the CER with live rats. The basic idea behind the suppression ratio is to compare the rate of bar pressing (the number of bar presses per minute) during the CS (Rate During CS) to the rate of

[2]See Chapter 12.

bar pressing during the period of time immediately preceding presentation of the CS (Rate Pre CS). When the Pre-CS and During-CS time periods are of equal duration (as in Sniffy Pro), comparing the bar-pressing rates is equivalent to comparing the number of bar presses during the CS (Bar Presses During CS) to the number of bar presses during the period preceding the CS (Bar Presses Pre CS). If the CS elicits no fear response, the number of bar presses during these two time periods should be about the same. However, if the CS suppresses bar pressing, then Bar Presses During CS will be less than Bar Presses Pre CS. To get a quantitative measure of suppression of bar pressing in response to the CS, the suppression ratio is expressed as the ratio between the Bar Presses During CS and the sum of Bar Presses During CS plus Bar Presses Pre CS. Written as an equation, the suppression ratio is defined as follows:

$$\text{Suppression ratio} = \frac{\text{Bar Presses During CS}}{\text{Bar Presses During CS} + \text{Bar Presses Pre CS}}$$

Let's think a bit about how this equation works. If presenting the CS does not affect the animal's bar pressing (if Bar Presses During CS = Bar Presses Pre CS), then the denominator of the fraction will be twice as large as the numerator; and the suppression ratio will be 0.5. However, if the CS suppresses bar pressing so that the rat presses less during the CS than during the Pre-CS period, the suppression ratio will be less than 0.5; if the rat doesn't press the bar at all during the CS, the suppression ratio will be 0. In a CER experiment in which the CS is being paired with an aversive US, Bar Presses During CS should rarely (and then only by chance) be greater than Bar Presses Pre CS, so that the suppression ratio should generally be less than or equal to 0.5. On the first training trial (before the animal has experienced the US), the suppression ratio should be about 0.5. Then as conditioning proceeds, the value of the suppression ratio should decline until it eventually levels off at an average value less than 0.5. To compute the suppression ratio, the Sniffy Pro program compares Sniffy's response rate during the 30 seconds preceding each CS presentation with the response rate during the CS.

With real rats and with Sniffy, CER conditioning is rather rapid. Maximal (or nearly maximal) conditioning is reached after about 10 CS–US pairings. The US that the Sniffy Pro program simulates is electric foot shock delivered through the parallel metal bars that form the floor of Sniffy's operant chamber. Shock duration is always 1 sec. CS duration is always 30 sec. When the shock US is being paired with the

CS, the shock US occurs during the last second of the CS.[3] Shocking Sniffy immediately interrupts Sniffy's behavior. He jumps and then freezes. When he begins to move around again, bouts of freezing are interspersed with bouts of grooming and exploratory behavior. After a few minutes, the effect of the shock wears off. If Sniffy has been trained to press the bar, bar pressing will resume. If Sniffy has not been trained to press the bar, he will resume moving around the cage and engaging in his other normal activities.

To animate Sniffy's UR to the shock US, we applied some tricks to sequences of animation frames derived from a videotape of a rat that had *not* been shocked or exposed to any other form of noxious stimulation. We think that the result looks plausible, but we do not know how realistic it is. Psychologists who study the CER virtually never give detailed descriptions of their animals' UR to the US. To create a realistic simulation of a rat's response to shock, we would have had to videotape a rat that was actually being shocked, but we did not do that.

In the Sniffy Pro program, the shock US has three levels of intensity: low, medium, and high. Sniffy's initial reaction to shocks of these three intensities is the same. The first time he is shocked, Sniffy will not take any longer to return to normal behavior after receiving a high-intensity shock than after receiving a low-intensity shock. In every case, after receiving an initial shock, Sniffy will require about 2 minutes before his behavior returns to its normal, pre-shock level. However, his reaction to *repeated* stimulation is different for the three shock levels:

- Sniffy's UR to the low-intensity shock **habituates.** As the number of shocks that he has received increases, his reaction to the low-intensity shock diminishes. After receiving about 25 low-intensity shocks, Sniffy no longer reacts to them at all.
- The duration of Sniffy's UR to the medium-intensity shock never changes no matter how many shocks he has received. Therefore, the medium setting is the one you should use except in experiments where you want Sniffy's UR to change.
- Sniffy's UR to the high-intensity shock **sensitizes.** As the number of shocks he has received increases, his reaction to the high-intensity shock gradually increases. After receiving a large number of high-intensity shocks, Sniffy will take about twice as long to return normal behavior.

[3]All stated times are in Sniffy program time. Program time is approximately equivalent to clock time when Sniffy's animation is set to run at a realistic-looking rate. However, program time and clock time will seldom be exactly equivalent.

The Sniffy Pro program simulates three different kinds of CS: a light, a tone, and a bell. The light and tone can be presented at three different intensity levels: low, medium, and high. The duration of the CS is always 30 seconds. On trials when the CS is paired with the US, the US occurs during the last second of the CS. In other words, the onset of the CS always precedes the onset of the US by 29 seconds.

None of the CSs initially has any effect on Sniffy's ongoing behavior. Neither the tone, the light, nor the bell is intense enough to have any tendency to act as a US capable of interrupting the flow of Sniffy's behavior. However, when a CS is paired with the shock US, the CS gradually acquires the capacity to suppress bar pressing and interrupt other aspects of Sniffy's behavior. When he is fully conditioned, Sniffy will begin showing bouts of freezing and other fear-related behaviors soon after the CS comes on. As was the case with the UR, although we think that Sniffy's CR looks plausible, we do not know how realistic it is because we did not videotape a rat that was actually being conditioned to manifest a CER.

## The Design Classical Conditioning Experiment Dialog Box

As noted earlier, one of the reasons for the CER's popularity among North American researchers is the fact that all aspects of CER experiments can be automated. A computer controls the presentation of stimuli, records the rat's behavior, and computes the movement ratio and/or suppression ratio. The Sniffy Pro program provides you with a simplified interface that enables you to set up and run a wide variety of classical conditioning experiments. Like a psychologist in a research lab, you will set up the experiment and then let your computer present the stimuli and record the data. When you choose the Design Classical Conditioning Experiment command from the Experiment menu, the dialog box at the top of the next page appears.[4]

Classical conditioning experiments consist of one or more **stages,** and each stage contains one or more **trial types.** A stage is a group of

---

[4] The dialog box is shown as it appears in Mac OS X 10.3. In earlier versions of the Mac OS and in Windows, the appearance of the dialog box is slightly different. All the program controls work in the same way in all versions of the Windows and Mac operating systems that the program supports. In this manual, we will sometimes illustrate dialog boxes and data windows as they appear in Mac OS X and sometimes illustrate them as they appear in Windows XP.

## Classical Conditioning Experiment Design

### Stage
View/Edit Experiment Stage 1

( Next Stage )  ( Previous Stage )

( **New Stage** )  ( Delete Stage )

Interval Between Trials [5] Minutes

Present Each Trial Type [1] Times

### Trial Types
View/Edit Trial Type    A

( Next Type )  ( Previous Type )

( **New Type** )  ( Delete Type )

### First Stimulus

|  | Intensity |  |  |
|  | Low |  | High |
| ☐ Light | ○ | ⊙ | ○ |
| ☑ Tone | ○ | ⊙ | ○ |
| ☐ Bell |  |  |  |

### Second Stimulus

|  | Intensity |  |  |
|  | Low |  | High |
| ⊙ Shock US | ○ | ⊙ | ○ |
| ○ CS used as US |  |  |  |
|   ⊙ Light | ○ | ⊙ | ○ |
|   ○ Tone | ○ | ⊙ | ○ |
|   ○ Bell |  |  |  |
| ○ None |  |  |  |

( Cancel )                    ( Save )

trials. All the trials in one stage are run before any trials in the next stage. A trial type specifies the stimulus events that occur during a trial. Each stage must have at least one trial type. However, a single stage may have two or more different trial types that define different kinds of stimulus events. If a stage has more than one trial type, the different kinds of trials occur in random order during the stage,[5] and each of the different trial types occurs an equal number of times.

To see the difference between stages and trial types more clearly, imagine that you set up an experiment in which Sniffy gets 10 trials during which the tone CS is paired with the shock US and 10 trials during which the tone CS occurs without the US. If you define the two kinds of trials as belonging to different stages of the experiment, Sniffy will receive a block of 10 trials of one kind followed by a block of 10 trials of the other kind. If you define the two kinds of trials as different trial types within the same 20-trial stage, the two kinds of trials will be randomly intermixed with each other.

Now let's examine the different parts of the Classical Conditioning Experimental Design dialog box.

---

[5] The order in which the trial types occur is randomized each time an experiment is run. If the experiment is repeated, the order in which the trial types occur will vary.

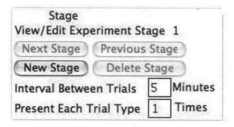

- In the Stage section of the dialog box, the number after View/Edit Experiment Stage indicates which stage of the experiment you are currently viewing. When you first open the dialog box by selecting the Design Classical Conditioning Experiment command from the Experiment menu, the numeral to the right of View/Edit Experiment Stage will always be 1, indicating that Stage 1 of the experiment is being displayed.

- You can edit (create or change) any stage that has not already been run, and you can add more stages to an experiment in which one or more early stages have already been run. You can also view the settings for stages that have been run. However, you cannot change the settings for any stage that has already been run or for a stage that is in the process of being run. When you view the settings for a stage that has already been run or for the stage currently being run, all command buttons are dimmed, and you cannot enter any information into the text boxes.

- The box labeled **Stage** contains four command buttons and two boxes into which you can type numerals.

- If you are viewing or editing Stage 1 of an experiment, the **Previous Stage** command button is dimmed. However, if you are working on Stage 2 or higher, the Previous Stage command is available. Executing the command by clicking your (left) mouse button while pointing at the command button will move you to the previous stage. For example, if you were working on Stage 3, clicking on the Previous Stage button would move you back to Stage 2, and clicking it a second time would move you back to Stage 1.

- The **Next Stage** button moves you from stage to stage in the opposite direction. For example, if you have created three stages and are currently working on Stage 2, clicking the Next Stage button moves you to Stage 3. The Next Stage button is dimmed when you are viewing or working on the last stage that you have defined.

- Clicking on the **New Stage** button creates a new stage, inserts it immediately after the stage that you were viewing when you clicked the button, and automatically moves you to the new stage. If necessary,

other stages of the experiment are automatically renumbered. For example, if you have already created three stages and are currently working on Stage 2, clicking on New Stage will create a new Stage 3 and insert it between Stage 2 and the stage that was previously called Stage 3. The former Stage 3 automatically becomes Stage 4.

- The **Delete Stage** button deletes the current stage and, if necessary, automatically renumbers the other stages. Suppose that you have already defined four stages in an experiment and are currently working on Stage 3. Clicking the Delete Stage button will eliminate the old Stage 3 and cause the stage that had previously been called Stage 4 to be renumbered as Stage 3.

- You specify the average time **Interval Between Trials** for the current stage by typing a number into the text box. Intervals between trials are measured in minutes. The number that you type must be an integer (a whole number without a decimal point). The shortest allowable average interval is 2 min; the longest is 20 min. Remember that you are specifying the *average* interval between trials. The actual intervals vary from trial to trial so that Sniffy cannot learn to anticipate when the next CS is going to occur.

- The number that you type into the box labeled **Present Each Trial Type \_\_\_ Times** is the number of times that each trial type will be presented in the stage of the experiment that you are currently editing. If the stage has more than one trial type, the total number of trials for the stage will be equal to the number of trials specified for Present Each Trial Type \_\_\_ Times multiplied by the number of trial types. For example, if the stage contains two trial types and you specify 10 for Present Each Trial Type \_\_\_ Times, the total number trials for that stage will be $2 \times 10 = 20$ trials.

Now let's examine the Trial Types panel in the dialog box:

- Trial Types are specified in sequence by letters: A, B, C, and so on. The letter that appears after **View/Edit Trial Type** tells you which trial type you are currently viewing or editing. Remember that trial types are defined within stages. Thus, Trial Type A for Stage 1 is likely to be different from Trial Type A for Stage 2. The box labeled **Trial Type** contains four command buttons. The **Previous Type,**

Next Type, New Type, and Delete Type buttons in the Trial Type panel of the dialog box work in a fashion analogous to the buttons with similar names in the Stage panel.

The panels labeled First Stimulus and Second Stimulus enable you to specify CS and US conditions, respectively, for the trial type of the stage that you are currently editing.

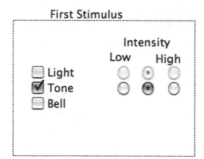
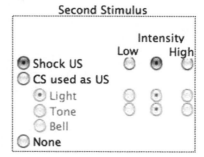

- *You must define a first stimulus (CS) and second stimulus (US) for each trial type in each stage of an experiment.*
- When the first stimulus (CS) is paired with the shock US, the duration of the first stimulus is always 30 seconds. Duration of a shock US is 1 second, and the shock occurs during the last second that the first stimulus is turned on.
- When the first stimulus (CS) is paired with another CS (light, tone, or bell) used as a second stimulus (CS used as US), the first stimulus lasts a total of 45 seconds; and the second stimulus occurs during the last 15 seconds of the first stimulus's presentation. The CS used as US settings for the second stimulus enable you to perform experiments on higher-order conditioning and sensory preconditioning. These varieties of classical conditioning are explained in Chapter 6.
- When the first stimulus (CS) is paired with another CS used as a US, the Sniffy Pro program measures Sniffy's movement ratio and/or suppression ratio during the 30-second period before the CS used as US comes on.
- To choose the light, tone, and/or bell as your first stimulus, click on one or more of the boxes just to the left of the words "Light," "Tone," and "Bell." If you choose the light or tone as a first stimulus, you must also specify a stimulus intensity (low, medium, or high) by clicking on the appropriate button. You should choose the medium intensity default unless you have a definite reason to choose another alternative.

- Choosing more than one kind of first stimulus (for example, both light and tone) will cause all the first stimuli selected to be presented together as a compound CS. The components of a compound CS come on and terminate simultaneously.

- If none of the boxes to the left of the words "Light," "Tone," and "Bell" is checked, no first stimulus will be presented. The only explicit second stimulus alternatives that you can choose when no first stimulus has been selected are the three intensities of the Shock US. When no first stimulus is selected, the shock occurs without warning.

- The second stimulus settings are in most ways analogous to the first stimulus settings except that only one kind of second stimulus can be chosen for each trial type.

- The default value for the shock US is medium. Remember that Sniffy's UR to the low-intensity US habituates and that his UR to the high-intensity US sensitizes. Choose the medium-intensity shock unless you want Sniffy's response to the shock to change as a function of the number of US presentations.

- As noted earlier, the CS used as US settings for the second stimulus enable you to perform experiments on higher-order conditioning and sensory preconditioning.

- The None alternative for second stimulus allows you to present the first stimulus (CS) without a second stimulus. As explained in Chapter 3, this alternative allows you to study a phenomenon called extinction.

The following two command buttons appear at the bottom of the Classical Conditioning Experimental Design dialog box:

( Cancel )                                        ( Save )

- Choosing **Cancel** closes the Classical Conditioning Experimental Design dialog box without saving any of the experimental design settings or changes that you have made.

- Choosing **Save** saves the experimental design that you have created (or any changes that you have made to the design) as a part of the current Sniffy file.

- To run (execute) a classical conditioning experiment that you have designed, select the **Run Classical Conditioning Experiment** command from the Experiment menu.

- Once the Run Classical Conditioning Experiment command has been executed, the Sniffy Pro program will run the experiment. *Be sure that the experiment is designed the way you want it before you execute the Run Classical Conditioning Experiment command!*
- If you Quit (Exit) the program or Open another Sniffy file after executing the Run Classical Conditioning Experiment command, you will be asked whether you want to save the file. If you save it, the program will begin running the classical conditioning experiment exactly where it left off when you open the file the next time.
- If you realize that you have made a mistake in setting up a stage of the experiment that has not already started to execute, you can choose the Design Classical Conditioning Experiment command and change the unexecuted stage(s).

## The Sensitivity & Fear Mind Window

Below is a picture of the Sensitivity & Fear mind window:

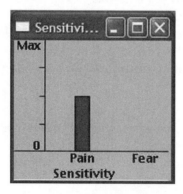

- Mind windows display some of the parameters of the Sniffy Pro program that affect Sniffy's behavior. You should view them as representing Sniffy's psychological states. They are *not* measures of Sniffy's behavior. All mind windows have a blue background.
- The column labeled **Pain Sensitivity** depicts Sniffy's sensitivity to the shock US and predicts the strength of his UR the next time the US occurs. This column will always be at its midpoint at the beginning of a classical conditioning experiment, and it will remain at the midpoint throughout experiments that employ the medium-intensity shock. If you are employing the high-intensity, sensitizing US, the height of the column will rise as Sniffy's UR becomes more intense as a result of repeated presentations of the US. If you are using the

low-intensity, habituating US, the height of the column will decrease as Sniffy's response to repeated presentations of the US decreases.

- The column labeled **Fear** shows the current intensity of Sniffy's fear. Remember that this is not a measure of Sniffy's behavior; it is a measure of an internal psychological process. The more intense Sniffy's internal fear, the more likely he is to display fear behaviors, such as freezing. If Sniffy has been trained to press the bar (or perform any other operantly conditioned response), he will be less likely to display that behavior when he is afraid. If Sniffy has not been trained to perform an operantly conditioned behavior, a high level of fear will reduce his exploratory and other movements that are not related to fear.

## The CS Response Strength Mind Window

In Sniffy Pro experiments, the light, tone, and bell can be used as CSs. The cage (the general operant chamber environment or background) can also function as a CS. The CS Response Strength mind window displays the strength of each possible CS's capacity to elicit a CR as a function of trials. In compound conditioning experiments, in which more than one CS is presented simultaneously, the CS Response Strength window displays each CS's response strength separately. The CS response strength of the compound stimulus is equal to the sum of the CS response strengths of the compound's component CSs. Below is the CS Response Strength mind window as it would be displayed at the end of the following compound conditioning experiment:

- Stage 1 of the experiment consisted of 10 trials during which the high-intensity tone and low-intensity light were presented as a compound CS paired with the medium-intensity shock US. Thus, Stage 1 had a single trial type that occurred 10 times.
- In Stage 2, each of two different trial types was presented once.
  - □ Trial Type B: The high-intensity tone CS occurred with no second stimulus.
  - □ Trial Type A: The low-intensity light CS occurred with no second stimulus.

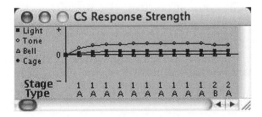

You should note the following features of this CS Response Strength mind window:

- The blue background color denotes that CS Response Strength window is a mind window, not a measure of Sniffy's behavior. The psychological state depicted is each possible CS's capacity to elicit a CR at the end of each trial. CS response strength thus predicts how strongly Sniffy will respond to a CS the *next* time it is presented.

- At the left-hand margin is the graph legend, which displays the data-point shapes associated with the light, tone, bell, and cage stimuli.

- The vertical axis of the graph indicates whether the CS response strength is excitatory or inhibitory. If a CS has an excitatory, positive tendency to elicit a fear-related CR, its response strength will be greater than 0. If a CS has an inhibitory, negative tendency to prevent the occurrence of a CR, its response strength will be less than 0. A response strength of 0 means that a stimulus has no capacity either to elicit or to inhibit a CR.

- Beneath the horizontal axis of the graph and to the right of the words "Stage" and "Type," respectively, are a row of numbers and a row of letters. The numbers denote the stage of the experiment in which each trial occurred, and the letters denote the trial type for each trial. In this example, the row of numbers consists of ten 1s followed by two 2s because Stage 1 of the experiment consisted of 10 trials and Stage 2 consisted of 2 trials. The letter A appears beneath each of the 1s because Stage 1 contained only one trial type. The letters B and A under the 2s indicate which trial type occurred during each of the two Stage 2 trials.

- During Stage 1, both the line connecting the black squares that denote the light CS and the line connecting the open circles that denote the tone CS increase to levels greater than 0. This change indicates that both the light and the tone CSs are acquiring a capacity to elicit the CR. The line for the tone CS rises higher than that for the light CS, and this difference indicates that the tone's capacity to elicit a CR is greater than the light's.[6] The lines for both the bell CS and the cage remain at approximately 0, indicating that neither of these stimuli is acquiring the capacity to elicit or inhibit a CR. Because the black-filled circles symbolizing the cage and the open triangles symbolizing the bell are superimposed on each other, only the black circles are clearly visible.

[6] In this experiment, the tone acquires more CER-eliciting power than the light because the tone is a high-intensity CS whereas the light is a low-intensity CS.

# The Movement Ratio Window

Below is the Movement Ratio window for this same experiment:

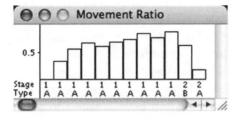

- The white background of this window indicates that it contains a measure of Sniffy's behavior. The movement ratio is the proportion of time during each CS presentation that Sniffy is frozen or manifesting other fear-related behaviors.
- At the bottom of the graph, the row of numbers that appears to the right of the word "Stage" denotes the stages of the experiment; and the row of letters that appears to the right of the word "Type" denotes the trial types.
- The movement ratio is 0 on the first trial. After Trial 1, the movement ratio increases rapidly and then levels out at around 0.7 during the remainder of Stage 1. Thus, during Stage 1, the light–tone compound CS acquires the capacity to elicit a strong CER.
- In Stage 2, Sniffy's responses to each of the components of the compound are tested during trials in which the shock US does not occur.
- On the first trial of Stage 2, Trial Type B (the high-intensity tone CS) is presented and elicits a strong CER (although not as strong as the light and tone together had been eliciting during late Stage 1 trials). This result is consistent with our observation in the CS Response Strength mind window that the tone CS had acquired a rather large amount of positive CS response strength during Stage 1 of the experiment.
- On the second trial of Stage 2, Trial Type A (the low-intensity light CS) is presented and elicits a weak CER. This result is consistent with our observation in the CS Response Strength mind window that the light CS had acquired only a small amount of positive CS response strength during Stage 1 of the experiment.

# The Cumulative Record During Classical Conditioning

We believe that most users will be using a file in which Sniffy has not previously been trained to bar-press for their classical conditioning experiments. However, for the benefit of those using files in which Sniffy has previously been trained to bar-press, we depict a cumulative record showing how the Sniffy Pro program records events during classical conditioning experiments. The cumulative record shown in this section depicts bar pressing during the last three trials of the experiment described above. In this case, prior to the classical conditioning experiment, Sniffy had been trained to press the bar in his operant chamber, and his bar-pressing behavior was being maintained on a VR-25 schedule of reinforcement, which means that he had to press the bar an average of 25 times to obtain a pellet of food.

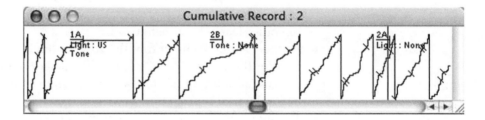

- The characteristics of the cumulative record as a measure of bar pressing and other operantly conditioned behaviors is described in detail in Chapter 10, Exercise 24.
- The cumulative record will not contain any useful information unless Sniffy has been trained to bar-press or perform another operant behavior. Users who are not using an operantly conditioned animal for their classical conditioning experiments should ignore this response measure.
- We strongly recommend that users who plan to use an operantly conditioned rat for studies of classical conditioning use an animal that is being maintained on a VR-25 schedule.
- At the left side of the record, the horizontal bar above the words "Light" and "Tone" mark the durations of the compound CS. The notation "1A" indicates that this trial occurred during Stage 1 and the event was an example of Trial Type A. The lettering below the horizontal bar indicates that both the light and tone CSs were presented and that they were followed by the shock US.

- In the center of the record, the notation "2B" indicates that the trial occurred in Stage 2 of the experiment and that it was the kind of event defined as Trial Type B. The words "Tone" and "None" indicate that the tone CS was presented and that it was *not* followed by the shock US.
- Finally, at the right-hand side of the record, the notation "2B" indicates that Trial Type B of Stage 2 was presented; and the words "Light" and "None" mean that the light CS was *not* followed by the shock US.

## The Suppression Ratio Window

Similarly, for the benefit of users who are using an operantly conditioned animal for their classical conditioning experiments, here is the Suppression Ratio window for the same experiment. This response measure produces useful information only for animals that have previously been operantly conditioned.

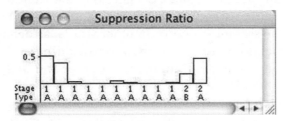

- The white background of this window indicates that it contains a measure of Sniffy's behavior.
- At the bottom of the graph, the row of numbers that appears to the right of the word "Stage" denotes the stages of the experiment; and the row of letters that appear to the right of the word "Type" denotes the trial types.
- The suppression ratio is about 0.5 on the first trial. After Trial 1, the suppression ratio decreases and then levels out at or just above 0 for the remainder of Stage 1. Thus, during Stage 1, the light–tone compound CS acquires the capacity to elicit almost complete suppression of bar pressing.
- In Stage 2, Sniffy's responses to each of the components of the compound are tested during trials in which the shock US does not occur.

- On the first trial of Stage 2, Trial Type B (the high-intensity tone CS) is presented and elicits strong suppression of bar pressing, but not as much as presenting both CSs. This result is consistent with our observation in the CS Response Strength mind window that the tone CS had acquired a rather large amount of positive CS response strength during Stage 1 of the experiment.
- On the second trial of Stage 2, Trial Type A (the low-intensity light CS) is presented and elicits very little suppression of bar pressing. This result is consistent with our observation in the CS Response Strength mind window that the light CS had acquired only a small amount of positive CS response strength during Stage 1 of the experiment.

## Types of Associations

As defaults, Sniffy associates the first stimulus with the second stimulus (learns an S–S association) whenever the shock US is used as the second stimulus, and associates the first stimulus with the response to the second stimulus (learns an S–R association) whenever a CS is used as the second stimulus. In other words, as defaults, Sniffy learns S–S associations for first-order conditioning and S–R associations for higher-order conditioning. First-order and higher-order conditioning and the difference between S–S and S–R associations are discussed fully in Chapter 7. These defaults simulate the kinds of associations that real rats are thought to learn in CER experiments (Domjan, 1998; Mazur, 1998).

Selecting the **Change Nature of Association** command from the Experiment menu brings up a dialog box that enables you to change the nature of the associations that Sniffy learns during classical conditioning experiments. The dialog box is shown below:

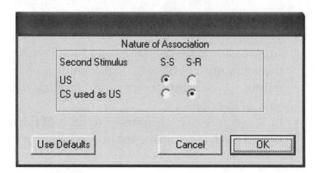

- Under the words "Second Stimulus" are two alternatives: US and CS used as US. There are two settings (S–S and S–R) for each kind of second stimulus. You change a setting by pointing the cursor at an unselected alternative and clicking your (left) mouse button.
- Under the panel in which settings are made are three command buttons:
- Clicking on the **Use Defaults** button restores the settings to the Sniffy Pro program's default values: S–S when the second stimulus is the shock US and S–R when the second stimulus is a CS used as a US.
- Clicking the **Cancel** button closes the dialog box without making any changes.
- Clicking the **OK** button closes the dialog box and puts whatever settings you have selected into effect.
- The Change Nature of Association command is always available so that you can see what settings are in effect. However, all the alternatives except Cancel will be dimmed after you have executed the Run Classical Conditioning Experiment command for the first time in a particular Sniffy Pro file. Thus, if you want anything other than the default settings to be in effect during a particular experiment, you must execute the Change Nature of Association command and select the settings that you want before you execute the Run Classical Conditioning Experiment command. This restriction on the Change Nature of Association command is necessary to ensure that the Sniffy Pro program gives consistent results with the different settings.
- **Warning:** We selected the Sniffy Pro program's default values for Nature of Association because they represent the ways in which most psychologists believe that real rats typically learn associations in a CER situation (Domjan, 1998, 2003; Mazur, 1998). Do not change these settings unless you have a specific reason to do so.

## How to Get Reliable, Comparable Results

The movement ratio is a very robust measure of Sniffy's classically conditioned fear behavior, so robust that it provides a useful response measure whether or not Sniffy has been operantly conditioned to press the bar in the operant chamber or to perform any of the other operantly conditioned behaviors that Sniffy is capable of learning.

However, the suppression ratio depends on measured changes in Sniffy's bar-pressing performance. The Sniffy Pro program computes the suppression ratio by comparing the number of responses that

Sniffy makes during the 30-second CS with the number of responses that he makes during the 30-second period just before the CS is presented. To make this measurement reliable, it is critically important that Sniffy be pressing the bar at a rapid, steady rate unless his response rate is being reduced because he is showing either a CR or a UR. If Sniffy is not pressing the bar at a steady rate, you will obtain erratic results because the value of the suppression ratio is affected by the number of bar presses that Sniffy makes during the 30 seconds prior to each CS presentation.

Variable ratio (VR) schedules produce rapid, steady bar-press performances that make ideal baselines against which to measure suppression ratios. Thus we strongly recommend that you use a VR-trained Sniffy as the starting point for all your classical conditioning experiments that use the suppression ratio as a response measure. Demonstrating many of the more advanced classical conditioning phenomena that the Sniffy Pro program simulates requires comparing the suppression ratios that Sniffy manifests under different experimental conditions. Whenever such a comparison is necessary, your results will be meaningful only if you use a Sniffy file with the same baseline performance characteristics (a Sniffy trained on the same reinforcement schedule) in each of the different experimental conditions.

The surest way to get predictable, comparable results both within and between experiments using the suppression ratio as a response measure is to use the same baseline Sniffy file as the starting point for all your classical conditioning experiments in which you want to use the suppression ratio as your response measure. The baseline that we used for calibrating the Sniffy Pro program is the VR-25 file located in the Sample Files folder. We recommend that you use it as your classical conditioning baseline in all experiments in which the suppression ratio is being used as your classical conditioning response measure. For experiments using the movement ratio as the response measure, we recommend that you start all your classical conditioning experiment with a new (that is, untrained) Sniffy file.

Your setting for the Average Interval Between Trials can also affect the reliability of both suppression ratio and movement ratio measurements. The default value for the average interval between trials is 5 minutes. When the low- or medium-intensity shock is being used as the US, that setting is almost always sufficient to ensure that Sniffy will have recovered from the effect of being shocked on the previous trial before the next trial occurs. However, recall that Sniffy's UR to the high-intensity shock sensitizes so that he requires longer to recover after he has experienced several high-intensity shocks. Thus, when the

high-intensity shock is being used as the US, it is a good idea to use a longer average interval between trials. A setting of 10 minutes should almost always be sufficient.

## Putting Everything Together to Understand Classical Conditioning

During a classical conditioning experiment, you can observe four things:

- **Occurrences of the CS and US.**
- **Changes in Sniffy's psychological states.** These changes are visible in the Sensitivity & Fear and in the CS Response Strength mind windows.
- **Sniffy's responses to the CS and US,** and especially how his response to the CS changes as a function of experience. You can observe Sniffy's responses to these stimuli by simply watching Sniffy's behavior during and after their presentation.
- **Response measures.** If Sniffy has been trained to bar-press or to perform any of several other automatically recordable operant behaviors, the Cumulative Record contains raw data about occurrences of the chosen operantly conditioned behavior throughout the experiment, shows when the different classical conditioning stimuli occur, and enables you to view the ways in which the stimuli affect Sniffy's operantly conditioned behavior. The Movement Ratio window shows the proportion of time during each conditioned stimulus that Sniffy is manifesting fear behaviors. The Suppression Ratio window contains the classical conditioning response measure that psychologists typically use in CER experiments.

Being able to see how stimulus events produce psychological changes that in turn produce behavior changes, which in turn are reflected in behavioral measurements, should enable you to develop a thorough understanding of the way in which psychologists believe classical conditioning works.

## Exporting Your Results to Other Programs

During a classical conditioning experiment, the Sniffy Pro program enters data into the Movement Ratio, Suppression Ratio, and CS Response Strength windows. These graphs are saved as part of the Sniffy

Pro file so that you can go back and examine your results after an experiment has been completed.

You can also export suppression ratio and CS response strength results to a spreadsheet or statistical analysis program, where you can perform additional data analyses or produce more sophisticated graphs. To export the numeric data on which both the CS Response Strength and Suppression Ratio graphs are based:

- Click your (left) mouse button once while pointing the cursor at the Movement Ratio, Suppression Ratio, or CS Response Strength window.
- Choose the Export Data command from the File menu. Executing the Export Data command will bring up the standard dialog box for creating and saving a new file.
- Choose an appropriate name and location on your hard drive for your data export file and click OK.

## Printing All the Contents of a Data Window

You can print the contents of any response measure or mind window that the Sniffy Pro program produces.[7] To print the contents of a window:

- Select the window by placing the cursor over it and clicking your (left) mouse button once.
- Execute the Print Window command in the File menu.
- Make the necessary selections in the printing dialog box that appears.

## Copying and Pasting the Visible Portion of a Window

With the exception of the Operant Chamber and the Lab Assistant, the visible portion of all the windows that the Sniffy Pro program produces can be copied and then pasted into a word processing or graphics program that accepts pasted images. To copy and paste the visible portion of a Sniffy window:

[7]The only window whose contents *cannot* be printed is the operant chamber, the window in which you see Sniffy moving around.

- Open your word processing or graphics program and determine where you want to paste the image that you are going to copy from Sniffy Pro. In a word processor, it's a good idea to go to the place in your document where you want to insert the image and create a blank line in the place you want to put it.
- Open the Sniffy Pro data file containing the window whose image you want to copy.
- If necessary, make the window that you want to copy visible by selecting it from the Windows menu.
- Make sure that the window that you want to copy is selected by clicking on it once.
- Execute the Copy Window command in the Sniffy Pro program's Edit menu.
- Move back to your word processor or graphics program.
- Execute the word processor's or the graphic program's Paste command, which will probably be under that program's Edit menu. (Some programs have a special Paste command for pasting images.)
- The graphic contents from the Sniffy Pro window will appear in the other program's document.

# 3

# Basic Phenomena of Classical Conditioning: Acquisition, Extinction, Spontaneous Recovery, and Stimulus Intensity Effects

## Important Technical Information

- ❖ In the following exercises, the instructions for saving Sniffy Pro files direct you to select an appropriate destination *on your computer's hard disk* for the Sniffy Pro file that you want to save. *It is extremely important that you get into the habit of saving your Sniffy Pro files on the hard disk of the computer that you are using.* **Never save a file on a floppy disk.** Sniffy files can grow to be quite large. If you try to save a large Sniffy file on a floppy disk that does not have enough room to accommodate it, the program will not be able to save the file successfully. As a consequence, the time and effort that you have invested in doing an exercise may be lost. This potential problem results from the limited storage capacity of floppy disks. It is *not* a problem with the Sniffy Pro program. Similar problems arise with any program that produces large files.
- ❖ If your instructor wants you to hand in your Sniffy Pro files on floppy disks, you should initially save the files on your computer's hard disk and then copy the saved files from the hard disk onto one or more floppy disks.
- ❖ If you do not have your own computer and must therefore store your Sniffy Pro files on floppy disks, you should initially save the file on the hard disk of the computer that you're using, then copy the files onto one or more floppy disks. You should then copy the files from the floppy disks back onto the hard disk of the computer that you're using before you try to work with the files again.
- ❖ You need to keep track of where you save your Sniffy Pro files on your computer's hard disk so that you can find them easily when you need to. A very good place to keep them is in the Sniffy Files

folder that was installed on your hard drive when you installed the program.

❖ If you require additional information about saving files, see the Appendix at the back of this manual.

## Accelerating Time

Some of the Sniffy Pro experiments that you will be performing require several hours of both clock time and program time to complete when your computer is displaying all Sniffy's movements. To enable you to run long experiments faster, we have made it possible for you to make Sniffy invisible so that your computer can run the experiments as fast as possible. Selecting the **Isolate Sniffy (Accelerate Time)** command from the Experiment menu simulates enclosing Sniffy's operant chamber in a soundproof, air-conditioned container of the type used in many laboratories to isolate an easily distractible live animal from extraneous stimuli that might divert the animal's attention from the experiment itself. When he is hidden, the window in which Sniffy is normally visible will look like this:

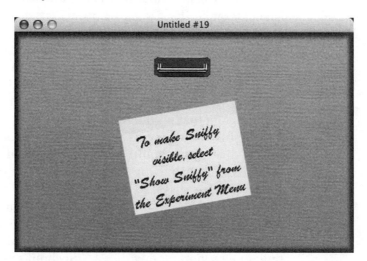

The amount of time acceleration that isolating Sniffy will achieve depends on the speed of your computer. With a relatively slow computer, 5 minutes of program time may pass in 90 seconds. With a fast computer, 5 minutes of program time may be compressed into 5 seconds or less. To make Sniffy visible again, click on the handle in the isolation window or choose the **Show Sniffy** command from the Experiment menu. The Isolate Sniffy (Accelerate Time) and Show Sniffy commands replace each other in the Experiment menu. The Isolate Sniffy (Accelerate Time) command is available whenever Sniffy is visible. The Show Sniffy command is available whenever Sniffy is isolated.

***Warning: Don't let accelerated time get away from you.*** If you are running an experiment using time acceleration and want to be able to add new stages to the experiment later, you need to keep an eye on things and stop the experiment when the exercise you are currently performing is complete. There is a time limit of 20 hours of program time for each Sniffy experiment, at which point no more data can be collected. If your computer can run an experiment 20 times faster than clock time when Sniffy is isolated, an hour of program time will elapse in 3 minutes. Unless you watch what's going on, it's easy to run an experiment for several "hours" longer than you intended.

The Sniffy Pro program includes two useful features to help you avoid running a time-accelerated experiment longer than you intended:

- The program signals the end of a classical conditioning experiment by beeping at the end of the last currently programmed classical conditioning trial. When you hear that sound, save the file and either quit (exit) the program or set up the next exercise that you want to perform.
- The Lab Assistant informs you about the status of your experiment. When a classical conditioning experiment is in progress, the Lab Assistant window provides several kinds of self-explanatory information about what is going on. When the classical conditioning experiment is complete, the Lab Assistant's message will change.

## Other Time-Saving Hints

Many of Sniffy's classical conditioning exercises require a considerable amount of time to run. Here are some tips about how to perform them as quickly and as efficiently as possible:

- Many of the classical conditioning exercises involve comparing two or more experimental conditions. If you follow our file-naming suggestions (so that you know which file to use), keep all your classical conditioning files in a single location on your hard drive (so that you know where to find them), and carefully follow our instructions about how to set up and run the experiments, you will often be able

to reuse a file from a previous exercise as the starting point for a later exercise or as one of the experimental conditions in a later exercise. We carefully planned the Sniffy Pro exercises in this way to make things as easy as possible for you.

■ If your computer has enough random access memory (RAM), you can set up a Sniffy exercise and let the program run the experiment in the background while you do something else on your computer. The program will run more slowly in the background than in the foreground, but that speed difference may be offset by the convenience of being able to do something else while the program is performing an experiment.

## Noise Control

Sniffy's classical conditioning exercises make frequent use of a tone as the CS. By default, that tone will be played at appropriate times whenever Sniffy is visible during classical conditioning experiments. If you, your family, or your roommates want peace and quiet, you can silence the sound by executing the Preferences command in the Sniffy menu in Mac OS X and in the File menu in Windows XP and selecting the Sound Proof Cage option.

## Background to the Exercises in This Chapter

**Acquisition** (learning) of a classically conditioned response is produced by repeatedly presenting the CS followed by the US. As a result of this acquisition procedure, the CS gradually acquires the capacity to elicit a new response (CR) that in most forms of classical conditioning resembles the UR. Once a classically conditioned response has been acquired, it can be eliminated by repeatedly presenting the CS alone—that is, without the US. Elimination of a CR by repeatedly presenting the CS without the US is called **extinction.** If the animal is removed from the experimental situation for a day or so after a CR has been extinguished and then returned to the experimental setting and given a second extinction session, it is likely that CR will occur again during the first few trials of the second extinction session. This reappearance of a previously extinguished CR is called **spontaneous recovery.** Early in the second extinction session, the CR is stronger than it was at the end of the first extinction session but weaker than it was at the end of acquisition.

# Exercise 1: Basic Acquisition of a CR

Acquisition is produced by setting up a series of trials in which a CS regularly precedes occurrences of the US. The steps outlined below describe how to set up and run an experiment in which Sniffy receives 10 pairings of the medium-intensity tone CS with the medium-intensity shock US.

- If you plan to use the movement ratio as your measure of classical conditioning, simply start the Sniffy Pro program or, if the program is already running, choose the New command from the File menu.
- If you want to use the suppression ratio as a response measure, open a file in which Sniffy has been fully trained to bar-press on a VR schedule. We recommend that you copy the file named VR-25 that is located in the Sample Files folder, and use it as the baseline file for this and all your classical conditioning experiments that use the suppression ratio as a response measure.
- Use the Save As command in the File menu to save the file under an appropriate new name (for example, Ex1-ClassAcq) on your computer's hard drive.
- **Select an appropriate destination for the file on your computer's hard disk.** If you are running the Macintosh version of the program, the Sniffy Files folder that we asked you to create on your hard drive when you installed the program is the best place to keep all your Sniffy files. If you are running the Windows version of the program, we suggest that you save this exercise and all future exercises in the Sniffy Pro for Windows folder that the installer program created. That folder is inside the Program Files folder at the root level of your hard drive. [1]
- Choose the Design Classical Conditioning Experiment command from the Experiment menu. In the Classical Conditioning Experimental Design dialog box, make the following settings:
  - □ In the Stage section, be sure the numeral 5 appears in the text box located to the right of Interval Between Trials, indicating that the average interval between trials will be 5 minutes.
  - □ In the text box located to the right of Present Each Trial Type, type 10.

[1]If you need additional information about how to save files, see the Appendix at the back of this manual.

- ▫ In the First Stimulus panel of the dialog box, check that the medium-intensity tone is selected. Make sure that no other first stimulus is selected.
- ▫ In the Second Stimulus panel of the dialog box, make sure that the medium-intensity shock US is selected.
- ▫ Carefully check to see that all the settings are correct.
- ▫ Click the Save command button.
- ■ After the Experimental Design dialog box has closed, choose the Run Classical Conditioning Experiment command from the Experiment menu.
- ■ If you want to speed up execution of the experiment, select the Isolate Sniffy (Accelerate Time) command from the Experiment menu. However, if you use this feature, be careful not to let the program run very long after the experiment is completed. You will need the file that this exercise creates in several future exercises. Thus you want to avoid inadvertently recording unneeded data about Sniffy's activities once the classical conditioning experiment is finished. Remember that the program beeps at the end of a classical conditioning experiment.
- ■ After the last acquisition trial, save your results by selecting the Save command from the File menu.

During the next 50 min of program time, the program will automatically run the experiment. While the program is running, the Movement Ratio window will draw a bar graph that shows Sniffy's movement ratio as a function of trials. At the same time, the CS Response Strength mind window will produce a line graph depicting changes in the CS's capacity to elicit a CR.

At the end of the experiment, your Movement Ratio and CS Response Strength windows should resemble the following windows.[2]

---

[2] The CS Response Strength mind window should look exactly like that shown if you are running Windows XP. If you are running another version of Windows or the Mac OS, the contents of the mind window should look exactly like that shown, but the format of the window borders will depend on your computer's operating system. The contents of mind windows depict processes that are parts of Sniffy's learning algorithm, and these parameters are completely determined by the settings that you make in the Design Classical Conditioning Experiment dialog box. However, the resemblance between the Movement Ratio window shown and the one you get will be less exact. The movement ratio is a measure of Sniffy's actual behavior. As Sniffy learns, the learning algorithm changes the *probability* that Sniffy will behave in certain ways but does not completely determine what Sniffy does. Because the learning algorithm only changes the probabilities with which behaviors occur, the details of the movement ratio result will be different each time the experiment is performed.

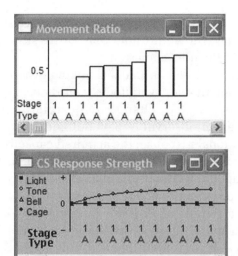

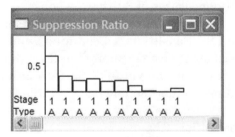

During acquisition, the movement ratio starts at 0 on the first trial, then rises and levels off at about 0.7. This increase in the movement ratio means that the tone CS is acquiring the capacity to induce freezing and other fear-related behaviors. As the movement ratio increases, the CS Response Strength mind window shows that the tone's capacity to elicit fear as a psychological process is increasing. Remember that the Movement Ratio window depicts a change in Sniffy's behavior, whereas the CS Response Strength mind window depicts the change in Sniffy's psychological state that influences the behavioral change.

If you performed the experiment with a file in which Sniffy had previously been trained to bar-press, the Suppression Ratio window should resemble that shown below:

During acquisition, the suppression ratio starts out at around 0.5 on the first trial, then declines and levels off at an average value a little above 0. This decrease in the suppression ratio means that the tone CS is acquiring the capacity to suppress Sniffy's bar pressing. You could verify this fact by examining the cumulative record. During the last several trials, you would note that Sniffy stops pressing the bar very quickly after the tone comes on.

With a real rat, the animal's changing response to the CS would be the only thing that a psychologist could observe. Many psychologists explain this behavior change by postulating that it results from a change in an unobservable psychological process. With the conditioned emotional response, the acquired capacity of a CS to elicit freezing and to suppress bar pressing or other operantly conditioned behaviors is thought to be the result of an increasingly intense fear response. During CS presentations, Sniffy's Sensitivity & Fear mind window displays the strength of Sniffy's current fear; and the CS Response Strength mind window shows how strong the fear response will be when the CS is presented the next time. With Sniffy Pro, you can observe both the behavior change and the change in the Sniffy Pro program's classical conditioning algorithm—Sniffy's psychological state—that causes Sniffy's behavior to change. We have designed Sniffy's classical conditioning algorithm to resemble theoretical processes that psychologists (for example, Guthrie, 1960; Hull, 1943, 1952; Rescorla & Wagner, 1972) have postulated in an effort to explain classical conditioning. However, nobody has ever seen anything closely analogous to CS response strength in a rat's brain; and many psychologists assert that it's impossible, even in principle, to observe the psychological (mental) processes of real animals. We believe that the Sniffy Pro program's mind windows will help you understand psychological explanations of classical conditioning, but it's important to remember that they do not provide any deep insights into the workings of the "animal mind."

An interesting thing to note is that the movement ratio and suppression ratio measures of Sniffy's response to the CS are not a perfect reflection of Sniffy's internal fear response. As the CS Response Strength and the Sensitivity & Fear mind windows show, Sniffy's fear response is at an almost constant high level during the last several acquisition trials. Yet the value of Sniffy's movement ratios and suppression ratios fluctuate somewhat from trial to trial. These behavioral measures vary because Sniffy's behavior is determined by a complex set of probabilities. Changes in Sniffy's learning algorithm (Sniffy's psychological state) change the *probabilities* with which fear-related behaviors occur, but Sniffy's behavior is always probabilistic and thus somewhat variable.

These variations in Sniffy's movement ratio and suppression ratio are somewhat analogous to the results that you obtain if you repeat-

edly perform an experiment in which you toss a coin 10 times. On any given coin toss, the probability that the coin will come up heads is equal to the probability that it will come up tails. For this reason, if you perform a great many 10-toss experiments, the average number of heads will be 5. However, the exact number of heads will vary from experiment to experiment. Sometimes you will get 5 heads, sometimes 7 heads, sometimes 4 heads. The operation of similar processes accounts for the variation that you see in Sniffy's response measures. The response measures vary because Sniffy's behavior is probabilistic. After every movement Sniffy makes, there are several things that he could do next. His experiences in the operant chamber change the probabilities of his behaviors, but the program is designed in a way that ensures that we can never know in advance exactly what Sniffy will do next. Even under very similar conditions, Sniffy doesn't always do the same thing. This variability in Sniffy's behavior is what accounts for the variability that we see in the classical conditioning response measures. The behavioral measures that psychologists obtain with real animals vary in a similar fashion and possibly do so for somewhat similar reasons.

## Exercise 2: Extinction

These instructions assume that you have already run the acquisition experiment described in Exercise 1. To set up a series of 30 extinction trials, you should follow the steps listed. You need to give more extinction than acquisition trials because the CER extinguishes much more slowly than it is acquired.

- Start the Sniffy Pro program and open the file that we suggested you name Ex1-ClassAcq in which Sniffy acquired a CR to the medium-intensity tone CS.[3]
- Use the Save As command to save the file under a new name (e.g., Ex2-ClassExt) in the Sniffy Files folder on your computer's hard drive. ***Saving the file under a new name preserves the original file in which Sniffy has been classically conditioned for future use. You will need it for several future exercises.***

[3]If you need help opening the file, see the Appendix at the end of this manual.

- Choose the Design Classical Conditioning Experiment command from the Experiment menu. The Classical Conditioning Experimental Design dialog box opens to Stage 1. All the options for defining conditions are dimmed because Stage 1 has already been run.
- In the Design Classical Conditioning Experiment dialog box, make the following settings to define Stage 2, which will contain your extinction trials:
  - In the Stage section, click on the command button labeled New Stage. The number after View/Edit Experimental Stage changes from 1 to 2 to indicate that you are now working on Stage 2 of the experiment. Because this is a new stage that has not yet been run, all the options for defining trial types are available.
  - In the Stage section, be sure that the numeral 5 appears in the text box after Interval Between Trials, and type 30 in the text box located to the right of Present Each Trial Type. These settings indicate, respectively, that the average interval between trials will be 5 minutes and that there will be 30 trials for each Trial Type.
  - In the First Stimulus panel, choose the medium-intensity tone.
  - In the Second Stimulus panel, choose None.
  - Carefully check your settings.
  - Click on the Save button at the bottom of the dialog box to save the experimental design.
- After the Classical Conditioning Experimental Design dialog box closes, choose the Run Classical Conditioning Experiment command from the Experiment menu.
- If you want to speed up the experiment, select the Isolate Sniffy (Accelerate Time) command from the Experiment menu. Because you will need to use the file from this exercise as the starting point for the next exercise, you want to avoid inadvertently letting the program run for very long after this exercise is complete.
- When the program has finished running the experiment, choose the Save command from the File menu to save your results.

During the next 150 minutes of program time, the Sniffy Pro program will automatically give Sniffy 30 extinction trials—that is, 30 tri-

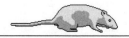

als during which the CS occurs without the US. As the program executes, the Sniffy Pro program will draw a graph showing Sniffy's movement ratio on each trial in the Movement Ratio window and the strength of the tone's capacity to elicit fear at the end of each trial in the CS Response Strength window. At the end of extinction, your Movement Ratio and CS Response Strength windows should resemble the following:

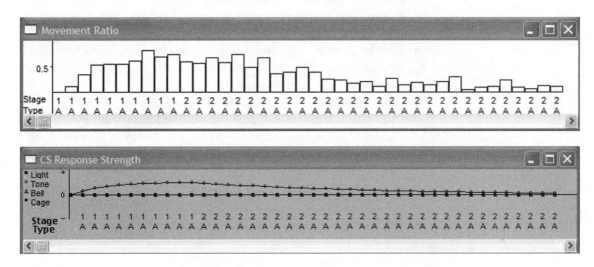

The Movement Ratio window shows that repeatedly presenting the CS without the US causes the CS to gradually stop eliciting freezing and other fear-related behaviors. The CS Response Strength mind window shows that this behavior change is the result of the CS's losing its capacity to elicit a fear response. Once again note the variability in the movement ratio that reflects the probabilistic nature of Sniffy's behavior. If your experiment was performed on a file in which Sniffy had been trained to bar-press, the Suppression Ratio window should look something like that shown below:

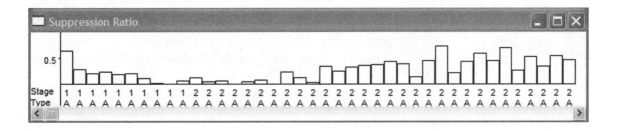

## Exercise 3: Spontaneous Recovery

Here are the steps that you need to follow to observe spontaneous recovery:

- Open the file that we suggested you call Ex2-ClassExt from Exercise 2, in which Sniffy was first conditioned in Stage 1 and then extinguished in Stage 2.
- Use the Save As command to save the file under an appropriate new name (e.g., Ex3-ClassSponRec) in the Sniffy Files folder on your computer's hard drive.
- Under the Experiment menu, choose Remove Sniffy for Time Out. This operation simulates removing Sniffy from the operant chamber and leaving him in his home cage for 24 hours; a dialog box will appear telling you that Sniffy has left the chamber. To return Sniffy to the experiment on the next simulated day, click the OK button in the dialog box.
- Choose Design Classical Conditioning Experiment from the Experiment menu and make the following settings in the Classical Conditioning Experimental Design dialog box to give Sniffy a second 15-trial extinction session:
  - ☐ The dialog box opens (as always) to Stage 1. All alternatives for defining trials and stimuli are dimmed because Stage 1 has already been run.
  - ☐ To define a new Stage 3, you must first move to Stage 2 because new stages are always inserted immediately after the stage currently being displayed. In the Stage section of the dialog box, click on Next Stage to move to Stage 2, which has also already been run.
  - ☐ When you reach Stage 2, click on New Stage to create the new Stage 3 after Stage 2. Note that the numeral 3 is now present after View/Edit Experiment Stage.
  - ☐ Make sure that the Interval Between Trials is set at 5 minutes.
  - ☐ Set Present Each Trial Type to 15 times.
  - ☐ In the First Stimulus panel, choose the medium-intensity tone.
  - ☐ In the Second Stimulus panel, choose None.
  - ☐ Carefully check your settings.

> □ Click on the Save command button at the bottom of the dialog box to save the experimental design.
> ■ After the dialog box closes, choose the Run Classical Conditioning Experiment command from the Experiment menu.
> ■ If you want to speed up the experiment, select the Isolate Sniffy (Accelerate Time) command from the Experiment menu.
> ■ When the experiment has finished running, save the file.

As Stage 3 executes, the movement ratio will be graphed as a function of trials in the Movement Ratio window, and the strength of the tone's capacity to elicit a fear response will be graphed in the CS Response Strength mind window. At the end of the experiment, these two windows should resemble those shown next:

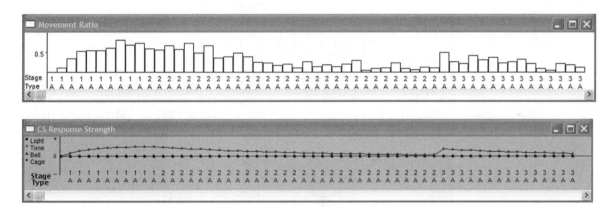

From here on, we assume that most users will be using the movement ratio as the response measure for classical conditioning and will no longer illustrate suppression ratio results.

## Exercise 4: Varying the Strength of the CS

The strength of the CS is a major determinant of the speed with which acquisition occurs in classical conditioning (for example, see Imada, Yamazaki, & Morishita, 1981). In the acquisition experiment described in Exercise 1, we used the medium-intensity tone as the CS. To study the effect of varying the intensity of the CS, repeat that experiment twice: once with the low-intensity tone CS and a second time with the high-intensity tone as the CS. The procedure for creating the two new Sniffy files is exactly the same as in Exercise 1 except that in one instance you will select the low-intensity tone as the first stimulus, whereas in the other instance you will select the high-intensity tone as the first stimulus. We suggest that you call your two new Sniffy files Ex4-LoToneCS and Ex4-HiToneCS, respectively.

After the two additional acquisition experiments have been completed, you can compare the movement ratio and CS response strength results in your three Sniffy files. We'll examine the movement ratios first.

Your Movement Ratio window for the low-intensity CS should look something like this:

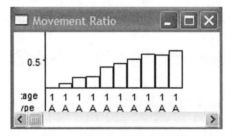

For the medium-intensity CS, your movement ratio results (from Exercise 1) should resemble these:

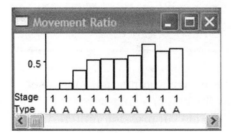

Here are our movement ratio results for the high-intensity CS:

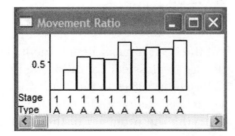

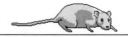

As expected, the movement ratio results suggest that the stronger the CS, the faster the CR is acquired. The situation is even clearer when we compare the results in the CS Response Strength mind windows.

First, here's the CS Response Strength mind window for the low-intensity CS:

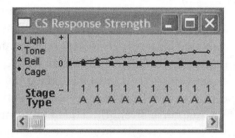

Here is the mind window for the medium-intensity CS:

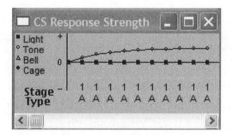

Finally, here is the mind window for the high-intensity CS:

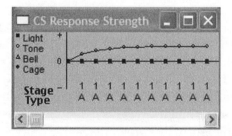

Comparing the three mind windows shows clearly that the stronger the CS, the faster conditioning occurs. In addition, note that the asymptote of the curves (the eventual level of conditioning reached when the curves level off) remains approximately the same. In other words, changing the intensity of the CS affects the speed with which

conditioning occurs but not the level of conditioning eventually reached. (Conditioning with the low-intensity CS is so slow that 10 conditioning trials are not enough for the CS response strength to reach its maximum level.)

You can obtain an even clearer picture of the effect of manipulating CS intensity by exporting your results to a spreadsheet program and plotting the CS response strength results on a single graph. We will conclude our discussion of this exercise by illustrating how this can be done. In this example, we will create data export files from the three acquisition experiments, open those files with a spreadsheet program, copy the relevant information into a single spreadsheet file, and finally draw a graph that shows the effect of manipulating CS intensity on acquisition of CS response strength. The general procedures that we outline will work with virtually any spreadsheet program. However, the details will vary from one program to another. This illustration uses Microsoft Excel Version X for Macintosh OS X.

- The first step is to create the three data export files that we will subsequently open with our spreadsheet program. To create each of the three data export files:
  - Open a relevant Sniffy Pro file in which the acquisition experiment has been completed.
  - Display the CS Response Strength mind window. (If necessary, make it visible by selecting it from the Mind Windows section of the Windows menu.)
  - Point the cursor at the CS Response Strength mind window and click your (left) mouse button once to make sure that the window is selected.
  - Choose the Export Data command from the File menu.
  - In the file-saving dialog that appears, Save your export file with an appropriate name in the place on your computer's hard drive where you keep the rest of your Sniffy files.
- Repeat this process to create data export files for all three acquisition experiments.
- Quit the Sniffy Pro program.
- Start your spreadsheet or statistical analysis program.
- If the program automatically creates a new file when it opens, Save the file under an appropriate name (e.g., CS Intensity). Otherwise, choose the New command and name the file.
- Enter row and column headings to create a group of cells that resembles the following:

| ◇ | A | B | C | D | |
|---|---|---|---|---|---|
| **1** | Trials | Weak CS | Medium CS | Strong CS | |
| **2** | 1 | | | | |
| **3** | 2 | | | | |
| **4** | 3 | | | | |
| **5** | 4 | | | | |
| **6** | 5 | | | | |
| **7** | 6 | | | | |
| **8** | 7 | | | | |
| **9** | 8 | | | | |
| **10** | 9 | | | | |
| **11** | 10 | | | | |
| **12** | | | | | |

- Open your three Sniffy data export files. To open each file in your spreadsheet program:
  - Choose the Open command from that program's file menu.
  - In the dialog box that appears, go to the location on your hard drive where you saved the Sniffy Pro data export files.
  - If the Sniffy Pro data export files are not visible, choose the Show All Files option in the file-opening dialog box.
  - If no Show All Files option is available or if the program does not open the file successfully when you select it, check to see whether the program has a special data import command. If necessary, read your spreadsheet program's manual or search its online Help files to determine how to import a tab-delimited text file.
  - Repeat this process for the other two data export files.
- Each of the three data export files will resemble the next figure when opened in your spreadsheet program:

HighToneDataExport

| ◇ | A | B | C | D | E | F | G | H | I | J | K | L | M |
|---|---|---|---|---|---|---|---|---|---|---|---|---|---|
| **1** | Stage | Trial | S/R | Light | Tone | Bell | Background | BP during CS | BP pre-CS | Freeze Durin | Active During | Movement Ratio | |
| **2** | 1 | A | 0.5222 | 0 | 0.45 | 0 | 0.0149 | 47 | 43 | 0 | 300 | 0 | |
| **3** | 1 | A | 0.1224 | 0 | 0.6907 | 0 | 0.023 | 6 | 43 | 96 | 211 | 0.3127 | |
| **4** | 1 | A | 0.2222 | 0 | 0.8195 | 0 | 0.0273 | 8 | 28 | 174 | 126 | 0.5799 | |
| **5** | 1 | A | 0 | 0 | 0.8884 | 0 | 0.0296 | 0 | 21 | 234 | 74 | 0.7597 | |
| **6** | 1 | A | 0 | 0 | 0.9253 | 0 | 0.0308 | 0 | 21 | 213 | 91 | 0.7006 | |
| **7** | 1 | A | 0.125 | 0 | 0.945 | 0 | 0.0315 | 2 | 14 | 222 | 85 | 0.7231 | |
| **8** | 1 | A | 0 | 0 | 0.9556 | 0 | 0.0318 | 0 | 20 | 249 | 60 | 0.8058 | |
| **9** | 1 | A | 0.0476 | 0 | 0.9612 | 0 | 0.032 | 2 | 40 | 225 | 82 | 0.7328 | |
| **10** | 1 | A | 0.0357 | 0 | 0.9642 | 0 | 0.0321 | 1 | 27 | 228 | 74 | 0.7549 | |
| **11** | 1 | A | 0.1 | 0 | 0.9658 | 0 | 0.0321 | 4 | 36 | 228 | 76 | 0.75 | |
| **12** | | | | | | | | | | | | | |

- The data are presented in vertical columns headed by the letters A through L and in horizontal rows headed by the numbers 1 through 11.
- There are 12 columns of data. In Row 1 of each column is a label that tells you what kind of data appears below.

- The column labeled **Stage** lists the stage of the experiment for each trial. Because this experiment had only one stage, the numeral 1 is entered for every trial.
- The column headed **Trial** gives the trial type for each trial. Because this experiment had only one trial type, the letter A appears for every trial.
- The column called **S/R** gives the suppression ratio for each trial.
- The columns called **Light**, **Tone**, **Bell**, and **Background** give the CS response strength values, respectively, for the light CS, tone CS, bell CS, and background (cage) CS for each trial.
- The column labeled **BP During CS** tells how many times Sniffy pressed the bar while the CS was on during each trial.
- The column labeled **BP Pre-CS** tells how many times Sniffy pressed the bar during the 30-sec period before the CS came on during every trial.
- The column labeled **Freeze During CS** tells how many units of freezing and other fear-related behaviors Sniffy produced during the CS.
- The column labeled **Active During CS** tells how many units of active, "non-frozen" behavior Sniffy produced during the CS.
- The column labeled **Movement Ratio** is the proportion of freeze units during the CS: Movement Ratio = Freeze During CS / (Freeze During CS + Active During CS).
- Starting with Row 2, each row of data contains the information about a particular classical conditioning trial.
- Each of your three data export files contains information about a particular intensity of the tone CS. The data that we need to draw our graph showing the effect of CS intensity on CS response strength appears in the column labeled Tone in each of the three data export files.
- To draw a single graph in which we compare CS response strength as a function of trials for the three different CS intensities, we need to copy the tone data from the three data export files and paste those data into the spreadsheet file that we named CS Intensity.
- The columns on the CS Intensity spreadsheet are labeled Trials, Weak CS, Medium CS, and Strong CS. First, we will copy the data from the low-intensity tone data export file into the column called Weak CS on the spreadsheet. To do this:

- ◻ Go to the LoCS data export file. Most spreadsheet programs have a pull-down menu called Windows. Your already open LoCS data file should be one of the menu choices under the Windows menu.
- ◻ Select the numbers in the column labeled Tone. In most programs, you can select a group of numbers in a column by pointing the cursor at the top number, clicking your (left) mouse button and then keeping the button depressed while dragging down to the bottom number. When all the numbers have been selected, release the mouse button.
- ◻ Choose the Copy command, which will probably be located under the Edit menu.
- ◻ Move back to the spreadsheet file into which you want to paste the numbers. To move back to the spreadsheet file, select it from the Windows menu.
- ◻ Select the cells for Trials 1 through 10 under the heading Weak CS. To select these cells, click on the cell for Trial 1, drag down to the cell for Trial 10 while holding down the (left) mouse button, then release the mouse button.
- ◻ Select the Paste command from the Edit menu.
- The numbers that you copied from the Ex23-LoCS data export file should appear in the spreadsheet so that your spreadsheet now looks something like this:

| | A | B | C | D |
|---|---|---|---|---|
| | Trials | Weak CS | Medium CS | Strong CS |
| 1 | 1 | 0.15 | | |
| 2 | 2 | 0.2752 | | |
| 3 | 3 | 0.3798 | | |
| 4 | 4 | 0.4671 | | |
| 5 | 5 | 0.54 | | |
| 6 | 6 | 0.6009 | | |
| 7 | 7 | 0.6518 | | |
| 8 | 8 | 0.6942 | | |
| 9 | 9 | 0.7297 | | |
| 10 | 10 | 0.7593 | | |

- Repeat the Copy–Paste process just outlined to copy data from the medium- and high-intensity tone data export files into the

spreadsheet columns labeled Medium CS and Strong CS, respectively.

- Your spreadsheet should now look like this:

| | A | B | C | D | E |
|---|---|---|---|---|---|
| 1 | Trials | Weak CS | Medium CS | Strong CS | |
| 2 | 1 | 0.15 | 0.3 | 0.45 | |
| 3 | 2 | 0.2752 | 0.5055 | 0.6907 | |
| 4 | 3 | 0.3798 | 0.6462 | 0.8195 | |
| 5 | 4 | 0.4671 | 0.7426 | 0.8884 | |
| 6 | 5 | 0.54 | 0.8087 | 0.9253 | |
| 7 | 6 | 0.6009 | 0.8539 | 0.945 | |
| 8 | 7 | 0.6518 | 0.8849 | 0.9556 | |
| 9 | 8 | 0.6942 | 0.9062 | 0.9612 | |
| 10 | 9 | 0.7297 | 0.9207 | 0.9642 | |
| 11 | 10 | 0.7593 | 0.9307 | 0.9658 | |

- Now you are ready to draw your graph. From this point on, we can give only sketchy instructions because different spreadsheet programs, and even different versions of the same program, take somewhat different approaches to graph drawing. You will very likely have to read the manual and/or consult the online Help files for the program that you are using.
- The next step is to select the data that you want to include in the graph. Some programs want you to select just the numeric data to be plotted (cells B2 through D11). Others want you also to select the column headers for the numeric data (cells B1 through D11), whereas still others want you to include the column labeled Trials (cells A1 through D11) as well.
- Once you have selected the right cells, you will choose a graph-drawing command from one of the pull-down menus and then make a series of decisions about what kind of graph you want to draw. These commands and choices vary considerably from program to program. In general, we can say that you want to draw a **line graph** and that you will want to create a **legend** to differentiate the different CS intensities. You will almost certainly need to consult the manual and/or the online Help to determine what to do.
- Eventually, your finished graph should resemble the following:

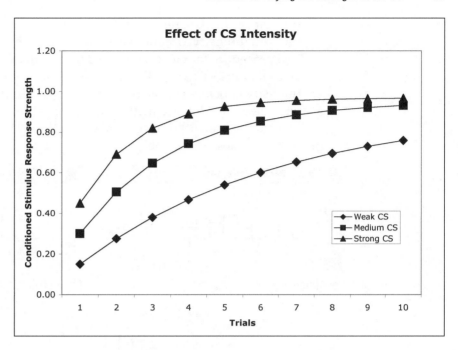

## Exercise 5: Varying the Strength of the US

The intensity of the US affects both the speed of acquisition and the level of classical conditioning that can ultimately be obtained (for example, Annau & Kamin, 1961; Polenchar, Romano, Steinmetz, & Patterson, 1984). The stronger the US, the faster conditioning occurs. The stronger the US, the greater the level of conditioning that can eventually be obtained. In addition, Sniffy's UR and hence the potential level of classical conditioning that the US can maintain changes as a function of repeated presentations for low-intensity and high-intensity US settings. The UR to the low-intensity US habituates, whereas the UR to the high-intensity US sensitizes. Thus, for the low-intensity US, not only is conditioning slower than for the medium- or high-intensity US, but the level of conditioning that the US can maintain also diminishes with repeated US presentations. For the high-intensity US, not only is the rate at which conditioning occurs faster, but the potential level of conditioning also increases.

In the acquisition experiment described in Exercise 1, we used the medium-intensity shock as the US. To study the effect of varying the

intensity of the US, repeat the acquisition experiment twice: once with the low-intensity US and a second time with the high-intensity US. The procedure for creating the two new Sniffy files is exactly the same as in Exercise 1 except that in one instance you will select the low-intensity shock as the second stimulus and in the other instance you will select the high-intensity shock as the second stimulus.

Your movement ratio results for the three shock intensities should resemble those shown below:

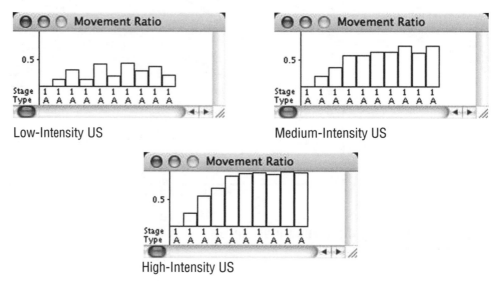

Low-Intensity US                    Medium-Intensity US

High-Intensity US

Your CS Response Strength mind window results should resemble those shown next:

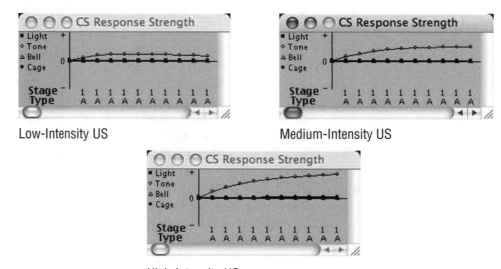

Low-Intensity US                    Medium-Intensity US

High-Intensity US

For the medium-intensity shock, the movement ratio curve levels off at an average around 0.7. For the high-intensity shock, the movement ratio curve rises higher to an average level of almost 1.0. However, the results with the low-intensity US are perhaps the most interesting. When an animal's response to a US habituates, the maximum level of conditioning that the US can maintain declines. When you start conditioning with an habituating US, CS response strength begins to build up; however, a point is reached where the declining effectiveness of the US overtakes the buildup in response strength. As a result, with an habituating US, there is always an optimal number of CS–US pairings beyond which conditioning declines. Both the CS Response Strength mind window and the movement ratio curves show this effect.

You can also export the CS response strength results to a spreadsheet or statistical analysis program to compare your acquisition results with the three different intensities of the US. The procedures for exporting the results and producing a graph to show the effect of varying US intensity are analogous to those just given for the effects of varying CS intensity. The resulting graph should resemble the following:

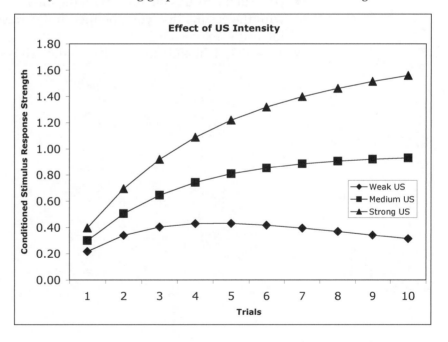

## Some Questions

- Compare and contrast the movement ratio and the suppression ratio as response measures in classical conditioning.

- As the strength of an animal's fear response increases, the value of the movement ratio increases but the value of the suppression ratio decreases. Why? How can two measures of the same thing move in opposite directions as the strength of the thing measured increases?
- Why do you think that most psychologists studying live rats use the suppression ratio and not the movement ratio as their response measure?
- Compare and contrast the effects of manipulating the strength of the CS and the strength of the US.

## Something to Do

Repeat Exercise 1 using the low-intensity, medium-intensity, and high-intensity light and the bell, respectively, as the CS. Export the data to text files, and compare the results in a spreadsheet program.

- How do the results obtained with the three light intensities compare with the results that you obtained in Exercise 4 for the three tone intensities?
- To which light and tone results are the bell results most similar?

# 4

# Compound Conditioning, Blocking, Overshadowing, and Overexpectation

So far, we have looked at examples of classical conditioning in which a single CS is paired with the US. This chapter deals with compound conditioning and three related phenomena: blocking, overshadowing, and overexpectation. In compound conditioning, two (or more) CSs are presented simultaneously—that is, they come on and go off at the same times. This paradigm is analogous to many real-life situations in which events produce stimuli in more than one sense modality. For example, when a car passes you on the street, you both see and hear and maybe even smell it. When a compound CS is paired with a US, the question of interest is the degree to which each of the component stimuli acquires the capacity to elicit a CR.

## Exercise 6: Compound Conditioning Compared With Separate CS Pairings

Exercise 6 involves comparing two experimental treatments. In both conditions, the light and tone CSs are presented 10 times during acquisition. In the compound conditioning treatment, the medium-intensity tone and medium-intensity light CSs will be presented simultaneously as a compound CS paired with the medium-intensity shock US. You will compare this compound conditioning procedure with a separate pairing control procedure in which Sniffy will receive 10 trials during which the medium-intensity tone is paired with the US and another 10 trials during which the medium-intensity light is paired with the US. The purpose of comparing compound conditioning with a separate pairing control is to determine whether these two different methods of presenting the two CSs produce different amounts of conditioning to the two CSs. After both experimental treatments, you will test the strength of Sniffy's CR to each CS by presenting the CSs separately during extinction test trials.

In this exercise, we introduce a method of summarizing classical conditioning experiments with charts. The compound conditioning experiment can be charted as follows:

| Condition | Stage 1 | Stage 2 | Stage 2 Expected Result |
|---|---|---|---|
| Compound Conditioning | 10: $CS_{ML}$&$CS_{MT}$–$US_M$ | 1: $CS_{ML}$–None | $CS_{ML}$–Moderate CR |
| | | 1: $CS_{MT}$–None | $CS_{MT}$–Moderate CR |
| Separate Pairing | 10: $CS_{ML}$–$US_M$ | 1: $CS_{ML}$–None | $CS_{ML}$–Strong CR |
| | 10: $CS_{MT}$–$US_M$ | 1: $CS_{MT}$–None | $CS_{MT}$–Strong CR |

In this and future charts:

- $CS_{ML}$ means the medium-intensity light used as a CS (first stimulus).
- $CS_{MT}$ means the medium-intensity tone used as a CS (first stimulus).
- $CS_{ML}$&$CS_{MT}$ means that the medium-intensity tone and medium-intensity light are presented simultaneously as a compound CS.
- $US_M$ means the medium-intensity shock used as the US (second stimulus).
- The numbers followed by a colon designate the number of trials during which a specified set of stimulus events will occur. Thus, "10: $CS_{ML}$&$CS_{MT}$–$US_M$" means that the compound of the medium-intensity tone and medium-intensity light is paired with the medium-intensity US 10 times during the designated stage of the experiment.

If you follow our directions carefully, the compound conditioning treatment can serve as the control condition for the blocking and overshadowing exercises. Being able to use your compound conditioning results as the control condition for the other two experiments will save time.

## The Compound Conditioning Experimental Condition

To set up the compound conditioning experimental condition, follow these steps:

- Start with a new Sniffy file.[1]

---

[1]If you want to use the suppression ratio as a response measure, open a file in which Sniffy has been fully trained to bar-press on a VR schedule.

- Use the Save As command in the File menu to save the file under an appropriate new name (e.g., Ex6-CompCon) in the Sniffy Files folder on your computer's hard drive.
- Choose Design Classical Conditioning Experiment from the Experiment menu.
- In the dialog box, make the following settings:
  - Be sure that the Interval Between Trials setting is 5 minutes.
  - Set Present Each Trial Type to 10 times.
  - In the First Stimulus section of the dialog box, click on the boxes to the left of the words "Light" and "Tone" so that check marks appear in both boxes; be sure that the medium intensity is chosen for both stimuli.
  - In the Second Stimulus section of the dialog box, be sure that a check mark appears in the box to the left of the words "Shock US" and that the medium-intensity value of that stimulus is selected.
  - Carefully check to see that you have selected the correct settings.
  - In the Stage section of the dialog box, click the New Stage command button to create a new Stage 2.
  - Verify that you are now working on Stage 2, Trial Type A.
  - In the Stage section of the dialog box, set the Average Interval Between Trials to 5 minutes.
  - In the text box located to the right of Present Each Trial Type, type 1.
  - In the First Stimulus section of the dialog box, be sure that only the medium-intensity *light* CS is selected.
  - In the Second Stimulus section of the dialog box, select None.
  - Carefully check to see that you have selected the correct settings.
  - In the Trial Types section of the dialog box, click the command button labeled New Type. Verify that you are now editing Stage 2, Trial Type B.
  - In the First Stimulus section of the dialog box, be sure that only the medium-intensity *tone* CS is selected.
  - In the Second Stimulus section of the dialog box, select None.
  - Carefully check to see that you have selected the correct settings.

> □ Use the Previous Type, Next Type, Previous Stage, and Next Stage buttons to scroll around and make sure that all your settings are correct.
> □ Click the command button labeled Save at the bottom of the dialog box.
> ■ After the Experimental Design dialog box has closed, choose Run Classical Conditioning Experiment from the Experiment menu.
> ■ If you want to speed up the experiment, select the Isolate Sniffy (Accelerate Time) command from the Experiment menu.
> ■ When the experiment has finished running, save the file again.

When the program has finished executing the experiment, your Movement Ratio and CS Response Strength windows should resemble the following:

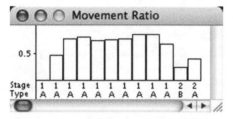

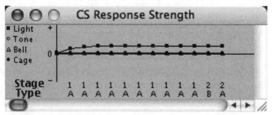

The Movement Ratio window shows that Sniffy acquired a strong CR to the compound CS over the course of the 10 Stage 1 conditioning trials. If you were running a compound conditioning experiment with real rats, these behavioral data would be the only information available to you. You would have no information about the individual response strengths of the two component CSs. However, in the Sniffy Pro program, the CS Response Strength mind window lets you see what is going on. During Stage 1, the CS Response Strength window shows that the response strengths of both the tone and the light components rise to moderate levels before leveling off. Because the two component stimuli acquire exactly equal amounts of response strength, their curves lie one on top of the other so that only a single curve is visible.

This mind window result predicts that when each of the two component CSs is presented separately during Stage 2 of the experiment, each component should produce a moderate movement ratio. The movement ratio results for Stage 2 of the experiment confirm this prediction. When presented alone, both the light and the tone elicit moderate, but not strong, CRs. In the example, the movement ratios for the light and tone CSs in Stage 2 are not exactly the same. The difference is a matter of chance. If you performed the experiment repeatedly, the differences would eventually average out.

So far we have discovered that during compound conditioning, the compound CS (both component stimuli presented together) acquires the capacity to elicit a strong CR, and each component of the compound acquires the capacity to elicit a moderate CR. This result suggests that the strong CR to the compound CS is equal to the sum of the CRs to the component CSs.

## The Compound Conditioning, Separate Pairing Control Condition

The next question is whether we will obtain the same or a different result if the two components of the compound are paired separately with the US. To find out, you will set up the control experiment in which Sniffy receives 10 trials during which the medium-intensity tone is paired with the US. These trials will be intermixed with another 10 trials during which the medium-intensity light is paired with the US.

To set up the separate pairing experiment, follow these steps:

- Start with a new Sniffy file.
- Use the Save As command in the File menu to save the file under an appropriate new name (e.g., Ex6-SepPair) in the Sniffy Files folder on your computer's hard drive.
- Choose Design Classical Conditioning Experiment from the Experiment menu.
  - Note that you are working with Stage 1, Trial Type A.
  - Ascertain that the Interval Between Trials setting is 5 minutes.
  - Set Present Each Trial Type to 10 times.
  - In the First Stimulus section of the dialog box, select the medium-intensity *light*. Make certain that the medium-intensity light is the only first stimulus selected.
  - In the Second Stimulus section of the dialog box, be sure that the medium-intensity shock US is selected.

- □ Carefully check to see that you have selected the correct settings.
- □ In the Trial Types section of the dialog box, click the New Type command button. Verify that you are now working on Stage 1, Trial Type B.
- □ In the First Stimulus section of the dialog box, be sure that only the medium-intensity *tone* is selected.
- □ In the Second Stimulus section of the dialog box, be sure that the medium-intensity shock US is selected.
- □ Carefully check your selections.
- □ In the Stage section of the dialog box, click the New Stage command button to create a new Stage 2.
- □ Make sure that the Average Interval Between Trials is set to 5 minutes.
- □ In the text box located to the right of Present Each Trial Type, type 1.
- □ Note that you are editing Stage 2, Trial Type A.
- □ In the First Stimulus section of the dialog box, select the medium-intensity *light*.
- □ In the Second Stimulus section of the dialog box, select None.
- □ Carefully check to see that you have selected the correct settings.
- □ Click the command button labeled New Type. Verify that you are now editing Stage 2, Trial Type B.
- □ In the First Stimulus section of the dialog box, be sure that only the medium-intensity *tone* CS is selected.
- □ In the Second Stimulus section of the dialog box, select None.
- □ Carefully check to see that you have selected the correct settings.
- □ Use the Previous Type, Next Type, Previous Stage, and Next Stage command buttons to scroll back and forth and make sure that *all* your settings are correct.
- □ Click the command button labeled Save at the bottom of the dialog box.
- ■ After the Experimental Design dialog box has closed, choose Run Classical Conditioning Experiment from the Experiment menu.
- ■ If you want to speed up the experiment, select the Isolate Sniffy (Accelerate Time) command from the Experiment menu. Be-

cause you will need to use this file as the starting point for Exercise 9, be alert and stop the experiment shortly after the last Stage 2 trial.
■ When the experiment has finished running, save the file again.

At the end of the compound conditioning control experiment, your results in the Movement Ratio and CS Response Strength windows should look somewhat like those that follow:

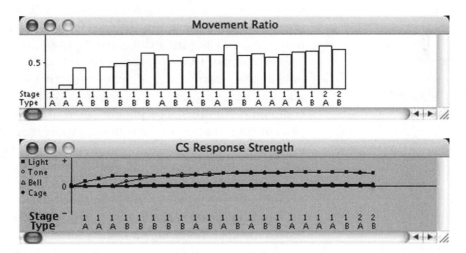

The movement ratio results show that during Stage 1, each of the CSs acquired the capacity to elicit strong suppression of Sniffy's ongoing behavior. In the CS Response Strength mind window, the acquisition curves for the two CSs mostly lie on top of each other so that only one curve is visible in most places. This curve also shows that both CSs have acquired large amounts of response strength.

During Stage 2, we see that, when presented alone, each of the two CSs elicits a strong CR. You might wonder why we include the Stage 2 test trials in this condition when we already know that each of the two CSs is eliciting a strong CR. In fact, the test trials are not absolutely essential. However, we included them to make the conditions under which the movement ratio is measured exactly equivalent for the experimental and control conditions.

The Sniffy Pro program presents trial types in random order. Hence, the order with which the trial types A and B occur during Stage 1 in your experiment will almost surely be different from the order in our example, and there's a 50% chance that the order will also be different

in Stage 2. These differences in trial type ordering will also affect the details of the CS response strength graph. These same chance effects and the randomness of Sniffy's behavior will also affect your movement ratio results.

## Exercise 7: Blocking

Exercise 6 showed that when a compound CS composed of the medium-intensity tone and medium-intensity light is paired with the US, the compound CS acquires the capacity to elicit a CR, and each component stimulus acquires the capacity to elicit moderate suppression. This is the result that psychologists normally obtain when each component of the compound is equally effective as a CS and when the animal has had no previous experience with either component of the compound stimulus. The phenomenon of blocking looks at what happens during compound conditioning trials if one of the components of the compound has already been paired with the US often enough to have acquired the capacity to elicit a strong CR.

The phenomenon of blocking is defined by the Stage 3 results of the experiment described in the following chart.[2] In other words, if you perform the two-treatment experiment that the diagram specifies and obtain the specified Stage 3 results for both experimental conditions, you have obtained the phenomenon that psychologists call **blocking.** The design for this experiment is similar to that of Kamin (1968).

| Condition | Stage 1 | Stage 2 | Stage 3 Expected Result |
|---|---|---|---|
| Blocking Experimental Condition | 10: $CS_{MT}$–$US_M$ | 10: $CS_{ML}$&$CS_{MT}$–$US_M$ | 1: $CS_{ML}$–None<br><br>$CS_{ML}$ elicits little or no CR<br><br>1: $CS_{MT}$–None<br><br>$CS_{MT}$ elicits a strong CR |
| Compound Conditioning Control | Rest | 10: $CS_{ML}$&$CS_{MT}$–$US_M$ | 1: $CS_{ML}$–None<br><br>$CS_{ML}$ elicits a moderate CR<br><br>1: $CS_{MT}$–None<br><br>$CS_{MT}$ elicits a moderate CR |

[2]In this chart, the symbols have the same meaning as those in the compound conditioning diagram given at the beginning of this chapter.

In Stage 1 of the blocking experimental condition, Sniffy receives 10 trials in which the medium-intensity tone is paired with the medium-intensity US. For the control condition, which is standard compound conditioning, Sniffy "rests" during Stage 1. In other words, Stage 1 is omitted for the control condition. In Stage 2, both conditions receive 10 standard compound conditioning trials in which the compound CS composed of the medium-intensity tone and medium-intensity light is paired with the medium-intensity US. Finally, in Stage 3, both conditions receive a compound conditioning test consisting of one presentation each of the tone and light CSs. During Stage 3, the US is omitted.

If you closely followed our suggestions when setting up Exercise 6, your compound conditioning results can be used as the blocking control condition and your original classical conditioning acquisition experiment from Exercise 1, in which the medium-intensity tone CS was paired with the medium-intensity US for 10 trials, can be used for Stage 1 of the blocking experimental condition. To set up the blocking experimental condition, follow these steps.

## Blocking Stage 1

- If you still have the file that we suggested you call Ex1-ClassAcq, open it. Choose Design Classical Conditioning Experiment from the Experiment menu, and verify that the following conditions were in effect for Stage 1:
  - □ The average Interval Between Trials was 5 minutes.
  - □ The number following Present Each Trial Type was 10.
  - □ The First Stimulus was the medium-intensity tone.
  - □ The Second Stimulus was the medium-intensity shock US.
  - □ Stage 1 is the only stage that has been run (i.e., the file that you are looking at is *not* the file in which Sniffy was subsequently extinguished in Stage 2). The file should have no stage except Stage 1. The easiest way to verify this is to look at the Next Stage command button. It should be dimmed because no Stage 2 has yet been created.
- If you have the right file, use the Save As command to save the file under an appropriate new name (e.g., Ex7-Blocking) in the Sniffy Files folder on your computer's hard drive and skip down to the next heading, "Blocking Stages 2 and 3." If you do not have your original conditioning file, go back to Exercise 1 and follow the instructions given there to create Stage 1 of the current experiment.

## Blocking Stages 2 and 3

Whether or not you had your original conditioning file, we assume that you are now working with a Sniffy file called Ex6-Blocking in which during Stage 1, Sniffy received 10 pairings of the medium-intensity tone with the medium-intensity US with an average interval between trials of 5 minutes. Follow the next series of steps to set up Stages 2 and 3 of the blocking experimental condition.

- Choose Design Classical Conditioning Experiment from the Experiment menu.
- In the dialog box, make the following settings:
  □ In the Stage section, click on the New Stage command button to create a new Stage 2 after Stage 1.
  □ Make sure that the Interval Between Trials is set at 5 minutes.
  □ Set Present Each Trial Type to 10 times.
  □ In the First Stimulus section, select *both* the medium-intensity light *and* the medium-intensity tone.
  □ In the Second Stimulus section, select the medium-intensity shock US.
  □ Check carefully to be sure that your settings are correct.
  □ Click the New Stage button to insert a new Stage 3 after Stage 2.
  □ Verify that you are now working with Stage 3, Trial Type A.
  □ Make sure that the Interval Between Trials setting is 5 minutes.
  □ Type 1 in the text box to the right of Present Each Trial Type.
  □ In the First Stimulus section of the dialog box, be sure that only the medium-intensity *light* CS is selected.
  □ In the Second Stimulus section of the dialog box, select None.
  □ Carefully check to see that you have selected the correct settings.
  □ In the Trial Types section of the dialog box, click the command button labeled New Type. Verify that you are now editing Stage 3, Trial Type B.
  □ In the First Stimulus section of the dialog box, be sure that only the medium-intensity *tone* CS is selected.
  □ In the Second Stimulus section of the dialog box, select None.

□ Carefully check to see that you have selected the correct settings.

□ Use the Previous Type, Next Type, Previous Stage, and Next Stage command buttons to scroll back and forth to make sure that *all* your settings are correct. *If you have made a mistake, NOW is the time when you want to find and correct it!*

□ Click the Save button at the bottom of the dialog box.

- Choose Run Classical Conditioning Experiment from the Experiment menu.

- If you want to speed up the experiment, select the Isolate Sniffy (Accelerate Time) command from the Experiment menu.

- When the experiment finishes running, save the file again.

At the end of the experiment, your Movement Ratio and CS Response Strength windows should resemble those shown here:

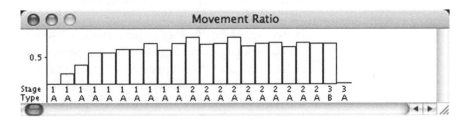

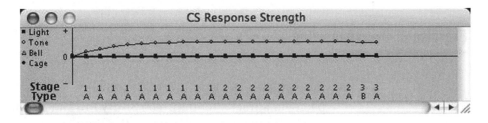

The CS Response Strength Window shows that, during Stage 1, the 10 pairings of the tone with the shock caused the tone to acquire a large amount of CS response strength. Thus, as the Movement Ratio window shows, the tone was eliciting strong fear CR by the end of Stage 1. Because of the tone's response strength, the tone–light compound already elicited a strong CR at the beginning of Stage 2, and the compound continued to elicit strong suppression of ongoing behavior throughout Stage 2. If you were a psychologist working with a real animal, the question would be: What was happening to the tone's and the light's CS response strengths during Stage 2? With a real animal, you

would not be able to tell because all you would see was that the compound of the two stimuli continued to elicit strong suppression of ongoing behavior. However, with Sniffy, we can look at the CS Response Strength mind window and observe that during Stage 2, although the tone's already high CS response strength remains high, the light acquires virtually no CS response strength. In Stage 3, this mind window result from Stage 2 is confirmed by the movement ratio results. When the tone and light are presented separately, the tone (Trial Type B) elicits a strong CR, whereas the light (Trial Type A) elicits little or no response.

Going back to the definition of blocking presented at the beginning of this exercise, we see that we have demonstrated the phenomenon. The control condition is the compound conditioning experiment from Exercise 6. As specified in the definition of blocking, when Sniffy has had no previous experience with either stimulus, 10 presentations of the compound CS composed of the medium-intensity tone and medium-intensity light paired with the medium-intensity shock produce test results in which each component stimulus elicits a moderate CR. However, if Sniffy has experienced 10 pairings of the tone with the shock before he receives the 10 compound conditioning trials, test results show that the tone elicits a strong CR but the light elicits little or no response. In other words, the previous tone–shock pairings block the light's capacity to acquire response strength during compound conditioning.

## Exercise 8: Overshadowing

The **salience** of a stimulus can be roughly defined as the stimulus's capacity to attract attention. The Sniffy Pro simulation of classical conditioning equates the salience of the light and tone CSs. For any given level of intensity, the light and the tone are equally salient and equally effective as a CS.[3] The phenomenon of **overshadowing** asks what happens during compound conditioning when the components of a compound CS are of unequal salience. For example, suppose you had a compound CS composed of a high-intensity tone and a low-intensity light. Like compound conditioning itself and blocking, overshadowing is defined by a two-treatment experimental design that can be charted as follows.

[3] An avid student might want to figure out how to compare the salience of the medium-intensity light and tone with the salience of the bell CS.

| Condition | Stage 1 | Stage 2 | Stage 2 Expected Result |
|---|---|---|---|
| Overshadowing Experimental Treatment | 10: $CS_{HT}$&$CS_{LL}$–$US_M$ | 1: $CS_{ML}$–None<br>1: $CS_{MT}$–None | $CS_{ML}$–Weak CR<br>$CS_{MT}$–Strong CR |
| Compound Conditioning Control | 10: $CS_{MT}$&$CS_{ML}$–$US_M$ | 1: $CS_{MT}$–None<br>1: $CS_{ML}$–None | $CS_{MT}$–Moderate CR<br>$CS_{ML}$–Moderate CR |

The symbols in this chart mean the same as those in the two previous charts, with two additions:

- $CS_{HT}$ means the high-intensity tone CS.
- $CS_{LL}$ means the low-intensity light CS.

Once again, the control condition is basic compound conditioning, in which Sniffy gets 10 trials in which the compound of medium-intensity light and medium-intensity tone CSs is paired with the medium-intensity US, followed by a single extinction trial each with the medium-intensity tone and the medium-intensity light. As we saw in Exercise 6, this control condition produces the Stage 2 result specified in the definition of overshadowing: Each of the component stimuli elicits a moderate CR.

In the overshadowing experimental condition, Sniffy gets 10 trials in which the compound of the high-intensity tone and low-intensity light CSs is paired with the medium-intensity US. Then in the extinction test phase of the experimental condition, we give Sniffy a single extinction trial each with the medium-intensity tone and medium-intensity light CSs. We use medium-intensity CSs during the test phase of the experimental condition to make the experimental condition's test phase exactly equivalent to the control condition's test phase.

To set up the overshadowing experimental condition, follow these steps:

- If you want to use the suppression ratio as a response measure, open a file in which Sniffy has been fully trained to bar-press on a moderate-sized VR schedule. As always, we recommend that you copy the VR-25 file located in the Sample Files folder and use it. Otherwise, start with a new Sniffy file.

- Use the Save As command to save the file under an appropriate name (e.g., Ex8–Overshadow) in the Sniffy Files folder on your computer's hard drive.
- Choose Design Classical Conditioning Experiment from the Experiment menu.
- In the dialog box, make the following settings:
  - In the Stage section, make sure that the Interval Between Trials is set at 5 minutes.
  - Set Present Each Trial Type to 10 times.
  - In the First Stimulus section, select both the *low*-intensity light and the *high*-intensity tone.
  - In the Second Stimulus section, select the medium-intensity US.
  - Check carefully to be sure that your settings are correct.
- In the Stage section, click on New Stage to create a new Stage 2 and insert it after Stage 1.
- Ascertain that Interval Between Trials is set to 5 minutes.
- Set Present Each Trial Type to 1 time.
- Note that you are working on Stage 2, Trial Type A.
- Under First Stimulus, select the *medium-intensity light* and be sure that it is the only First Stimulus selected.
- Under Second Stimulus, select None.
- Carefully check your settings.
- In the Trial Type section, click on New Type.
- Note that you are now working on Stage 2, Trial Type B.
- Under First Stimulus, select the *medium-intensity tone* and be sure that it is the only First Stimulus selected.
- Under Second Stimulus, select None.
- Carefully check your settings.
- Use the Previous Type, Next Type, Previous Stage, and Next Stage command buttons to scroll back and forth and carefully check everything. *If you have made a mistake, now is the time to find it!*
- At the bottom of the dialog box, click on Save.
- Select Run Classical Conditioning Experiment from the Experiment menu.
- If you want to speed up the experiment, select the Isolate Sniffy (Accelerate Time) command from the Experiment menu.
- When the experiment finishes running, save the file again.

Your Movement Ratio and CS Response Strength windows should resemble those shown below:

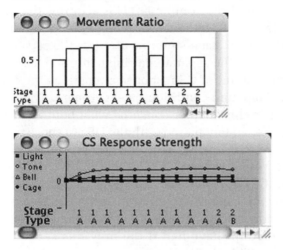

During Stage 1, the Movement Ratio window shows that the compound CS steadily acquires the capacity to elicit freezing as a CR. At the end of Stage 1, the compound is evoking a strong CR. Remember that these are the only data that would be available if you were working with a real rat. However, once again, the CS Response Strength mind window provides interesting information about Sniffy's psychological processes. It reveals that when the salience of two component CSs differs, the amount of CS response strength that the components develop also differs. The high-intensity tone CS develops more CS response strength than the low-intensity light CS. The Stage 2 movement ratio results confirm the predictions from the CS Response Strength mind window. The tone CS (Trial Type B) elicits a strong CR, but the light CS (Trial Type A) has little effect. Finally, going back to the definition of overshadowing, we note that the Stage 2 behavioral results for the experimental condition, when compared to the Stage 2 results for the compound conditioning control, enable us to conclude that we have demonstrated the phenomenon of overshadowing.

## Exercise 9: Overexpectation

In the first exercise in this chapter (Exercise 6), we compared compound conditioning with a separate pairing control condition. We

found that when two CSs occur together in a compound paired with a US, the compound stimulus attains the capacity to elicit a strong CR, but each of the component CSs acquires the capacity to elicit only a moderate CR. In contrast, when two CSs are each separately paired with the US, each stimulus acquires the capacity to elicit a strong CR. Indeed, in the separate pairing condition, each CS acquires about the same amount of CS response strength as the compound CS attains in the compound conditioning experiment. The last question that we address in this chapter concerns what happens when two CSs that have been separately paired with the US are subsequently placed together in a compound paired with the US. Does each component CS retain its high response strength? Or does the response strength of the component CSs decline? The answer is that, although the compound CS retains the capacity to elicit a strong CR, the response strength of the component CSs declines to approximately the level that each component would have had if the previous separate pairings had not occurred. This decline in the response strength of the component CSs is called the **overexpectation effect.**

The single condition of the experiment can be charted as follows:

| Stage 1 | Stage 2 | Stage 3 | Stage 4 | Stage 4 Expected Result |
|---|---|---|---|---|
| 10: $CS_{MT}$–$US_M$ | 1: $CS_{MT}$–None | 10: $CS_{ML}$&$CS_{MT}$–$US_M$ | 1: $CS_{ML}$–None | $CS_{ML}$–Moderate CR |
| 10: $CS_{ML}$–$US_M$ | 1: $CS_{ML}$–None | | 1: $CS_{MT}$–None | $CS_{MT}$–Moderate CR |

In Stage 1, Sniffy receives a total of 20 trials, 10 with the medium-intensity light paired with the medium-intensity shock and 10 with the medium-intensity tone paired with the medium-intensity shock. In Stage 2, we present single extinction test trials to determine the strength of the CR to the light and tone CSs presented by themselves. In Stage 3, the compound of the medium-intensity light and medium-intensity tone is paired with the medium-intensity shock. Finally, in Stage 4, we once again provide single extinction test trials to determine the strength of the CR to the light and tone CSs presented singly. The first two stages of the experiment are the same as the separate pairing control condition from Exercise 6. Thus, you will start out with that file and add the last two stages. Here are the detailed instructions:

■ Open the separate pairing control file that we suggested you call Ex6-SepPair in Exercise 6.

- Use the Save As command to save the file under a new name (e.g., Ex9-OE) in the Sniffy Files folder on your computer's hard drive.
- Choose the Design Classical Conditioning Experiment command from the Experiment menu.
- Make the following settings in the dialog box:
  - Note that the dialog box opens to Stage 1, with all settings dimmed because Stage 1 has already been run.
  - Click the Next Stage command button to move to Stage 2, which has also already been run.
  - Click the New Stage command button to create a new Stage 3.
  - Make sure that Average Interval Between Trials is set at 5 minutes.
  - Set Present Each Trial Type to 10 times.
  - In the First Stimulus section of the dialog box, select both the medium-intensity tone and the medium-intensity light CSs.
  - In the Second Stimulus section of the dialog box, select the medium-intensity shock US.
  - Carefully check your Stage 3 settings.
  - Click the New Stage command button to create a new Stage 4.
  - Verify that the Average Interval Between Trials is set at 5 minutes and that Present Each Trial Type is set at 1 time.
  - Note that you are currently editing Stage 4, Trial Type A.
  - In the First Stimulus section of the dialog box, select the medium-intensity *light*.
  - In the Second Stimulus section of the dialog box, select None.
  - Carefully check to see that you have selected the correct settings.
  - In the Trial Types section of the dialog box, click the command button labeled New Type. You are now editing Stage 4, Trial Type B.
  - In the First Stimulus section of the dialog box, be sure that only the medium-intensity *tone* CS is selected.
  - In the Second Stimulus section of the dialog box, select None.
  - Carefully check to see that you have selected the correct settings.

> □ Use the Previous Type, Next Type, Previous Stage, and Next
>   Stage command buttons to scroll back and forth and make
>   sure that *all* your settings are correct.
> □ Click the command button labeled Save at the bottom of the
>   dialog box.
> ■ After the Experimental Design Dialog box has closed, choose
>   Run Classical Conditioning Experiment from the Experiment
>   menu.
> ■ If you want to speed up the experiment, select the Isolate Sniffy
>   (Accelerate Time) command from the Experiment menu.
> ■ When the experiment has finished running, save the file again.

Your Movement Ratio and CS Response Strength windows should
resemble those shown below:

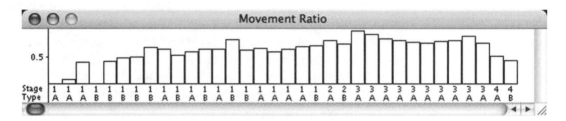

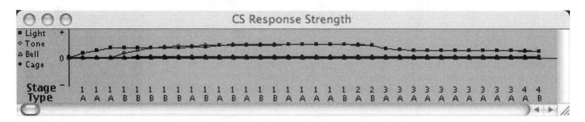

The Stage 3 movement ratio results show that Sniffy manifested a
strong fear-related freezing CR to the compound CS throughout the
stage. Remember that these behavioral results would be all the information available to you if you were studying a real rat. However, at the
same time, the CS Response Strength mind window reveals that the CS
response strength of each of the two CSs comprising the compound declined during the early Stage 3 trials. This drop in the CS response
strength predicts that Sniffy should manifest a moderate CR to the light
and tone CSs when they are tested individually during Stage 4. The
Stage 4 movement ratio results confirm this prediction.

## Summary

We can summarize the results of this chapter's four exercises as follows:

- When two novel CSs of equal salience are presented in a compound paired with the US, the compound CS acquires the capacity to elicit a strong CR, and each of the component stimuli acquires the capacity to elicit a moderate CR.
- When one of the CSs in a compound has previously been paired with the US, the novel member of the compound acquires little capacity to elicit a CR. This phenomenon is called *blocking.*
- When the two components of a compound CS are of unequal salience, the more salient component acquires a greater capacity to elicit a CR than the less salient component. This phenomenon is called *overshadowing.*
- When two CSs that have been separately paired with a US are subsequently placed together in a compound paired with the US, the response strength of each of the component CSs declines to approximately the level that it would have shown if the compound–US pairings had been the only pairings that occurred. Thus, compound conditioning erases the effect of previous separate pairings. This phenomenon is called the *overexpectation effect.*

## Some Questions

- The movement ratio results that you obtain when you do the exercises in this chapter probably will not look exactly like the results shown in the manual. At least two kinds of differences will occur. What are they? What accounts for them?
- The exercises on compound conditioning, blocking, and overshadowing involve comparisons between experimental and control conditions. What is the role of the control conditions in these exercises? Why are the control conditions needed?
- Why does the exercise on overexpectation *not* require a control condition?
- What is the difference between overshadowing and blocking?
- In what way is compound conditioning the basis for understanding both blocking and overshadowing?

## Something to Do

You might be interested in the results you get when you try some variations of the overexpectation experiment.

- Repeat the experiment using the high-intensity shock in Stages 1 and 3.
- Now try using the low-intensity shock in Stages 1 and 3.
- How do the results in Stage 4 compare with those obtained when the medium-intensity shock is employed in Stages 1 and 3?

# 5

## Inhibitory Conditioning

All the phenomena of classical conditioning that we have examined so far exemplify forms of **excitatory conditioning.** In excitatory conditioning, a CS is paired with a US, with the result that the CS acquires the capacity to elicit a CR. In the case of the CER with electric shock as the US, the CS comes to elicit freezing and the suppression of ongoing behavior as a CR. Another way of thinking about excitatory conditioning is that when a US regularly follows a CS, the CS comes to act as a "signal" that the US is going to occur. Conditioning in which a CS acquires the capacity to elicit a CR is called excitatory conditioning because the verbs *excite* and *elicit* are (more or less) synonymous.

In contrast, with **inhibitory conditioning,** a CS comes to act as a "signal" that a US that might otherwise be expected is *not* going occur. As a consequence, when presented by itself, an inhibitory CS elicits no CR. Moreover, when an inhibitory CS occurs in a compound with an excitatory CS, the inhibitory CS prevents or reduces the magnitude of the CR that the excitatory CS would otherwise elicit.

To set up a situation in which a CS signals that an otherwise expected US will not occur, we can give Sniffy some training with two trial types. In the first trial type, occurrences of the light CS (by itself) are followed by the shock US. As a consequence of this training, Sniffy will learn to show a CR (and thus manifest freezing) when the light occurs by itself. In the second trial type, occurrences of the light as part of a compound CS with the tone are not followed by shock. Because the tone is now acting as a signal that the shock that might otherwise be expected to follow the light will not occur, the tone becomes an inhibitory CS.

This situation is somewhat analogous to a scenario that occasionally arises at a traffic intersection. As a result of training, drivers learn both to obey traffic lights and to follow the instructions of police officers.

Ordinarily, when a traffic light is red, drivers stop. However, if a police officer is directing traffic and signals motorists to drive through a red light, the officer's signal inhibits the motorists' stopping responses that would otherwise occur.

Because inhibitory CSs elicit no CRs when presented by themselves, measuring inhibitory conditioning can be a bit tricky. Unless you are careful about how you design the experiment, the nonoccurrence of CRs as a consequence of inhibitory conditioning might be confused with non-occurrences of CRs that are the result of either a lack of training or extinction. To demonstrate inhibitory conditioning unambiguously, you need to show clearly that inhibitory conditioning produces certain expected effects on excitatory conditioning. In other words, inhibitory conditioning must always be measured against a background of excitatory conditioning. The two exercises in this chapter show you two simple ways that Pavlov (1927) described to demonstrate inhibitory conditioning.

## Exercise 10: Prior Inhibitory Conditioning Slows Excitatory Conditioning

In the first exercise, you will compare (1) the speed with which Sniffy learns an excitatory CR to the medium-intensity tone after the tone has been made inhibitory with (2) the speed with which he learns an excitatory CR to the same tone when the tone has not previously been made inhibitory. The following chart outlines the two experimental conditions:

| Condition | Stage 1 | Stage 2 | Stage 2 Expected Result |
|-----------|---------|---------|-------------------------|
| Experimental | 10: $CS_{ML}$–$US_M$<br>10: $CS_{MT}$&$CS_{ML}$–None | 10: $CS_{MT}$–$US_M$ | Slow conditioning |
| Control | Rest | 10: $CS_{MT}$–$US_M$ | Faster conditioning |

The experimental condition involves a two-stage experiment. In Stage 1, Sniffy receives 10 trials in which the medium-intensity light CS is paired with the medium-intensity shock, intermixed with 10 trials during which Sniffy receives the compound of the medium-intensity light and medium-intensity tone without the US. Because the shock follows occurrences of the light by itself, the light will become

an excitatory CS that elicits freezing. At the same time, because the shock does not follow occurrences of the light-and-tone compound, the tone will become an inhibitory CS that prevents the occurrence of the fear-related freezing CR that would ordinarily occur when the light is presented. Then in Stage 2, Sniffy receives 10 trials in which medium-intensity tone is paired with the medium-intensity shock. Because the US now follows occurrences of the tone, the Stage 2 training will make the tone excitatory—that is, capable of eliciting freezing. However, because the Stage 1 training made the tone inhibitory, during Stage 2 Sniffy must unlearn the inhibitory conditioning before the tone can become excitatory. This unlearning process should slow down acquisition of a CR to the tone.

Of course, when we say that prior inhibitory conditioning will slow down acquisition of excitatory conditioning, we need something with which we can make a comparison. That's where the control condition comes in. In the control condition, Sniffy receives 10 trials during which the medium-intensity tone CS is paired with the medium-intensity shock without any previous inhibitory training. If Sniffy learns a CR to the tone more slowly in Stage 2 of the experimental condition than in the control condition, you will have demonstrated a predicted behavioral effect of inhibitory conditioning and thus will have obtained behavioral evidence that inhibitory conditioning occurred in Stage 1 of the experimental condition.

## Setting Up the Experimental Condition

To set up the experimental condition, follow these steps:

- Start with a new Sniffy file.
- Use the Save As command to save the file under an appropriate new name (e.g., Ex10-Inhibitory 1) in the Sniffy Files folder on your computer's hard drive.
- Choose Design Classical Conditioning Experiment from the Experiment menu. In the Classical Conditioning Experimental Design dialog box, make the following settings:
  - □ Ascertain that the Interval Between Trials is set at 5 minutes.
  - □ Set Present Each Trial Type to 10 times.
  - □ Note that you are currently editing Stage 1, Trial Type A.
  - □ Select the medium-intensity light as the First Stimulus, and be sure that it is the only First Stimulus selected.

- □ Select the medium-intensity shock US as the Second Stimulus.
- □ Carefully check your settings.
- □ Click on New Type.
- □ Verify that you are now working on Stage 1, Trial Type B.
- □ Select both the medium-intensity light and the medium-intensity tone in the First Stimulus section of the dialog box.
- □ Select None as the Second Stimulus.
- □ Carefully check your settings.
- □ Click on New Stage to create and move to a new Stage 2.
- □ Verify that you are now editing Stage 2, Trial Type A.
- □ Be sure that the Interval Between Trials is set at 5 minutes.
- □ Set Present Each Trial Type to 10 times.
- □ In the First Stimulus section of the dialog box, select the medium-intensity tone, and be sure that it is the only First Stimulus selected.
- □ In the Second Stimulus section, select the medium-intensity shock US.
- □ Carefully check your settings.
- □ Use the Previous Type, Next Type, Previous Stage, and Next Stage buttons to scroll around and carefully check all your settings.
- □ Click Save.
- ■ After the dialog box closes, choose Run Classical Conditioning Experiment from the Experiment menu.
- ■ If you want to speed up the experiment, select the Isolate Sniffy (Accelerate Time) command from the Experiment menu.
- ■ When the experiment finishes running, save the file.

## Setting Up the Control Condition

The control condition in which the medium-intensity tone is paired with the medium-intensity US during 10 conditioning trials is identical to Exercise 1 in Chapter 3. If you still have the file from that exercise (we recommended that you call it Ex1-ClassAcq), you can reuse it here. If not, you should go back and redo Exercise 1.

## Examining the Results

Your Movement Ratio and CS Response Strength windows for the Experimental Condition should resemble the following:

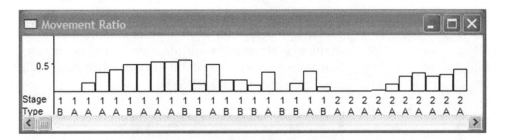

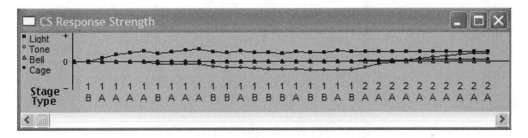

When examining the Stage 1 movement ratio results, you need to look at the Type A and Type B trials separately. Remember that the Type A trials are those in which the light is paired with the shock US, and the Type B trials are the ones in which the light–tone compound occurred without the US. Because the two kinds of trials occur in a different random order each time the experiment is run, your results will not be exactly like those shown. However, as Stage 1 progresses, your Type A trials should show an overall trend toward higher movement ratios, and that trend should not be apparent in your Type B trials. Depending on the random ordering of Type A and Type B trials in your experiment, you may see either no trend at all in the movement ratio results for the Type B trials or a trend for the Type B movement ratios to decrease. In any case, by the end of Stage 1, you should be seeing higher average movement ratios on the Type A than on the Type B trials. During Stage 1, the CS Response Strength window shows that the light CS is acquiring excitatory (above zero) response strength while the tone CS acquires inhibitory (below zero) response strength.

Of course, if you were working with a real rat whose psychological processes are invisible, Stage 1 would not provide a convincing demonstration of inhibitory conditioning because the only data at hand would be the movement (or suppression) ratios. To demonstrate clearly that the tone has become inhibitory on the basis of behavioral data, you would need to show that the events of Stage 1 make it more difficult to condition an excitatory response to the tone during Stage 2 of the experimental condition than would have been the case if Stage 1 had not occurred. Our excitatory conditioning results for the control condition are shown next:

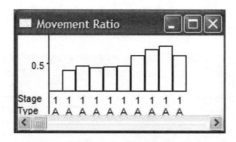

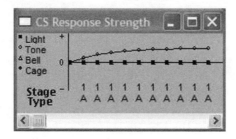

When you compare the movement ratio results from the control condition with the movement ratio results from in Stage 2 of the experimental condition, it is apparent that the predicted difference occurs. The excitatory CR to the tone is in fact acquired more slowly and less completely in Stage 2 of experimental condition than in the control condition. Comparing the CS response strength results for the two conditions reveals why this is so. The CS response strength results for Stage 2 of the experimental condition show that the excitatory CR to the tone is acquired slowly because several tone–shock pairings are required to overcome the inhibitory conditioning that the tone had previously acquired during Stage 1. In contrast, conditioned fear is acquired faster in the control condition because the CS response strength starts out at zero and not at a negative inhibitory value.

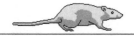

# Exercise 11: Inhibitory Conditioning Measured by Response Summation

In this exercise, you will show that an inhibitory CS not only inhibits responding to the CS with which it originally occurred in a compound; an inhibitory CS can also inhibit responding to another excitatory CS with which it has never previously occurred in a compound. The experimental design is charted next. In the chart, we introduce a new abbreviation: $CS_B$ means the bell CS.

| Stage 1 | Stage 2 | Stage 2 Expected Results |
|---|---|---|
| 10: $CS_{ML}$–$US_M$ | 1: $CS_B$–None | $CS_B$ elicits strong CER |
| 10: $CS_{MT}$&$CS_{ML}$–None | 1: $CS_{MT}$&$CS_B$–None | $CS_{MT}$&$CS_B$ elicits weak CER |
| 10: $CS_B$–$US_M$ | | |

The experiment involves two stages, with three trial types in Stage 1. The first two Stage 1 trial types are the same as in the previous exercise's experimental condition. There are 10 trials during which the medium-intensity light is paired with the medium-intensity shock, intermixed with 10 trials during which the medium-intensity light and medium-intensity tone occur in a compound without the shock. However, in this experiment, there is also a third trial type in which the bell is paired with the medium-intensity shock. Thus, Stage 1 involves a total of 30 trials, 10 for each of the three trial types. During Stage 1, both the light and the bell should come to elicit excitatory CRs because they are paired with the shock, and the tone should acquire the capacity to inhibit CRs to the light because on trials when the tone occurs in a compound with the light, no shocks occur. Then in Stage 2, we test the response-inhibiting power of the tone by presenting the bell by itself and in a compound with the tone. Because the bell is an excitatory stimulus, it should elicit a strong CR when presented alone. However, when the tone and bell occur together for the first time in a compound, the inhibitory power of the tone CS should prevent or greatly reduce expression of the CR that the bell would otherwise elicit. When the bell–tone compound is presented, we should see little or no suppression of Sniffy's ongoing behavior.

Here are the steps you need to follow to set up the experiment:

- Start with an new Sniffy file.

- Use the Save As command to save the file under a new appropriate name (e.g., Ex11-Inhibitory 2) in the Sniffy Files folder on your computer's hard drive.
- Choose Design Classical Conditioning Experiment from the Experiment menu.
- In the Classical Conditioning Experimental Design dialog box, make the following settings:
  - □ Make sure that the Average Interval Between Trials is set to 5 minutes.
  - □ Set Present Each Trial Type to 10 times.
  - □ Note that you are currently editing Stage 1, Trial Type A.
  - □ Select the medium-intensity light as the First Stimulus, and be sure that it is the only First Stimulus selected.
  - □ Select the medium-intensity shock US as the Second Stimulus. Carefully check your settings.
  - □ Click on New Type.
  - □ Verify that you are now working on Stage 1, Trial Type B.
  - □ Select both the medium-intensity light and the medium-intensity tone in the First Stimulus section of the dialog box.
  - □ Select None as the Second Stimulus. Carefully check your settings.
  - □ Click on New Type.
  - □ Verify that you are now working on Stage 1, Trial Type C.
  - □ Select the bell in the First Stimulus section of the dialog box, and be sure that it is the only First Stimulus selected.
  - □ Select the medium-intensity shock as the Second Stimulus.
  - □ Carefully check your settings.
  - □ Click on New Stage to create and move to a new Stage 2.
  - □ Verify that you are now editing Stage 2, Trial Type A.
  - □ Set the Average Interval Between Trials to 5 minutes.
  - □ Set Present Each Trial Type to 1 time.
  - □ In the First Stimulus section of the dialog box, select the bell, and make sure that it is the only First Stimulus selected.
  - □ In the Second Stimulus section, select None. Carefully check your settings.
  - □ Click on New Type.
  - □ Verify that you are now working on Stage 2, Trial Type B.
  - □ In the First Stimulus section of the dialog box, select both the bell and the medium-intensity tone.
  - □ In the Second Stimulus section, select None. Carefully check your settings.

□ Use the Previous Type, Next Type, Previous Stage, and Next Stage buttons to scroll around and carefully check all your settings.

□ Click Save.

■ When the Design Classical Conditioning Experiment dialog box disappears, select the Run Classical Conditioning Experiment command from the Experiment menu.

■ If you want to speed up the experiment, select the Isolate Sniffy (Accelerate Time) command from the Experiment menu.

■ When the experiment finishes running, save the file.

At the end of the experiment, your Movement Ratio and CS Response Strength windows should look something like those shown next:

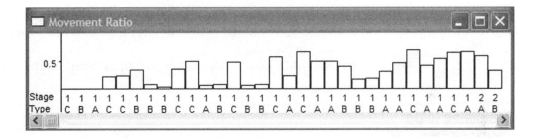

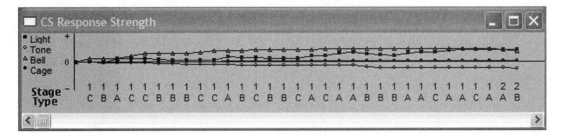

In this experiment, you once again need to examine the movement ratio results for each trial type separately. Remember that during Stage 1, the Type A trials are those in which the light is paired with the shock, the Type B trials are those in which the tone–light compound occurs without the shock, and the Type C trials are those in which the bell is paired with the shock. Because the Type A, B, and C trials occur in different random orders each time the experiment is run, your results will look somewhat different from those shown. However, during Stage 1, you should observe trends toward larger movement ratios in

both the Type A and Type C trials; this trend should not be apparent in the Type B trials. At the very least, by the end of Stage 1, you should be seeing larger average movement ratios on Type A and C trials than on Type B trials.

During Stage 2, the Type A trial was the one in which the bell was presented by itself; and the Type B trial was the crucial test in which for the first time the inhibitory tone CS was presented in a compound with the bell. During Stage 2, the movement ratio on the Type A trial should be higher than that on the Type B trial. Throughout the course of the experiment, the CS Response Strength mind window should show that Sniffy is acquiring excitatory response strength to the light and bell and inhibitory response strength to the tone.

## Some Questions

- Compare and contrast the behavioral effects of inhibitory conditioning and extinction.
- How is inhibitory conditioning related to compound conditioning?

## Something to Do

- Examine how manipulating the intensity of the lights and tones employed in Exercise 11 affects the manifestation of inhibitory conditioning.

# 6

## Associative Structures in Classical Conditioning: Sensory Preconditioning and Higher-Order Conditioning

## Background

So far, we have examined conditioning phenomena in which associations are established as a consequence of pairing one or more CSs with the shock US. Another name for conditioning in which one or more CSs are paired with a US is **first-order conditioning.** The phenomena of sensory preconditioning and higher-order conditioning, which we will define shortly, show that learning also occurs as a result of pairing two CSs.

As we noted in Chapter 2, one difference between a CS and a US is that a US initially elicits an obvious, easy-to-measure response called the unconditioned response (UR), whereas a CS initially elicits a much less obvious response called an orienting response (OR). In fact, ORs are so inconspicuous that psychologists usually do not try to measure them. When a CS is paired with a US, the CS acquires the capacity to elicit a new learned response, called a conditioned response (CR). Because the CR and UR typically resemble each other, the CR is also an obvious, easy-to-measure response. In fact, the main practical advantage of pairing a CS with a US is the obviousness of the resulting CR, whose occurrence demonstrates that the animal has learned an association.

In contrast, if all you do is to pair two CSs, nothing obvious happens. The animal does not respond in an apparent way to either stimulus; and you thus have no behavioral evidence that any learning has occurred. Sensory preconditioning and higher-order conditioning are two procedures for overcoming this problem of showing that pairing CSs results in learning.

In ordinary first-order classical conditioning, the CS acquires the capacity to elicit a CR *because* the CS precedes the US. Imagine that we are pairing two CSs (for example, a light and a tone) in a sequence so that one CS regularly precedes the other. Let's call the CS that comes first $CS_1$ and the CS that comes second $CS_2$. When $CS_1$ and $CS_2$ are paired in sequence, $CS_2$ is playing the role of the US in ordinary classical conditioning. When two CSs are paired, the reason why $CS_1$ ordinarily fails to acquire an obvious CR is that $CS_2$ elicits no obvious "UR." If $CS_2$ could somehow be made to elicit an obvious, easy-to-measure response and if learning occurs when $CS_1$ and $CS_2$ are paired, then $CS_1$ should also come to elicit an obvious response that would probably resemble the response to $CS_2$.

A simple way to get $CS_2$ to elicit an easy-to-measure response is to condition an easy-to-measure CR to $CS_2$ by pairing $CS_2$ with a US. Interestingly, it doesn't matter very much whether the conditioning of a CR to $CS_2$ occurs before or after $CS_1$ and $CS_2$ are paired. Both orderings work. However, psychologists have given the resulting behavioral phenomena different names. If $CS_1$ and $CS_2$ are paired *before* a CR is conditioned to $CS_2$, psychologists call the resulting behavioral phenomenon in which $CS_1$ acquires the capacity to elicit a CR **sensory preconditioning.** If $CS_1$ and $CS_2$ are paired *after* a CR is conditioned to $CS_2$, psychologists call the resulting behavioral phenomenon in which $CS_1$ comes to elicit a CR **higher-order conditioning.**

## Exercise 12: Sensory Preconditioning

The following chart outlines a two-condition experiment for demonstrating sensory preconditioning:

| Condition | Stage 1 | Stage 2 | Stage 3 | Stage 3 Expected Result |
|---|---|---|---|---|
| Experimental | 5: $CS_{ML}$–$CS_{MT}$ | 10: $CS_{MT}$–$US_M$ | 3: $CS_{ML}$–None | $CS_{ML}$ elicits a CR |
| Unpaired Control | 5: $CS_{ML}$–None  5: $CS_{MT}$–None | 10: $CS_{MT}$–$US_M$ | 3: $CS_{ML}$–None | $CS_{ML}$ elicits no CR |

In the experimental condition, the medium-intensity light ($CS_1$) precedes the medium-intensity tone ($CS_2$) during 5 Stage 1 trials, then the medium-intensity tone ($CS_2$) is paired with the medium-intensity

shock US 10 times in Stage 2, and finally we test by presenting the medium-intensity light ($CS_1$) during 3 extinction trials in Stage 3. Because the light ($CS_1$) precedes the tone ($CS_2$) in Stage 1 and the tone ($CS_2$) precedes the shock in Stage 2, we expect the light ($CS_1$) to elicit a CR in Stage 3.

Sensory preconditioning is the first phenomenon in which we need to consider the type of association that Sniffy is learning. We will discuss the nature of the association learned in classical conditioning much more fully in Chapter 7. Here we simply note that a stimulus–response (S–R) association is one in which the first stimulus (CS) becomes associated with the response to the second stimulus. If the second stimulus is a US, the first stimulus becomes associated with the UR. If the second stimulus is a CS used as a US, then the first stimulus becomes associated with the OR or the CR elicited by the CS used as a US. In contrast, a stimulus–stimulus (S–S) association is one in which the first stimulus (CS) becomes associated with the second stimulus. In sensory preconditioning, we pair the light with the tone before conditioning a CR to the tone by pairing the tone with shock. Because the tone does not elicit an obvious CR during Stage 1 when the tone is used as the second stimulus in the series of light–tone pairings, Sniffy must learn an S–S association in order for any behaviorally measurable learning to occur.

The control condition is designed to show that the light–tone pairings in Stage 1 are crucial. The unpaired control, in which the tone and light occur unpaired in Stage 1, shows that the $CS_1$ and $CS_2$ must be paired for sensory preconditioning to occur. To equate the conditions under which learning occurs in the experimental and control conditions, we will use the same association model in both the experimental and the control conditions.

## The Experimental Condition

To set up the experimental condition, you should follow these steps:

- Start with a new Sniffy file.
- Use the Save As command located under the File menu to save the file under an appropriate new name (e.g., Ex12-SPC) in the Sniffy Files folder on your computer's hard drive.
- Choose the Change Nature of the Association command from the Experiment menu. In the dialog box that appears, select the

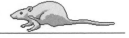

S–S association for CS used as US and click the OK command button at the bottom of the dialog box.

- Choose Design Classical Conditioning Experiment from the Experiment menu.
- Make the following settings in the Classical Conditioning Experimental Design dialog box:
  - In the Stage section of the dialog box, make certain that the Interval Between Trials is set to 5 minutes.
  - Set Present Each Trial Type to 5 times.
  - In the First Stimulus section of the dialog box, select the medium-intensity light.
  - In the Second Stimulus section of the dialog box, select the medium-intensity tone as the CS used as US.
  - Carefully check your settings.
  - Click the New Stage command button, and verify that you are now editing Stage 2, Trial Type A.
  - Ascertain that the Interval Between Trials is set at 5 minutes.
  - Set Present Each Trial Type to 10 times.
  - In the First Stimulus section of the dialog box, select the medium-intensity tone.
  - In the Second Stimulus section of the dialog box, select the medium-intensity shock US.
  - Carefully check your settings.
  - In the Stage section of the dialog box, click the New Stage command button to create a new Stage 3, and verify that you are now editing Stage 3, Trial Type A.
  - Be sure that the Interval Between Trials is set to 5 minutes.
  - Set Present Each Trial Type to 3 times.
  - In the First Stimulus section of the dialog box, select the medium-intensity light.
  - In the Second Stimulus section of the dialog box, select None.
  - Carefully check your settings.
  - Use the Previous Stage and Next Stage buttons to scroll around and be sure that all your settings are correct.
  - Click the Save command button at the bottom of the dialog box.
- After the dialog box closes, execute the Run Classical Conditioning Experiment command in the Experiment menu.
- If you want to speed up the experiment, select the Isolate Sniffy (Accelerate Time) command from the Experiment menu.
- When the experiment has finished running, save the file again.

When the experiment is completed, your Movement Ratio window and CS Response Strength mind window should resemble the following:

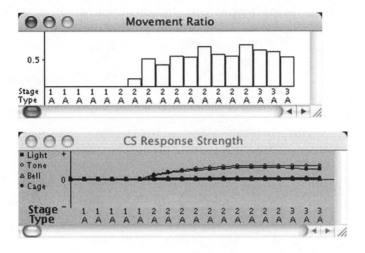

The Movement Ratio window shows that the light acquires no capacity to elicit a CR during Stage 1, that the tone acquires the capacity to elicit a CER in Stage 2, and that the light elicits a CR in the Stage 3 test trials. The fact that the light does not elicit a CR in Stage 1 but does do so in Stage 3 supports the idea that sensory preconditioning has occurred. The CS Response Strength mind window clarifies the learning process that enables the light to elicit a CR in Stage 3. The mind window shows that the light acquires no CS response strength during Stage 1. However, the interesting thing is that the light's CS response strength increases during Stage 2, even though the light is not being presented during that stage. The light's CS response strength (its potential ability to elicit a CER) increases during Stage 2 because Sniffy learned the tone–light S–S association during Stage 1. Because of this Stage 1 learning, the light's capacity to elicit a CR increases in parallel with the tone's capacity to elicit a CR during Stage 2.

## The Unpaired Control Condition

To set up the unpaired control condition, you should follow these steps:

- Start with a new Sniffy file.
- Use the Save As command located under the File menu to save the file under an appropriate new name (e.g., Ex13-SPCUPC, for

"sensory preconditioning unpaired control") in the Sniffy Files folder on your computer's hard drive.

- Choose Change Nature of the Association from the Experiment menu. In the dialog box that appears, select the S–S association for CS used as US and click the OK command button at the bottom of the dialog box.
- Choose Design Classical Conditioning Experiment from the Experiment menu.
- Make the following settings in the Classical Conditioning Experimental Design dialog box:
  - Make sure that the Interval Between Trials is set to 5 minutes.
  - Set Present Each Trial Type to 5 times.
  - In the First Stimulus section of the dialog box, select the medium-intensity light CS.
  - In the Second Stimulus section of the dialog box, select None.
  - Carefully check your settings.
  - Click the New Type command button and verify that you are now editing Stage 1, Trial Type B.
  - In the First Stimulus section of the dialog box, select the medium-intensity tone CS.
  - In the Second Stimulus section of the dialog box, select None.
  - Carefully check your settings.
  - In the Stage section of the dialog box, click the New Stage command button to create a new Stage 2, and verify that you are now editing Stage 2, Trial Type A.
  - Make sure that the Interval Between Trials is set to 5 minutes.
  - Set Present Each Trial Type to 10 times.
  - In the First Stimulus section of the dialog box, select the medium-intensity tone.
  - In the Second Stimulus section of the dialog box, select the medium-intensity shock US.
  - Carefully check your settings.
  - In the Stage section of the dialog box, click the New Stage command button and verify that you are now editing Stage 3, Trial Type A.
  - Ascertain that the Interval Between Trials is set at 5 minutes.
  - Set Present Each Trial Type to 3 times.

> - In the First Stimulus section of the dialog box, select the medium-intensity light CS.
> - In the Second Stimulus section of the dialog box, select None.
> - Carefully check your settings.
> - Use the Previous Stage, Next Stage, Previous Type, and Next Type buttons to scroll around and be sure that all your settings are correct.
> - Click the Save command button at the bottom of the dialog box.
> - After the dialog box closes, execute the Run Classical Conditioning Experiment command in the Experiment menu.
> - If you want to speed up the experiment, select the Isolate Sniffy (Accelerate Time) command from the Experiment menu.
> - When the experiment has finished running, save the file again.

At the end of the experiment, your Movement Ratio and CS Response Strength windows should resemble the following:

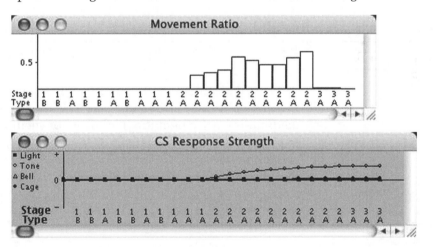

During Stage 1, when the tone and light are presented separately without a second stimulus, neither stimulus acquires any capacity to suppress ongoing behavior. When the tone is paired with shock during Stage 2, the tone acquires the capacity to elicit a CER. During the Stage 3 test trials, the light elicits no response. The CS Response Strength window shows that the light failed to elicit a CER during Stage 3 because the light acquired no CS response strength at any stage of the experiment. This is the result that we expect because the light and tone were never paired.

When the results from the sensory preconditioning experimental condition are combined with the results from the control condition, we see that the operational definition of sensory preconditioning has been fulfilled. In the experimental condition, the light–tone event sequence causes the light to acquire the capacity to "predict" the tone. In that case, when the tone is subsequently paired with shock, both the light and the tone acquire the capacity to elicit a CR. The control condition demonstrates that the light–tone pairings during Stage 1 are critical. If the two stimuli are unpaired during Stage 1, the light does not acquire the capacity to "predict" the tone. Unless the light "predicts" the tone, pairing the tone with shock fails to impart to the light any capacity to elicit a CR.

## Exercise 13: Higher-Order Conditioning

The following chart outlines an experiment that demonstrates higher-order conditioning:

| Stage 1 | Stage 2 | Stage 3 | Stage 3 Expected Result |
|---|---|---|---|
| 10: $CS_{MT}$–$US_M$ | 5: $CS_{ML}$–$CS_{MT}$ | 3: $CS_{ML}$–None | $CS_{ML}$ elicits a CR |

The medium-intensity tone ($CS_2$) is paired with the medium-intensity shock 10 times in Stage 1. Then the stimulus sequence of medium-intensity light ($CS_1$) followed by medium-intensity tone ($CS_2$) is presented during 5 trials in Stage 2. Finally, in Stage 3, we test by presenting the medium-intensity light ($CS_1$) during 3 extinction trials. Because the tone ($CS_2$) was paired with the shock in Stage 1 and then the light ($CS_1$) was paired with the tone ($CS_2$) in Stage 2, we expect Sniffy to exhibit a CR to the light ($CS_1$) in Stage 3.

### Stage 1 Higher-Order Conditioning

The file we suggested you call Ex1-ClassAcq can be used for Stage 1.

- If you have your Ex1-ClassAcq file, open it.
- Choose Design Classical Conditioning Experiment from the Experiment menu.

- Verify that the following conditions were in effect for Stage 1:
  - □ The average Interval Between Trials was 5 minutes.
  - □ The number following Present Each Trial Type was 10.
  - □ The First Stimulus was the medium-intensity tone.
  - □ The Second Stimulus was the medium-intensity US.
  - □ Stage 1 is the only stage that has been run. The easiest way to verify this condition is to look at the Next Stage command button. It should be dimmed because no Stage 2 has yet been created.
- If you have the right file, use the Save As command to save the file under an appropriate new name (e.g., Ex13-HOC) in the Sniffy Files folder on your computer's hard drive and skip down to the next heading.
- If you do not have your original conditioning file, go back to Exercise 1 and follow the instructions given there to recreate it.

## Stages 2 and 3 of Higher-Order Conditioning

Whether or not you had your original conditioning file, we assume that you are now working with a Sniffy file called Ex13-HOC in which during Stage 1 Sniffy received 10 pairings of the medium-intensity tone with the medium-intensity shock US with an average interval between trials of 5 minutes.

Follow these steps to set up Stages 2 and 3 of the experimental condition:

- Click the New Stage button and verify that you are now editing Stage 2, Trial Type A.
- Make sure that the Interval Between Trials is set to 5 minutes.
- Set Present Each Trial Type to 5 times.
- In the First Stimulus section of the dialog box, select the medium-intensity light.
- In the Second Stimulus section of the dialog box, select the medium-intensity tone as a CS used as US.
- Carefully check your settings.
- Click the New Stage button, and verify that you are now editing Stage 3, Trial Type A.
- Ascertain that the Interval Between Trials is set to 5 minutes.

- Set Present Each Trial Type to 3 times.
- In the First Stimulus section of the dialog box, select the medium-intensity light.
- In the Second Stimulus section of the dialog box, select None.
- Carefully check your settings.
- Use the Previous Stage and Next Stage buttons to scroll around and make sure that all your settings are correct.
- Click the Save button at the bottom of the dialog box.
- After the dialog box closes, select Run Classical Conditioning Experiment from the Experiment menu.
- If you want to speed up the experiment, select the Isolate Sniffy (Accelerate Time) command from the Experiment menu.
- When the experiment finishes running, save the file.

At the end of the experiment, your Movement Ratio window and CS Response Strength mind window should resemble the following:

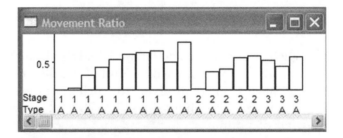

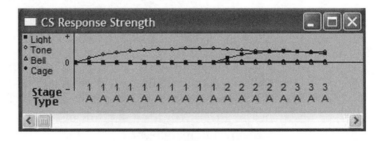

The Movement Ratio window shows that Sniffy acquired a CR to the tone in Stage 1. During Stage 2, when the light–tone sequence was presented 5 times, the light acquired the capacity to elicit a CR, and this capacity carried over into the light-only test trials during Stage 3. The CS Response Strength mind window shows that the tone acquired CS response strength during Stage 1 when it was paired with the shock. During Stage 2, the light–tone pairings caused the light to acquire CS

response strength, but the tone lost CS response strength because the shock no longer followed the tone. In Stage 3, the CS response strength of the light diminished because the tone no longer followed the light.

## Some Things to Do

- Compare the effect of manipulating the number of light–tone pairings in the sensory preconditioning and higher-order conditioning exercises. Why is there an optimal number of light–tone pairings that produces the strongest higher-order conditioning? Why does a similar effect not occur in sensory preconditioning?
- In sensory preconditioning, the light comes on and remains on for a time by itself before the tone comes on. Try a variant of the sensory preconditioning in which, during Stage 1, the light and tone are presented as a compound stimulus (the two stimuli both come on and go off simultaneously) with None selected as the US. Why do you think the result is different from that obtained with the standard sensory preconditioning procedure?

# 7

# The Nature of the Association in Classical Conditioning

## Background

Historically, psychologists have proposed two major theories about the nature of the association learned during classical conditioning. The **stimulus–response** (or **S–R**) **theory** postulates that the first stimulus (CS) becomes associated with the response to the second stimulus (that is, with UR if the second stimulus is a US or with the OR or CR elicited by a CS used as a US). In contrast, the **stimulus–stimulus** (or **S–S**) **theory** proposes that the CS becomes associated with the second stimulus itself. When the difference between S–S and S–R associations is stated in this scientifically correct but abstract way, many people have trouble understanding the importance and implications of the difference. As an aid to understanding the difference, let's imagine the difference between the psychological status of an animal that has learned either an S–S or an S–R association in simple excitatory CER conditioning in which the first stimulus is a tone and the second stimulus is the shock US. Because no one can actually look inside an animal's mind, the speculations that we are about to describe have no scientific basis. However, such speculations are harmless so long as we remember that they are just speculations. With that proviso in mind, imagine that you are Sniffy (or a real rat) in a CER conditioning situation.

Getting shocked upsets you and stops you from doing whatever you were doing until you somewhat recover your composure. When the tone is paired with the shock, you learn fear as a response to the tone CS, and this fear can also suppress your ongoing behavior. Now let's imagine the difference between an S–S and an S–R association.

If you are learning an S–S association, repeated presentations of the shock after the tone cause you to learn to expect the shock whenever the tone occurs. The tone acquires the capacity to elicit fear because you expect the shock to follow the tone, and you're afraid of the shock. An implication of this state of affairs is that if you've learned an S–S association, the tone will elicit a fear response only so long as you are afraid of the shock. If you were not afraid of the shock, the tone would elicit no fear even though you expected the shock to follow the tone.

In contrast, if you are learning an S–R association as a result of tone–shock pairings, the tone comes to elicit fear directly without any kind of expectation about the shock. The tone elicits fear; but because you have not learned to expect the shock to follow the tone, you don't know why the tone makes you afraid. It just does. For this reason, if you've learned an S–R association, the tone would continue to elicit fear even if you were no longer afraid of the shock. To put the matter in a slightly different way, when you learn an S–S association, you know what you're afraid of. However, when you learn an S–R association, you are just afraid.

We began this speculation about the difference between S–S and S–R associations by saying that it was unscientific; and we close it by reminding you about why it is unscientific. The speculation is unscientific because we can never observe what goes on inside an animal's mind. All we can say with scientific respectability is that an S–S association is an association between the first stimulus and the second stimulus, whereas an S–R association is an association between the first stimulus and the response to the second stimulus.

The S–S and the S–R theories seem equally plausible. For hundreds of years, philosophers and later psychologists have believed that one of the main factors involved in learning associations is temporal proximity. When two events occur close together in time, and especially if one event reliably precedes the other, people and animals learn to associate the events. In classical conditioning, the CS is presented shortly before the US, and the US reliably and swiftly elicits the UR. This procedure means that CS reliably precedes both the US and the UR. Thus, we might suppose that people and animals would learn to associate the CS with either the US or the UR (or maybe with both).

Moreover, most basic facts about classical conditioning do not help us distinguish between the two theories. For example, in most forms of classical conditioning, the CR resembles the UR in the sense that some of the same response elements occur in both responses. According to S–R theory, the reason for this resemblance is obvious. If the CR is the product of a learned association between the CS and the UR, the CR certainly ought to contain elements of the UR. However, S–S theory can also easily explain the similarity between the two responses. If the ani-

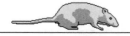

mal learns to associate the CS and US so that it expects the US to follow the CS, then it also seems natural that the response to the CS should resemble the response to the US. In some exceptional kinds of classical conditioning, the CR does not resemble the UR. However, because both theories say that the CR should resemble the UR, both theories have trouble explaining these exceptions. In addition, both theories are equally able to explain phenomena such as acquisition, extinction, compound conditioning, blocking, overshadowing, and higher-order conditioning. Thus these phenomena provide no information about the nature of the association. For these reasons, it has not been easy for psychologists to figure out which kind of association people and animals actually learn. Nevertheless, some progress has been made in recent years (for example, see Rescorla, 1973).

The Sniffy Pro program simulates both S–S and S–R associations. In this chapter, we will show you three experimental designs in which the S–S and S–R theories predict different results. Because you can determine how Sniffy learns associations, you will obtain different results when you run these experiments with the program set to learn associations in different ways.

In the Sniffy Pro program, you determine the nature of the associations that Sniffy learns in classical conditioning by making settings in the dialog box that appears when you select the Change Nature of Association command from the Experiment menu. The Change Nature of Association command is always available so that you can check which association model is in effect in any Sniffy Pro file, but you are allowed to change the settings only until you choose the Run Classical Conditioning Experiment command for the first time. Once you have started to run a classical conditioning experiment, you can no longer change the nature of the associations. This restriction is necessary in order to get the Sniffy Pro program to give consistent results with particular settings. Here is what the dialog box looks like:

| Nature of Association | | |
|---|---|---|
| Second Stimulus | S-S | S-R |
| US | ⦿ | ○ |
| CS used as US | ○ | ⦿ |

| Use Defaults | | Cancel | OK |
|---|---|---|---|

The illustration shows the default setting. There are four association models. These models are denoted by two pairs of letters, with the first letter pair describing how Sniffy learns the association when a CS is paired with shock US (that is, during first-order conditioning) and the second letter pair indicating how Sniffy learns the association when a CS is paired with another CS used as a US. The four models are:

- The Default (S–S, S–R) model, in which Sniffy learns an S–S association when a CS is paired with the shock US and an S–R association when a CS is paired with another CS used as a US. We chose this model as the Sniffy Pro default setting (that is, as the model in effect unless you change the setting) because data suggest that real rats generally learn S–S associations when a CS is paired with a US and S–R associations in higher-order conditioning (Domjan, 1998, 2003; Mazur, 1998; Rizley & Rescorla, 1972; Tarpy, 1997).
- The S–S, S–S model, in which Sniffy always learns S–S associations.
- The S–R, S–S model, in which Sniffy learns an S–R association when a CS is paired with the shock US and an S–S association when a CS is paired with another CS used as a US.
- The S–R, S–R model, in which Sniffy always learns S–R associations.

## Exercise 14: Basic Acquisition Under the Four Models

The first exercise demonstrates that the four models produce comparable acquisition results. The experimental design is charted as follows:

| Condition | Stage 1 |
|-----------|---------|
| S–S, S–R | 10: $CS_{MT}$–$US_M$ |
| S–S, S–S | 10: $CS_{MT}$–$US_M$ |
| S–R, S–S | 10: $CS_{MT}$–$US_M$ |
| S–R, S–R | 10: $CS_{MT}$–$US_M$ |

The four experimental conditions are the four different classical conditioning models that the Sniffy Pro program simulates. In each case, Sniffy receives 10 trials in which the medium-intensity tone is paired with the medium-intensity shock. Because S–S, S–R is Sniffy Pro's default model, if you still have the file that we recommended you

call Ex1–ClassAcq when you performed Exercise 1, you can use that file for the Default (S–S, S–R) model. If you don't have it, you can recreate it with the following directions for setting up the experiment. Here are the steps that you need to follow for each of the four classical conditioning models:

- Start with a new Sniffy file.
- Immediately give the file an appropriate new name. We suggest that you include the name of the classical conditioning model in the file name. For example, if you are creating a file for the S–R, S–S model, we suggest you call the file Ex14-acqSRSS.
- Choose the Change Nature of Associations command from the Experiment menu. In the dialog box that appears, choose the settings appropriate for the model that you are setting up. For example, if you are setting up the S–R, S–S model, choose S–R for US and S–S for CS used as US.
- Choose the Design Classical Conditioning Experiment command from the Experiment menu, and make the following settings in the Classical Conditioning Experiment Design dialog box:
  - Set the Interval Between Trials to 5 minutes.
  - Set Present Each Trial Type to 10 times.
  - In the First Stimulus section of the dialog box, choose the medium-intensity tone.
  - In the Second Stimulus section of the dialog box, choose the medium-intensity shock.
  - Carefully check your selections.
  - At the bottom of the dialog box, click on the Save command button.
- After the dialog box disappears, choose the Run Classical Conditioning Experiment command from the Experiment menu.
- If you want to speed up the experiment, select the Isolate Sniffy (Accelerate Time) command from the Experiment menu. However, be careful not to let the program run very long after the exercise is completed. You will need the files from this exercise as starting points for the next two exercises.
- When the experiment has finished running, save the file.

For all four classical conditioning association models, your results should resemble the following:

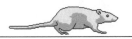

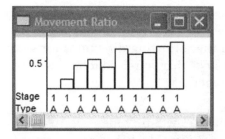

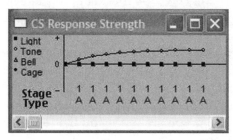

Because of the random factors that partially determine Sniffy's behavior, your movement ratio results will be somewhat variable; but all four models should produce movement ratio results resembling those shown. The CS response strength results will be identical for all four models.

## Exercise 15: Effect on First-Order Conditioning of Habituating the UR

Now we will consider the first experimental design in which the different models produce different results. Here is the chart of the experimental design:

| Condition | Stage 1 | Stage 2 | Stage 3 | Stage 3 Expected Result |
|---|---|---|---|---|
| S–S, S–R | 10: $CS_{MT}$–$US_M$ | 30: $US_L$ | 3: $CS_{MT}$–None | $CS_{MT}$ elicits no CR |
| S–S, S–S | 10: $CS_{MT}$–$US_M$ | 30: $US_L$ | 3: $CS_{MT}$–None | $CS_{MT}$ elicits no CR |
| S–R, S–S | 10: $CS_{MT}$–$US_M$ | 30: $US_L$ | 3: $CS_{MT}$–None | $CS_{MT}$ elicits CR |
| S–R, S–R | 10: $CS_{MT}$–$US_M$ | 30: $US_L$ | 3: $CS_{MT}$–None | $CS_{MT}$ elicits CR |

In the chart, $US_L$ means the low-intensity shock US. In this experiment, Stage 1 is the acquisition experiment you performed in Exercise 14. To set up this experiment, you will be adding two more stages to

that experiment. In Stage 2, Sniffy will receive 30 trials during which the low-intensity shock occurs by itself (that is, without a preceding first stimulus). Then in Stage 3, you will present three extinction test trials during which the medium-intensity tone is presented paired with the None Second Stimulus.

In this experiment, the Stage 2 CS response strength results and the Stage 3 movement ratio results that you obtain will depend on whether Sniffy learned an S–S or an S–R association during Stage 1 when the tone was paired with the shock. Because both the S–S, S–R and the S–S, S–S models cause Sniffy to learn an S–S association when a CS is paired with the shock US, these two models should produce similar results that differ from those produced by the S–R, S–S and the S–R, S–R models, both of which cause Sniffy to learn an S–R association when the tone is paired with shock.

To see why the two pairs of models produce different results, recall that repeated presentations of the low-intensity shock during Stage 2 will produce habituation of Sniffy's UR to the shock US. By the end of Stage 2, Sniffy will no longer be responding to the shock. When the shock occurs, he will just keep moving around as if nothing had happened. What this experiment shows us is that habituating the UR to the shock will have different effects depending on whether Sniffy learned an S–R or an S–S association when the tone was paired with the shock. Habituating the UR to the US should abolish the CR to the tone if Sniffy has learned an S–S association but not if he has learned an S–R association. To see why this should be so, we need to recall what we said earlier about the difference between S–S and S–R associations.

When Sniffy learns an S–R association, he learns a direct connection between the tone and a part of his UR to the shock (its capacity to interrupt his chain of behavior). However, when Sniffy learns an S–S association, he learns to associate the tone with the shock as a stimulus. This difference is crucial in determining whether Sniffy will respond to the tone after his response to the shock has habituated. When Sniffy has learned an S–R association, he will still respond to the tone because the tone directly elicits elements of Sniffy's original response to the shock. In contrast, learning an S–S association is learning an expectancy. After learning an S–S association, Sniffy will respond to the tone only if the shock itself would produce a response. Thus, habituating Sniffy's response to the shock abolishes his response to the tone if he has learned an S–S association,[1] but not if he has learned an S–R association.

---

[1] In the terms of our earlier unscientific discussion of the difference between S–S and S–R associations, we assume that when Sniffy stops responding to the shock, he is no longer afraid of it.

Here are the steps you need to go through to set up the experiment for each of Sniffy's four classical conditioning models:

- Open the acquisition file from the previous experiment for the association model that you want to study at the moment. For example, if you want to set up the experiment for the S–R, S–S model, open the file that we recommended you call Ex14-acqSRSS.
- Immediately use the Save As command to save the file under a new appropriate name (e.g., Ex15-HabSRSS, for "effects of habituation") in the Sniffy Files folder on your computer's hard drive.
- If you wish to check the association model settings, you can select the Change Nature of Associations command from the Experiment menu. The settings are dimmed because you cannot change them after the Run Classical Conditioning Experiment command has been executed for the first time in a particular Sniffy Pro file.
- Choose the Design Classical Conditioning Experiment command from the Experiment menu.
- In the Classical Conditioning Experiment Design dialog box:
  - Click on the command button labeled New Stage to produce Stage 2 of the experiment.
  - Verify that you are now editing Stage 2, Trial Type A.
  - Make sure that the Interval Between Trials is set to 5 minutes.
  - Set Present Each Trial Type to 30 times.
  - In First Stimulus section of the dialog box, click on the existing check mark to the left of the word "Tone" to *deselect* it. Make sure that *no* first stimulus is selected.
  - In the Second Stimulus section of the dialog box, select the *low-intensity* shock US.
  - Carefully check your Stage 2 selections.
  - Click on the New Stage command button to create a new Stage 3.
  - Note that you are now editing Stage 3, Trial Type A.
  - Be sure that the Interval Between Trials is set to 5 minutes.
  - Set Present Each Trial Type to 3 times.
  - In the First Stimulus section of the dialog box, choose the medium-intensity tone CS.

□ In the Second Stimulus section of the dialog box, choose None.
□ Carefully check your Stage 3 selections.
□ Use the Previous Stage and Next Stage command buttons to scroll around and make sure that all your settings are correct.
□ Click on the Save command button at the bottom of the dialog box.
■ Select the Run Classical Conditioning Experiment command from the Experiment menu.
■ If you want to speed up the experiment, select the Isolate Sniffy (Accelerate Time) command from the Experiment menu.
■ When the experiment has finished running, save the file.

If you keep an eye on the Sensitivity & Fear mind window during Stage 2, you will note that with all four models, Sniffy's pain sensitivity progressively declines to zero during the 30 presentations of the low-intensity shock US. The declining pain sensitivity indicates that Sniffy's UR to the low-intensity shock is habituating. At the end of the experiment, your CS Response Strength and Movement Ratio windows for the S–R, S–S and S–R, S–R models will resemble the following:

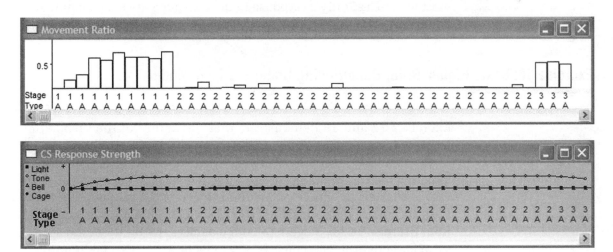

The Stage 2 CS Response Strength mind window results show that CS response strength for the tone did not change. The Stage 2 movement ratio results are meaningless because no CS was presented during Stage 2. However, the movement ratio results show that Sniffy responds

to the tone during Stage 3. This result agrees with the CS Response Strength mind window's prediction about what the movement ratio results should be.

In contrast, your results for the Default (S–S, S–R) and S–S, S–S models should resemble the following:

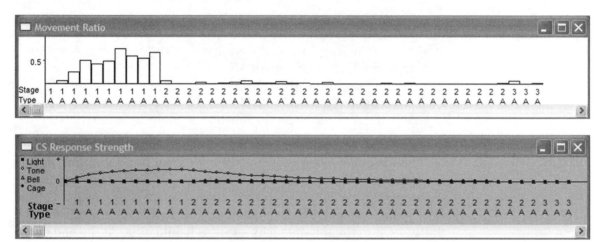

Here, during Stage 2, the tone's CS response strength diminishes almost to zero as Sniffy's response to the low-intensity shock habituates, and Sniffy does not respond to the tone during the Stage 3 test trials.

## Exercise 16: Basic Higher-Order Conditioning Under the Four Models

Exercises 17 and 18 demonstrate that the nature of the association learned during higher-order conditioning affects the results of experiments that test the effects of extinguishing the first-order CR and habituating the UR. In both exercises, the first stage of the experiment involves 10 trials in which the medium-intensity tone is paired with the medium-intensity shock. Thus, you can use the files that you obtained from Exercise 14 for Stage 1 in both exercises. In addition, the second stage for both exercises consists of 5 trials in which the medium-intensity light is paired with the medium-intensity tone to establish basic higher-order conditioning. Therefore, the most efficient way to perform Exercises 17 and 18 is to start with your files from Exercise 14, add the common Stage 2, save the result, and then add the later stages, which are different for the two subsequent exercises. In other words, to

save time, we recommend that you perform a preparatory exercise before going on to do the two different exercises on higher-order conditioning. The design of the preparatory exercise is charted as follows:

| Condition | Stage 1 | Stage 2 | Stage 2 Expected Result |
|-----------|---------|---------|-------------------------|
| S–S, S–R | 10: $CS_{MT}$–$US_M$ | 5: $CS_{ML}$–$CS_{MT}$ | $CS_{ML}$ comes to elicit a CR |
| S–S, S–S | 10: $CS_{MT}$–$US_M$ | 5: $CS_{ML}$–$CS_{MT}$ | $CS_{ML}$ comes to elicit a CR |
| S–R, S–S | 10: $CS_{MT}$–$US_M$ | 5: $CS_{ML}$–$CS_{MT}$ | $CS_{ML}$ comes to elicit a CR |
| S–R, S–R | 10: $CS_{MT}$–$US_M$ | 5: $CS_{ML}$–$CS_{MT}$ | $CS_{ML}$ comes to elicit a CR |

The four experimental conditions are the four different classical conditioning models. In all conditions, Sniffy receives 10 Stage 1 trials in which the medium-intensity tone is paired with the medium-intensity shock. Then in Stage 2, Sniffy receives 5 trials in which the medium-intensity light is paired with the medium-intensity tone. To set up the preparatory experiment for each of the four models, you should follow these steps:

- Open the acquisition file from Exercise 14 for the association model that you want to study at the moment. For example, if you want to set up the experiment for the S–R, S–S model, open the file that we recommended you call Ex14-acqSRSS.
- Immediately use the Save As command to save the file under a new appropriate name (e.g., Ex16-HOCSRSS, for "higher-order conditioning with S–R, S–S model") in the Sniffy Files folder on your computer's hard drive.
- Choose the Design Classical Conditioning Experiment command from the Experiment menu.
- In the Classical Conditioning Experiment Design dialog box, make the following settings:
  - Note that the dialog box opens to Stage 1, Trial Type A. Most of the settings are dimmed because Stage 1 has already been run.
  - Click on the command button labeled New Stage to create Stage 2 of the experiment.
  - Note that you are now editing Stage 2, Trial Type A.
  - Make sure that the Interval Between Trials is set to 5 minutes.

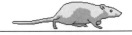

□ Set Present Each Trial Type to 5 times.
□ In First Stimulus section of the dialog box, select the medium-intensity light.
□ In the Second Stimulus section of the dialog box, select the medium-intensity tone under CS used as US.
□ Carefully check your Stage 2 selections.
□ Click on the Save command button at the bottom of the dialog box.

- Select the Run Classical Conditioning Experiment command from the Experiment menu.
- If you want to speed up the experiment, select the Isolate Sniffy (Accelerate Time) command from the Experiment menu. However, be careful not to let the program run for long after the exercise is complete. You need the files from this exercise as the basis for the next two exercises, so you want to avoid inadvertently filling up cumulative records with unneeded data.
- When the experiment has finished running, save the file.

Your results for all four conditioning models will be similar and should resemble the following:

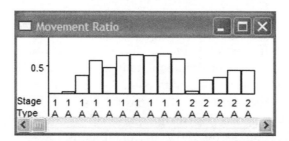

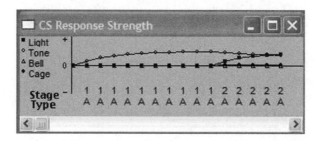

During Stage 2, the CS response strength for the light increased because it was being paired with the tone; and the CS response strength

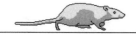

for the tone decreased because the tone was being presented without the shock. The movement ratio results show that Sniffy acquired a CR to the light.

## Exercise 17: Effect on Higher-Order Conditioning of Extinguishing the First-Order CR

This exercise examines the effect on higher-order conditioning of extinguishing the first-order association. The experimental design is shown as follows:

| Condition | Stage 1 | Stage 2 | Stage 3 | Stage 4 and Predicted Result |
|---|---|---|---|---|
| S–S, S–R | 10: $CS_{MT}$–$US_M$ | 5: $CS_{ML}$–$CS_{MT}$ | 20: $CS_{MT}$–None | 2: $CS_{ML}$–None $CS_{ML}$ elicits CR |
| S–S, S–S | 10: $CS_{MT}$–$US_M$ | 5: $CS_{ML}$–$CS_{MT}$ | 20: $CS_{MT}$–None | 2: $CS_{ML}$–None $CS_{ML}$ elicits no CR |
| S–R, S–S | 10: $CS_{MT}$–$US_M$ | 5: $CS_{ML}$–$CS_{MT}$ | 20: $CS_{MT}$–None | 2: $CS_{ML}$ –None $CS_{ML}$ elicits no CR |
| S–R, S–R | 10: $CS_{MT}$–$US_M$ | 5: $CS_{ML}$–$CS_{MT}$ | 20: $CS_{MT}$–None | 2: $CS_{ML}$ –None $CS_{ML}$ elicits CR |

The experimental conditions are the four associative models for classical conditioning. In Stage 1, Sniffy receives 10 trials in which the medium-intensity tone is paired with the medium-intensity shock. Thus Stage 1 establishes first-order conditioning. In Stage 2, Sniffy receives 5 trials in which the medium-intensity light is paired with the medium-intensity tone to establish higher-order conditioning. In Stage 3, the first-order CR is extinguished by presenting the tone 30 times with no second stimulus. Finally, in Stage 4 we present the light CS twice during extinction test trials to see what effect extinguishing the first-order CR has had on the higher-order CR.

The S–S model of higher-order conditioning predicts that extinguishing the first-order CR should abolish the higher-order CR. The S–R model of higher-order conditioning predicts that extinguishing the first-order CR should have no effect on the higher-order CR. Thus, during Stage 4, we expect that Sniffy will respond to the light if he has

learned higher-order conditioning under either the S–S, S–R model or the S–R, S–R model, but not if he has learned higher-order conditioning under the S–S, S–S or the S–R, S–S models.

To see the logic behind these expectations, we must again consider the difference between S–S and S–R associations. When Sniffy learns higher-order conditioning under the S–S model, he is learning an association between the light and the tone as a stimulus. He learns to expect the tone to follow the light. For this reason, he should make a CR to the light only if he would make a CR to the tone. Thus, when we extinguish Sniffy's response to the tone, we also abolish his response to the light if Sniffy's higher-order association is an S–S association. In contrast, when Sniffy learns an S–R association during higher-order conditioning, he learns a direct connection between the light and the CR to the tone. Under the S–R model, the tone's only role in the acquisition process is as a means of getting the CR to occur shortly after presentations of the light. Because the tone as a stimulus plays no role in an S–R association to the light, extinguishing the response to the tone has no effect on the second-order association.

To set up the experiment, follow these steps for each of the four classical conditioning models:

- Open a higher-order conditioning acquisition file from Exercise 16. For example, to set up the experiment for the S–R, S–S model, open the file that we recommended you call Ex16-HOCSRSS.
- Immediately use the Save As command to save the file under a new appropriate name (e.g., Ex17-HOCExtSRSS) in the Sniffy Files folder on your computer's hard drive.
- Choose Change Nature of the Association from the Experiment menu and verify that you have the right setting for the model that you are currently studying.
- Choose the Design Classical Conditioning Experiment command from the Experiment menu.
- Make the following settings in the Classical Conditioning Experiment Design dialog box:
  □ When you first open the dialog box, it displays settings for Stage 1. All the Stage 1 settings are dimmed because Stage 1 has already been run.
  □ Click on the command button labeled Next Stage to move to Stage 2 of the experiment. The Stage 2 settings are also dimmed because Stage 2 has also been run.

- □ Click the New Stage command button to create a new Stage 3. Note that you are now editing Stage 3, Trial Type A. The Stage 3 settings are active because Stage 3 has not yet been run.
- □ Ascertain that the Average Interval Between Trials is set at 5 minutes.
- □ Set Present Each Trial Type to 30 times.
- □ In the First Stimulus section of the dialog box, select the medium-intensity tone.
- □ In the Second Stimulus section of the dialog box, select None.
- □ Carefully check your Stage 3 settings.
- □ Click the New Stage command button to create a new Stage 4. Verify that you are now editing Stage 4, Trial Type A.
- □ Make sure that the Average Interval Between Trials is set to 5 minutes.
- □ Set Present Each Trial Type to 2 times.
- □ In the First Stimulus section of the dialog box, select the medium-intensity light.
- □ In the Second Stimulus section of the dialog box, select None.
- □ Carefully check your Stage 4 settings.
- □ Use the Previous Stage and Next Stage buttons to scroll back and forth to make sure that your settings for all four stages match those shown in the experimental design chart at the beginning of this exercise.
- □ Click the Save command button at the bottom of the dialog box.
- ■ Choose the Run Classical Conditioning Experiment command from the Experiment menu.
- ■ If you want to speed up the experiment, select the Isolate Sniffy (Accelerate Time) command from the Experiment menu.
- ■ When the experiment has finished running, save the file.

Your CS Response Strength and Movement Ratio windows for the S–R, S–S and S–S, S–S models should resemble those shown next:

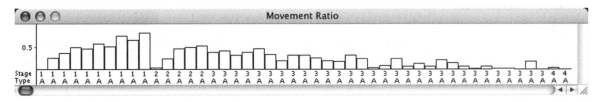

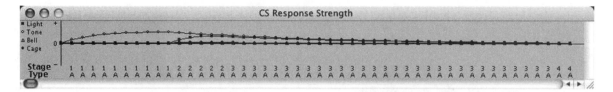

During Stage 3, as the CR to the tone was extinguished, the CS response strength for both the tone and the light declined, even though only the tone was being presented. The declining strength of the light's CR response strength predicts that Sniffy will not respond to the light during the Stage 4 test trials. The movement ratio results for Stage 4 confirm this prediction.

In contrast, your CS Response Strength and Movement Ratio windows for the S–R, S–R and S–S, S–R models should resemble the following:

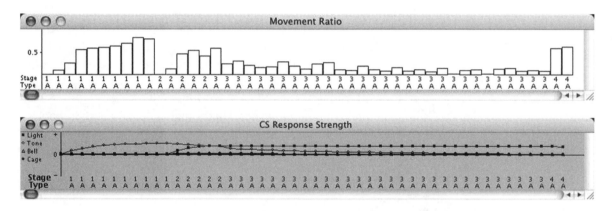

During Stage 3, as the CR to the tone is extinguished, only the CS response strength for the tone declines; the CR response strength for the light is unaffected. This observation predicts that Sniffy will still respond to the light during the Stage 4 test trials. The movement ratio results for Stage 4 confirm this prediction.

## Exercise 18: Effect on Higher-Order Conditioning of Habituating the UR

The experimental design for the final exercise in this chapter is charted as follows:

| Condition | Stage 1 | Stage 2 | Stage 3 | Stage 4 | Stage 4 Predicted Result |
|-----------|---------|---------|---------|---------|--------------------------|
| S–S, S–R | 10: $CS_{MT}$–$US_M$ | 5: $CS_{ML}$–$CS_{MT}$ | 30: $US_L$ | 2: $CS_{ML}$–None | $CS_{ML}$–CR |
|           |         |         |         | 2: $CS_{MT}$–None | $CS_{MT}$–No CR |
| S–S, S–S | 10: $CS_{MT}$–$US_M$ | 5: $CS_{ML}$–$CS_{MT}$ | 30: $US_L$ | 2: $CS_{ML}$–None | $CS_{ML}$–No CR |
|           |         |         |         | 2: $CS_{MT}$–None | $CS_{MT}$–No CR |
| S–R, S–S | 10: $CS_{MT}$–$US_M$ | 5: $CS_{ML}$–$CS_{MT}$ | 30: $US_L$ | 2: $CS_{ML}$–None | $CS_{ML}$–CR |
|           |         |         |         | 2: $CS_{MT}$–None | $CS_{MT}$–CR |
| S–R, S–R | 10: $CS_{MT}$–$US_M$ | 5: $CS_{ML}$–$CS_{MT}$ | 30: $US_L$ | 2: $CS_{ML}$–None | $CS_{ML}$–CR |
|           |         |         |         | 2: $CS_{MT}$–None | $CS_{MT}$–CR |

After establishing higher-order conditioning in Stage 2, we habituate Sniffy's UR to the shock in Stage 3 and then present both the light and the tone during extinction test trials in Stage 4. A very interesting thing about this exercise is that the S–S, S–R model—the model that many psychologists think applies to real rats in the CER conditioning situation—produces a unique and somewhat counterintuitive prediction about the Stage 4 results. The S–S, S–R model says that after Sniffy's UR to the shock has habituated, he will respond to the higher-order light CS but not to the first-order tone CS. To see how this and the other predicted outcomes in the experimental table work, we need to recall several things that we have already noted about S–S and S–R associations.

First, recall what we said about first-order associations. When Sniffy learns an S–R association as a result of tone–shock pairings, he learns a direct connection between the tone and the fear response to the shock. That direct connection between the tone and its CR means that Sniffy will respond to the tone even if he no longer responds to the shock. Thus, both the S–R, S–R and the S–R, S–S models predict that habituating the response to the shock will have no effect on Sniffy's response to the tone. In contrast, when Sniffy learns an S–S association as a result of tone–shock pairings, he learns to expect the shock to follow the tone, and his response to the tone depends on what his response to the shock would be. If he would respond to the shock, he will respond to the tone. If he would not respond to the shock, he will not respond to

the tone Thus, habituating the UR to the shock abolishes the CR to the tone under the S–S, S–S and S–S, S–R models.

Similar arguments can be made with respect to higher-order conditioning. When Sniffy learns an S–R association as a result of light–tone pairings, he acquires a direct connection between the light and the tone's CR so that he will continue to respond to the light even if the CR to the tone no longer occurs. However, when Sniffy learns an S–S association as a result of light–tone pairings, he learns to expect the tone to follow the light and will respond to the light only if he would respond to the tone.

Now let's put the two conditioning stages together and look at the effect of habituating the UR to the shock on Sniffy's response to both the first-order tone CS and the higher-order light CS. We'll go through each of the models:

- The S–S, S–R model says that habituating the UR to the shock will abolish the first-order response to the tone because Sniffy has learned an S–S association between the tone and the shock and thus will not respond to the tone unless he would respond to the shock. However, abolishing Sniffy's response to the tone should have no effect on his response to the light because Sniffy learned a direct S–R connection between the light and the tone's CR. Thus, Sniffy should respond to the light even though he does not respond to the tone.

- The S–S, S–S model says that habituating the UR to the shock will abolish the response to both the tone and the light because both responses depend on S–S associations. Sniffy will not respond to the tone unless he would respond to the shock; he will not respond to the light unless he would respond to the tone. Thus, when habituation abolishes the response to the shock, it eliminates the CR to the tone, and eliminating the CR to the tone also eliminates the CR to the light.

- Finally, both the S–R, S–S and the S–R, S–R models predict that habituating the response to the shock will affect neither the CR to the tone nor the CR to the light. Both models say that the tone–shock pairings produce an S–R association for the tone. Thus habituating the response to the shock will have no effect on the CR to the tone. So long as the CR to the tone is intact, the CR to the light will remain intact, whichever kind of association the light–tone pairings produced.

To set up the experiment, you should follow these steps for each of the four classical conditioning models:

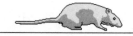

- Open a higher-order conditioning acquisition file from Exercise 16. For example, to set up the experiment for the S–R, S–S model, open the file that we recommended you call Ex16-HOCSRSS.
- Immediately use the Save As command to save the file under a new appropriate name (e.g., Ex18-HOCHabUSSRSS, for "higher-order conditioning after US habituation") in the Sniffy Files folder on your computer's hard drive.
- Choose the Change Nature of the Association command from the Experiment menu and verify that (in this example) the S–R, S–S model is already chosen. The options in the dialog box are dimmed because part of the experiment has already been run.
- Choose the Design Classical Conditioning Experiment command from the Experiment menu.
- In the Classical Conditioning Experiment Design dialog box, make the following settings:
  - □ When you first open the dialog box, it displays settings for Stage 1. All the Stage 1 settings are dimmed because Stage 1 has already been run.
  - □ Click on the command button labeled Next Stage to move to Stage 2 of the experiment. All the Stage 2 settings are also dimmed because Stage 2 has also been run.
  - □ Click the New Stage command button to create a New Stage 3. Note that you are now editing Stage 3, Trial Type A. All the Stage 3 settings are active because Stage 3 has not yet been run.
  - □ Make sure the Average Interval Between Trials is set to 5 minutes.
  - □ Set Present Each Trial Type to 30 times.
  - □ In the First Stimulus section of the dialog box, click on the check box next to the word "Tone" to *deselect* the tone; make sure that no other first stimulus is selected.
  - □ In the Second Stimulus section of the dialog box, select the *low-intensity* shock US.
  - □ Carefully check your Stage 3 settings.
  - □ Click the New Stage command button to create a new Stage 4. Note that you are now editing Stage 4, Trial Type A.
  - □ Make sure that the Average Interval Between Trials is set to 5 minutes.

- ☐ Set Present Each Trial Type to 2 times.
- ☐ In the First Stimulus section of the dialog box, select the medium-intensity light.
- ☐ In the Second Stimulus section of the dialog box, select None.
- ☐ Click the New Type command button to create a new trial type. Note that you are now working on Stage 4, Trial Type B.
- ☐ In the First Stimulus section of the dialog box, select the medium-intensity tone.
- ☐ In the Second Stimulus section of the dialog box, select None.
- ☐ Use the Previous Stage, Next Stage, Previous Type, and Next Type buttons to scroll around and make sure that your settings for all four stages match those shown in the experimental design diagram at the beginning of this section.
- ☐ Click the Save command button at the bottom of the dialog box.
- ■ Choose the Run Classical Conditioning Experiment command from the Experiment menu.
- ■ If you want to speed up the experiment, select the Isolate Sniffy (Accelerate Time) command from the Experiment menu.
- ■ When the experiment has finished running, save the file.

Your results for the S–S, S–R model should resemble the following:

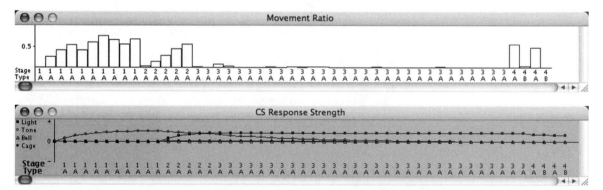

As habituation to the low-intensity shock proceeds during Stage 3, the CS response strength for the first-order tone CS declines, but the CS response strength for the higher-order light CS is unchanged.[2] These

[2]If you're using the suppression ratio as your response measure, during Stage 3, the suppression ratio results are meaningless because no CS is being presented.

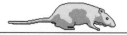

CS response strength results predict that Sniffy will respond to the light but not to the tone during the Stage 4 test trials. The movement ratio results for Stage 4 confirm this prediction.

Your results for the S–S, S–S model should resemble those shown next:

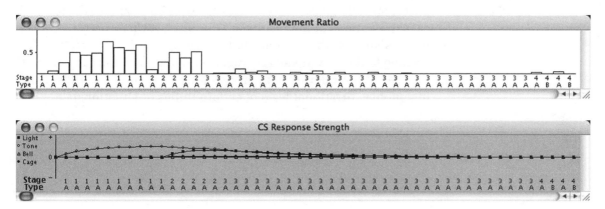

During Stage 3, the CS response strength for both the first-order tone and the higher-order light CSs decline. These CS response strength results predict that Sniffy will not respond to either CS during the Stage 4 test trials. The movement ratio results for Stage 4 confirm this prediction.

Finally, your results for both the S–R, S–S and the S–R, S–R models should resemble the following:

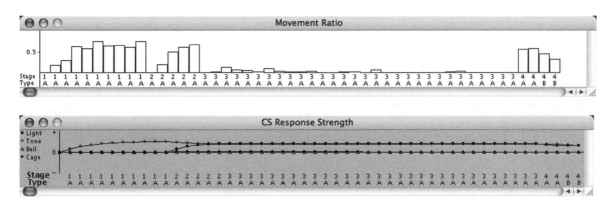

During Stage 3, the CS response strength for both the first-order tone and the higher-order light CSs remain unchanged. These CS response strength results predict that Sniffy will respond to both CSs during the Stage 4 test trials. The movement ratio results for Stage 4 confirm this prediction.

## Some Questions

- What is the difference between an S–S and an S–R association?
- The exercises and theoretical explanations in this chapter are complex. Carefully go over Exercises 17 and 18 and explain the theoretical explanations of the results in your own words.
- Results suggest that real animals learn first-order associations according to the S–S model and higher-order associations according to the S–R. What relevance might this difference have for understanding phobias (irrational fears of certain things or situations)?

# 8

# Habituation, Sensitization, Background Conditioning, and the CS and US Pre-exposure Effects

## Background

When Sniffy is shocked without a preceding CS, two different things may happen. The first thing is that Sniffy's response to the shock may change. As we have seen in previous exercises, with the low-intensity shock, Sniffy's UR to the shock US habituates. The more often he is shocked, the less he responds. After about 25 low-intensity shocks, Sniffy's UR is gone. He just keeps on doing whatever he is doing as if nothing had happened. With the medium-intensity shock, Sniffy's UR never changes. Every shock interrupts Sniffy's ongoing behavior for about 2 minutes. With the high-intensity shock, Sniffy's UR sensitizes. Up to a point, each successive shock suppresses Sniffy's normal ongoing behavior for longer and longer periods. The first high-intensity shock will suppress Sniffy's ongoing behavior for about 2 minutes, but the 20th shock will suppress his ongoing behavior for about 4 minutes. These effects of repeated US presentation occur whether or not a CS precedes the US.

When medium- or high-intensity shocks occur without a preceding CS, a new phenomenon that we call **background conditioning** emerges. Background or contextual stimuli (the walls and floor of the operant chamber, the bar, and so on) come to act as the CS. Because these stimuli are always present and never change, they are not very salient, so the conditioning process is quite slow. However, if Sniffy experiences enough medium- or high-intensity shocks with no preceding tone, light, or bell, the background stimuli eventually come to elicit a more or less nonstop fear response. Given enough unsignaled shocks, Sniffy will exhibit freezing much of the time because he is continuously manifesting a CR to the background stimuli. In other words, after enough unsignaled medium- or high-intensity shocks, Sniffy will become "paralyzed by fear." If he has been operantly conditioned to press the bar or perform some other behavior, he will rarely do so because he spends so much time frozen. When you recall that ordinary classical conditioning in which a CS precedes the US never leaves Sniffy in a state of "fear paralysis," it's easy to appreciate the fact that signaled shock is much less stressful to a real rat than unsignaled shock. Real rats subjected to unsignaled shock sometimes succumb to stress, an effect that signaled shock almost never produces (Seligman, 1968; Seligman, Maier, & Solomon, 1971).

The phenomenon of background conditioning raises a couple of interesting questions:

- *Why doesn't background conditioning occur with the low-intensity shock?* In fact, it starts to occur with the first few low-intensity shocks. However, because habituation of the UR to the low-intensity US is going on simultaneously, the background stimuli never acquire enough response strength to produce much freezing.
- *Why doesn't background conditioning occur when an explicit CS (tone, light, or bell) precedes the shock?* A little background conditioning does occur.[1] However, in part because the tone, light, and bell CSs are not continuously present, they are much more salient than the background stimuli. As a consequence, an explicit CS almost completely overshadows the contextual stimuli. (If you need a review of the phenomenon of overshadowing, reread Chapter 4.)

---

[1] The simplest way to convince yourself that a little contextual conditioning always occurs is to go back and open some of your old classical conditioning files in which the conditioning experiment has been completed. Almost any completed classical conditioning experiment will show the effect. To see the background conditioning, examine the Sensitivity & Fear mind window. Even though no CS is currently being presented, the Fear bar will be slightly above the zero level. That little bit of residual fear is the result of background conditioning. However, it is not enough to produce very much freezing. A slightly more complicated way to see that a little background conditioning always occurs is to do the following:

- Open one of your previous classical conditioning files.
- Make the CS Response Strength mind window visible by selecting it from the Windows menu.
- Make sure that the CS Response Strength mind window is selected by clicking on it.
- Select the Export Data command from the file window, give the exported data file an appropriate name, and save it on your hard disk.
- Look at the exported data file in a spreadsheet program.
- In the spreadsheet, the column headed "Cage" shows the CS Response Strength for background stimuli. During any classical conditioning experiment in which a US is presented, the "Cage" always acquires a little response strength.

# Exercise 19: Habituation, Sensitization, and Background Conditioning

The first exercise in this chapter simultaneously demonstrates habituation, sensitization, and background conditioning. The exercise can be charted as follows:

| Condition | Stage 1 | Result |
|---|---|---|
| Low-Intensity US | 50: $US_L$ | UR habituates<br>No significant background conditioning |
| Medium-Intensity US | 50: $US_M$ | UR does not change<br>Moderate background conditioning |
| High-Intensity US | 50: $US_H$ | UR sensitizes<br>Strong background conditioning |

The three conditions differ in the intensity of the US that Sniffy receives. In all conditions, Sniffy is shocked 50 times without any preceding explicit CS.

Because each of the experimental conditions will require more than 8 hours of program time to run, we suggest that you use the Isolate Sniffy (Accelerate Time) command to speed things up. To set up the experiment, you should follow these steps:

- Start with a new Sniffy file.
- Immediately give the file an appropriate new name and save it in the Sniffy Files folder on your computer's hard drive. We suggest that you call the files for the low-, medium-, and high-intensity USs, respectively, Ex19-BkgrL, Ex19-BkgrM, and Ex19-BkgrH.
- Choose the Design Classical Conditioning Experiment command from the Experiment menu.
- Make the following settings in the Design Classical Conditioning Experiment dialog box:
  - □ Set the average interval between trials to 10 minutes.[2]
  - □ Set Present Each Trial Type to 50 times.

[2] Since Sniffy will require longer than usual to recover from high-intensity shock, we suggest that you set the average interval between trials to 10 minutes, instead of the usual 5 minutes. Setting this value to 10 minutes for all three shock intensities ensures that the only difference between the three experimental conditions is shock intensity.

- ◻ In the First Stimulus section of the dialog box, click on the check mark that appears to the left of the word "Tone" to de-select that stimulus, and make sure that no other First Stimulus is selected.
- ◻ In the Second Stimulus section of the dialog box, choose the low-, medium-, or high-intensity shock US.
- ◻ Carefully check your selections.
- ◻ At the bottom of the dialog box, click on the Save command button.
- ■ Before running the experiment, examine the Sensitivity & Fear mind window. In all cases, it should look like this:

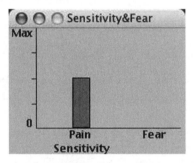

- ■ Sniffy's pain sensitivity is a measure of his sensitivity to the shock US. Because he has not yet received any shocks, his pain sensitivity is at its midpoint and his fear level is zero.
- ■ Choose the Run Classical Conditioning Experiment from the Experiment menu.
- ■ Select the Isolate Sniffy (Accelerate Time) command from the Experiment menu to speed up execution of the experiment.
- ■ Let the program run at least 5 minutes of program time after the last US presentation.
- ■ Save the file.

To evaluate the effects of habituation and sensitization, we will examine the Sensitivity & Fear mind windows for the three experimental conditions. The three mind windows should look like those that follow.

### Low Shock

The zero-level pain sensitivity indicates that Sniffy's response to the shock has completely habituated.

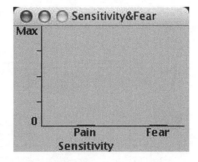

### Medium Shock

The mid-level pain sensitivity indicates that Sniffy's response to the shock has remained unchanged.

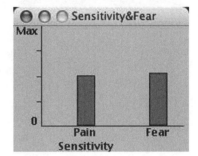

### High Shock

The maximum-level pain sensitivity indicates that Sniffy's response to the shock has become much stronger than it was at the beginning of the experiment.

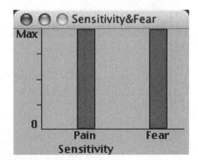

To assess the effects of background conditioning, we can examine the movement ratio results for the three experimental conditions. Even though no CS is being presented before each shock, the movement ratio provides a useful measure of conditioning because it records the proportion of time that Sniffy was exhibiting freezing during the 30 seconds before each shock occurred. Finally, the CS Response Strength mind window provides a view of Sniffy's changing fear state.

For the low-intensity shock condition, the movement ratio results and CS Response Strength mind window should resemble these:

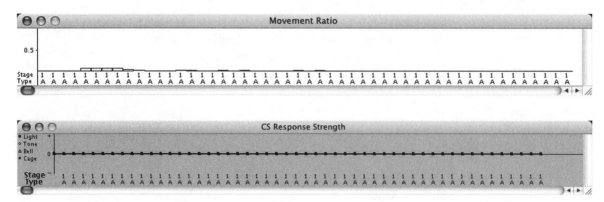

The Movement Ratio window shows that the only time he manifested any fear at all during 30-second periods before shock presentation was during the early part of the experiment before the response to the shock had completely habituated. The CS Response Strength mind window shows no substantial conditioning at any stage of the experiment.

For the medium-intensity shock condition, your movement ratio and CS response strength results should look something like this:

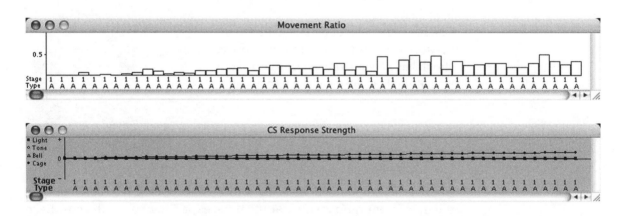

The movement ratio results show that during the experiment the proportion of time that Sniffy was frozen during 30-second intervals before shock presentation gradually increased to moderate levels. The CS Response Strength mind window shows that moderate fear of the "Cage" CS very gradually built up throughout the experiment.

For the high-intensity shock condition, your movement ratio and CS response strength results should resemble those shown next.

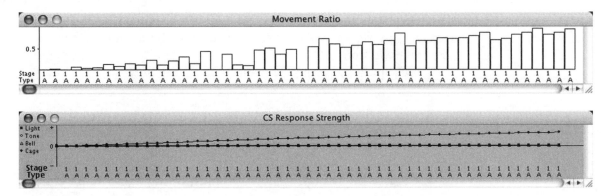

The movement ratio shows that the proportion of time during which Sniffy was frozen during 30-second intervals before shock presentation rose to high levels during the course of the experiment; and the CS Response Strength mind window shows that the "Cage" CS developed the capacity to elicit a high level of fear.

## Exercise 20: CS Pre-exposure Effect

At least in terms of the procedures employed to produce it, the phenomenon called the **CS pre-exposure effect** (also sometimes known as **latent inhibition**) is related to the other phenomena discussed in this chapter. The essence of the phenomenon is this: If an animal has been repeatedly exposed to a CS before that CS is paired with a US, conditioning is slowed down. Demonstrating the phenomenon involves the following two-condition experimental design:

| Condition | Stage 1 | Stage 2 | Stage 2 Expected Result |
|---|---|---|---|
| Experimental | 10: $CS_{MT}$–None | 10: $CS_{MT}$–$US_M$ | Conditioning slower than usual |
| Control | Rest | 10: $CS_{MT}$–$US_M$ | Conditioning at normal rate |

In the experimental condition, Sniffy receives 10 presentations of the medium-intensity tone without a second stimulus during Stage 1, and 10 pairings of the medium-intensity tone with the medium-intensity shock during Stage 2. The control condition receives only the 10 pairings of the medium-intensity tone and medium-intensity shock.

The CS pre-exposure effect is successfully produced if the CR to the tone is acquired more slowly in the experimental condition than in the control condition.

To set up the experimental condition, follow these steps:

- Start with a new Sniffy file.
- Use the Save As command to save the file under an appropriate new name (e.g., Ex20-CSPE) in the Sniffy Files folder on your computer's hard drive.
- Choose the Design Classical Conditioning Experiment command from the Experiment menu and make the following settings in the dialog box:
  - Ascertain that the Interval Between Trials is set at 5 minutes.
  - Set Present Each Trial Type to 10 times.
  - In the First Stimulus section of the dialog box, select the medium-intensity tone.
  - In the Second Stimulus section of the dialog box, select None.
  - Carefully check your Stage 1 settings.
  - Click on the New Stage command button and verify that you are now editing Stage 2, Trial Type A.
  - Set the Interval Between Trials to 5 minutes.
  - Set Present Each Trial Type to 10 times.
  - In the First Stimulus section of the dialog box, select the medium-intensity tone.
  - In the Second Stimulus section of the dialog box, select the medium-intensity shock US.
  - Carefully check your Stage 2 settings.
  - Click on the Save command button at the bottom of the dialog box.
- When the dialog box disappears, select the Run Classical Conditioning Experiment command from the Experiment menu.
- If you want to speed up the experiment, select the Isolate Sniffy (Accelerate Time) command from the Experiment menu.
- When the experiment finishes running, Save the file.

At the end of the experiment, your Movement Ratio and CS Response Strength windows should resemble the following:

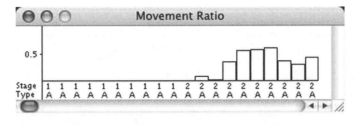

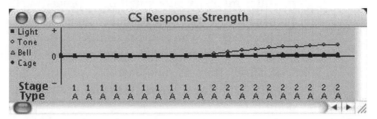

The Movement Ratio window shows that Sniffy gradually acquires a CR to the tone during Stage 2 of the experiment, and the CS Response Strength mind window shows that the tone's CS Response Strength increases during Stage 2.

The question is whether the acquisition that occurs during Stage 2 of the experimental condition is slower than it would have been if Sniffy had not experienced the 10 presentations of the tone by itself in Stage 1. The control condition for this experiment is the same as the basic classical conditioning acquisition experiment from Exercise 1. If you still have the file that we suggested you call Ex1-ClassAcq, open it and compare the results there with the results from the experimental condition in this exercise. That comparison will reveal that, in fact, the 10 tone-only trials during Stage 1 of the CS pre-exposure effect experimental condition do substantially slow the subsequent speed of acquisition.

## Exercise 21: US Pre-exposure Effect

The **US pre-exposure effect** is similar to the CS pre-exposure effect except that, during Stage 1, Sniffy receives a series of US-only trials. Demonstrating the effect involves the two-condition experimental design shown next:

| Condition | Stage 1 | Stage 2 | Stage 2 Expected Result |
|---|---|---|---|
| Experimental | 10: $US_M$ | 10: $CS_{MT}$–$US_M$ | Conditioning less efficient |
| Control | Rest | 10: $CS_{MT}$–$US_M$ | Conditioning normal |

In the experimental condition, Sniffy receives 10 presentations of the medium-intensity shock without a preceding CS during Stage 1, and 10 pairings of the medium-intensity tone with the medium-intensity shock during Stage 2. The control condition receives only the 10 pairings of the medium-intensity tone and medium-intensity shock. The US pre-exposure effect is successfully produced if the CR to the tone is acquired more efficiently in the control than in the experimental condition.

To set up the experimental condition, follow these steps:

- Start with a new Sniffy file.
- Use the Save As command to save the file under an appropriate new name (e.g., Ex21-USPE) in the Sniffy Files folder on your computer's hard drive.
- Choose the Design Classical Conditioning Experiment command from the Experiment menu and make the following settings in the dialog box:
  □ Make sure that the Interval Between Trials is set to 5 minutes.
  □ Set Present Each Trial Type to 10 times.
  □ In the First Stimulus section of the dialog box, make sure that *no* CS is selected.
  □ In the Second Stimulus section of the dialog box, select the medium-intensity shock.
  □ Carefully check your Stage 1 settings.
  □ Click on the New Stage command button and verify that you are now editing Stage 2, Trial Type A.
  □ Make sure that the Interval Between Trials is set to 5 minutes.
  □ Set Present Each Trial Type to 10 times.
  □ In the First Stimulus section of the dialog box, select the medium-intensity tone.
  □ In the Second Stimulus section of the dialog box, select the medium-intensity shock US.
  □ Carefully check your Stage 2 settings.
  □ Click on the Save command button at the bottom of the dialog box.

- When the dialog box disappears, select the Run Classical Conditioning Experiment command from the Experiment menu.
- If you want to speed up the experiment, select the Isolate Sniffy (Accelerate Time) command from the Experiment menu.
- When the experiment finishes running, save the file.

At the end of the experiment, your Movement Ratio and CS Response Strength windows should resemble the following:

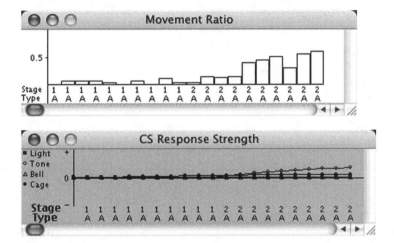

The Movement Ratio window shows that, during the first stage of the experiment, background conditioning starts to develop. However, the CS Response Strength mind window shows that 10 US-only trials produce a very low level of conditioning to the "Cage" CS. During Stage 2, both Movement Ratio and CS Response Strength windows show that Sniffy acquires a CR to the tone. Comparing these results with those for the control condition, which is once again the same as your original conditioning experiment from Exercise 1, reveals that, in fact, the CR was acquired somewhat less efficiently in the experimental condition than in the control condition.

## Comparing CS and US Pre-exposure With the Control

The following graph compares the acquisition of CS response strength in the CS and US pre-exposure conditions with each other and with their control:

**Pre-Exposure Comparisons**

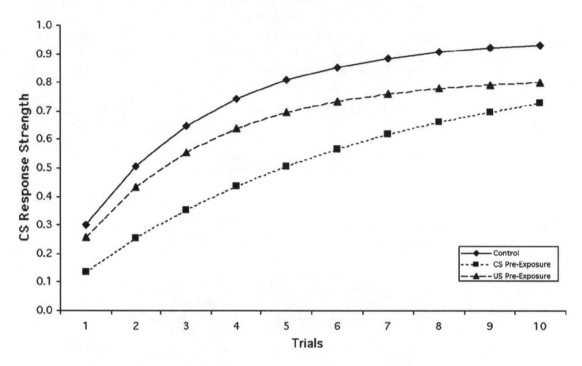

This graph indicates that both CS and US pre-exposure reduces the asymptote to which conditioning proceeds. In addition, CS pre-exposure slows down the rate of conditioning, but US pre-exposure seems to have little effect on the speed of conditioning. Although these subtle differences between the effects of CS and US pre-exposure are not readily apparent in the movement ratio results from any single run of the experiments, similar results for the movement ratio measure of Sniffy's behavior can be obtained if you run several replicates of each experimental condition and average the movement ratios. These results are based on Sniffy's classical conditioning model. We do not know whether these quantitative details would also turn out to be the same with real rats.

## A Question

The previous graph shows the comparative effects of CS and US pre-exposure according to Sniffy's classical conditioning algorithm. CS pre-exposure slows down the rate of subsequent classical condition-

ing, whereas US pre-exposure reduces the level of conditioning. Do you think that this result would actually be obtained with live animals? Why or why not?

## Something to Do

In Exercise 19, you examined the effect of repeated, unsignaled shocks (shocks that are not preceded by a CS that signals their occurrence). Repeated presentation of either the medium- or the high-intensity shock caused Sniffy to manifest more or less continuous fear. You might wonder whether an equivalent number of signaled shocks would produce a similar effect. To find out, set up the following experiment.

- Start with a new Sniffy file and give it an appropriate name, such as SignaledShock.
- In the Design Classical Conditioning Experiment dialog box:
- In Stage 1, set up 50 trials with the medium-intensity tone followed by the high-intensity shock.
- In Stage 2, set up 5 trials with no CS (uncheck all the First Stimulus options) followed by the None US. This will provide five 30-second samples of Sniffy's behavior to determine how much fearful behavior he is manifesting when no CS is present.
- Run the experiment and examine the results, paying particular attention to Stage 2. Compare the results with the last few trials of the high-shock condition in Exercise 19. If you want a completely comparable situation, add a 5-trial second stage like the one you set up for the signaled shock experiment to the high-shock condition from Exercise 19.
- What relevance does the result have to the phenomenon of overshadowing?
- Do you think that the different effects of signaled versus unsignaled shock might have any relevance to human abnormal psychology? Explain your answer.

# 9

## Introduction to Operant Conditioning

**Edward Thorndike**

The research that led to the study of what today we call operant conditioning began more than a century ago with the work of Edward Thorndike. Impressed by William James's classic textbook, *Principles of Psychology* (James, 1890), Thorndike enrolled at Harvard University and took courses with James. At Harvard, Thorndike began the first experimental study of learning in animals. At the time, there was no formal psychological laboratory at Harvard and very little money to support Thorndike's work. His first laboratory was in his home.

Thorndike (1898) described his early animal learning experiments in a classic monograph. In these experiments, Thorndike studied the way cats learned to escape from an apparatus that he called a **puzzle box.** The cats were locked inside the box and had to manipulate a mechanical device to open the box and escape. Initially, the cats behaved in many different ways, most of which did not lead to escape. However, gradually, by trial and error, the cats found the behaviors that led to escape. Thorndike recorded how long it took each cat to escape on each trial and found that the average time gradually decreased from several minutes to a few seconds. As the escape speeds increased, the cats were learning to eliminate useless behaviors, while retaining the much smaller number of successful behaviors. The form of learning that Thorndike studied is often called **instrumental conditioning.** Thorndike summarized the mechanism that strengthens and selects successful behaviors by stating what he called the **Law of Effect:**

> Of several responses made to the same situation, those which are accompanied or closely followed by satisfaction to the animal will, other things

being equal, be more firmly connected with the situation, so that, when it recurs, they will be more likely to recur; those which are accompanied or closely followed by discomfort to the animal will, other things being equal, have their connections with that situation weakened, so that, when it recurs, they will be less likely to occur. The greater the satisfaction or discomfort, the greater the strengthening or weakening of the bond. (quoted in Kimble, 1961, p. 10)

Thorndike's experiments showed that the effect—the consequence—of a behavior determines whether the behavior will be strengthened or weakened. Hitting the right combination of levers in Thorndike's puzzle box had the positive effect of opening the door and letting the cat out of the box. As with most pioneers, Thorndike's models of instrumental conditioning and his statement of the law of effect have been subject to many changes. However, they remain an important cornerstone of our understanding of the learning process.

## B. F. Skinner

B. F. Skinner formulated the methods and procedures that describe a variant of Thorndike's instrumental conditioning that Skinner called **operant conditioning.** In Thorndike's work with puzzle boxes, and subsequently in his studies of animals learning to run mazes, the learning tasks involved apparatus and procedures in which animals had the opportunity to make a correct response only at certain well-defined times called **trials.** Skinner developed a learning situation in which an animal is confined during training in a cage called an **operant chamber,** which contains a device on which responses can be made, as well as a mechanism, called the **magazine,** for the delivery of food. In an operant chamber, animals are trained in an experimental situation in which the opportunity to perform some response is continuously available. Like Thorndike, Skinner was interested in how the consequences of behaviors influence the frequency with which those behaviors are repeated. Skinner's work with operant conditioning is thus an extension of Thorndike's work with instrumental conditioning. Moreover, the same principles of learning seem to apply both when the animal has the opportunity to make a correct response only at certain times (as in Thorndike's puzzle boxes and mazes) and when the animal is able to respond at any time (as in Skinner's operant chamber).

Skinner (1938) made three fundamental assumptions about behavior:

- Animals are frequently active, a fact that means that organisms are continually **emitting** various behaviors.
- These emitted behaviors frequently have consequences that influence the frequency with which the behaviors are repeated in the future.
- The effects of the consequences are influenced by the animal's motivational state as well as by the physical and social environment. For example, the effect of presenting food as a consequence of performing some behavior depends upon whether the animal has been deprived of food.

Skinner studied animal learning, but he believed that it was possible to apply his findings to design more effective human institutions in which the planned, systematic application of reinforcement would make people happier and more productive (Skinner, 1953). Skinner not only called for the objective study of behavior, he also posited that behavior is often caused by events in the environment that can be discovered and manipulated to change behavior. In other words, he attempted to create a philosophical framework based on his findings; this effort generated a lot of excitement and controversy (Skinner, 1971).

Traditionally, people have believed that mental events cause many aspects of human behavior. In contrast, Skinner (1953, 1971) asserted that it is more useful to view feelings, thoughts, emotions, and most other mental events as covert behaviors. In Skinner's view, both overt behaviors and the mental events that accompany them occur because of current and past conditions of reinforcement, and both are subject to the same behavioral laws.

Although he recognized that behavior is produced by the interaction of genetic and environmental factors, Skinner and his followers have concerned themselves almost exclusively with environmental effects. The historical reasons for this emphasis on the environment are complex, but one important reason is that environmental factors are easier to manipulate than genetic factors, especially in human beings, in which genetic manipulations are usually considered to be unethical. Thus, for example, a child's genes and the environment in which the child grows up jointly determine how tall the child will grow to be. Although nothing can be done about a child's tallness genes once the embryo has been conceived, the diet that the child eats—an environmental factor—can significantly affect adult height.

Skinner (1938, 1953) stated that psychologists should be concerned with discovering the laws of behavior and emphasized the importance of relating environmental causes to behavioral effects. In addition, he believed it is often possible to discover behavioral laws without understanding what goes on inside the organism. Many psychologists have used the metaphor of a black box to characterize this aspect of Skinner's approach to psychology. The box, which represents the organism, is opaque. The inside is invisible, and we don't need to know what goes on inside the box. Understanding the rules that govern the box's behavior and controlling its actions do not require opening it. In fact, trying to understand what goes on inside the box may be confusing and misleading.

We can understand this "black box" view of the individual by considering the behavior of a television set. Few of us can produce or understand a circuit diagram that explains how a TV set works, but we can still operate one. We know that we must plug the set into an electric outlet. We know that when we manipulate the channel selector, the stations change. We know that a second control adjusts the volume, and other controls change the colors. The picture and sound are the behaviors that we want to predict and change, and we can predict and change these behaviors. If the set is not working properly, we also know that sometimes a sharp rap on the side of the case will improve the picture. None of this knowledge about how to change the behavior of a TV set requires understanding its internal workings. Skinner believed we can predict and change the behavior of organisms, including ourselves, in a similar way without needing to understand the internal workings of the body.

Skinner (1938) proposed that psychologists should seek to discover relationships between the environment and behavior without speculating about what goes on inside the organism. This "agnostic" approach to the workings of the organism was one of the most controversial aspects of Skinner's approach to psychology. A great many psychologists in Skinner's day (for example, Guthrie, 1960; Hull, 1943, 1952; Tolman, 1932) believed, and a majority of present-day psychologists still maintain, that understanding behavior requires understanding the psychological and/or physiological processes that go on inside the organism. A computer program manual is not the place to debate these profound issues in the philosophy of science. Suffice it to say that in designing a virtual animal that simulates the behavior of a real rat in an operant chamber, we had to endow Sniffy with certain psychological processes in order to reproduce the results that Skinner and others have obtained. Sniffy's psychological processes are modeled after

those discussed in many contemporary textbooks on the psychology of learning (for example, Domjan, 1998; Mazur, 1998; Tarpy, 1997). Nevertheless, there is no way of knowing how closely Sniffy's psychological processes resemble those of real rats. All we can say is that Sniffy's psychological processes, which we display in the various mind windows, illustrate the kinds of processes that many psychologists believe are characteristics of real rats.

Skinner (1935, 1938, 1953) distinguished between elicited and emitted behaviors. An elicited behavior is the specific result of presenting a particular stimulus. You studied how learning can affect elicited behaviors in the preceding experiments on classical conditioning. In contrast, emitted behaviors are responses that occur without any readily identifiable eliciting stimulus. For example, there is no stimulus that will reliably elicit grooming movements or barking from all normal dogs in the same way that placing food on a dog's tongue will elicit salivation.

Many of the behaviors that psychologists are interested in understanding are emitted, not elicited. Consider the behavior of students during class. They not only listen to the instructor and take notes, they also scratch, yawn, doodle, wiggle around in their seats, and exhibit a wealth of other behaviors. Almost all these behaviors are emitted in the sense that no single stimulus exists whose presentation will reliably elicit any of these behaviors from everyone.

The scientific question to which Skinner sought experimental answers was: What controls the frequency of emitted behaviors? To address this question, Skinner developed the operant chamber, a very simple environment in which he thought it would be possible to discover how the environment determines the frequency with which animals and people produce emitted behaviors.

## The Operant Chamber

Sniffy's operant chamber resembles those found in laboratories where psychologists do research on operant conditioning. A look at Sniffy's operant chamber reveals three particularly important objects on the back wall: a lever, or so-called **bar,** that you will train Sniffy to press; a water spout; and a food hopper. As in all operant conditioning situations, the bar is continuously available for Sniffy to press. The hopper is the device that you will use to provide a positive consequence, or **reinforcement,** when Sniffy does something that you want him to do more often. You can program the operant chamber to deliver food pellets

automatically when Sniffy presses the bar, or you can dispense pellets manually by hitting the space bar on your computer keyboard or clicking your computer's (left) mouse button while pointing at the bar. Other devices in Sniffy's operant chamber permit you to present other kinds of stimuli. These devices include a speaker through which sounds can be played, a light that can be turned on and off, and the parallel metal bars that form the floor through which electric shocks can be delivered.

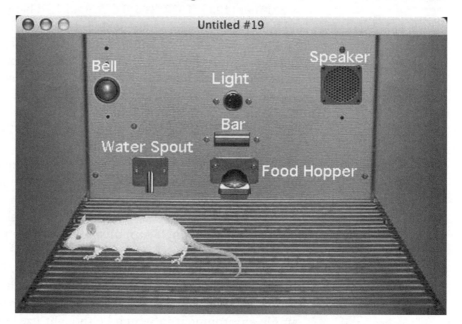

In this restricted environment, a real rat performs a limited subset of species-typical behaviors. As with a real rat, you can expect to see Sniffy rearing up, grooming himself, and exploring the chamber. You can observe and record many of Sniffy's behaviors. However, the response that psychologists generally study in an operant chamber is bar pressing. In research laboratories, psychologists use computers to control the presentation of food and other stimuli and to record bar presses; the Sniffy Pro program simulates these functions.

## Reinforcement and Punishment

Skinner (1938) defined **reinforcement** as a procedure that makes a behavior pattern, or **response,** more likely to be repeated under similar circumstances in the future. In operant conditioning, the term *rein-*

*forcement* refers to the procedure of presenting or removing a stimulus (called a **reinforcer**) as a consequence of performing a response. A **positive reinforcer** is a stimulus whose presentation as a consequence of a behavior causes that behavior to occur more frequently under similar circumstances in the future. The term **positive reinforcement** refers to the procedure of presenting a positive reinforcer as a consequence of a behavior pattern. You will use food as a positive reinforcer to train Sniffy to press the bar or do certain other things in the operant chamber. A **negative reinforcer** is a stimulus whose removal or termination as a consequence of a behavior makes that behavior more likely to occur under similar circumstances in the future. The term **negative reinforcement** refers to the procedure of removing a negative reinforcer as a consequence of a behavior. Uncomfortable environmental conditions (temperature extremes, rain) are examples of negative reinforcers—stimuli whose termination can strengthen behaviors. As the saying goes, most people are smart enough to learn to come in out of the rain. Both positive and negative reinforcement have the effect of increasing the rate (the number of times per minute or hour) at which the reinforced response will occur under similar circumstances in the future.

Skinner (1953, 1971) decried the fact that much of our society is controlled by negative reinforcement. If we have a noisy neighbor in an apartment building, we may bang on the wall to make the noise stop. Termination of the annoyance is negative reinforcement for wall banging and will increase the probability of banging the wall again under similar circumstances in the future. Children do homework to avoid parental nagging, a woman visits her mother to escape her husband's abusive behavior, a worker shows up for work on time to avoid unemployment. Skinner believed that this heavy reliance on negative reinforcement is a sign of a poorly planned society. He wrote several books and articles describing how society might be better organized based on knowledge of operant principles and extensive use of positive reinforcement.

Operant conditioning also defines two procedures for punishing behavior. **Punishment** is the mirror image of reinforcement. Whereas reinforcement causes behaviors to be repeated more often, punishment causes behaviors to occur less often. A **positive punisher** is a stimulus whose presentation following the occurrence of a response makes that response occur less often in the future. **Positive punishment** is the name of the procedure involved in presenting a positive punisher as a behavioral consequence. If you hit your puppy with a rolled-up newspaper when it has a toilet accident in the house, you are employing positive punishment. A **negative punisher** is a stimulus whose

removal following a response causes that response to occur less often in the future. **Negative punishment** is the procedure involved in removing a negative punisher to make a behavior occur less often. If your daughter misbehaves while watching her favorite television program and you send her to her room (thereby terminating access to the television program), you are employing negative punishment.

Note that the terms *negative* and *positive* have the same meaning when applied to punishment that they have when applied to reinforcement. Both positive reinforcers and positive punishers have their effects, respectively, of strengthening or weakening behaviors when you *apply* or *turn on* the stimuli following a behavior pattern. Thus, the term *positive* in this context refers to the presentation or application of a stimulus. Both negative reinforcers and negative punishers have their respective effects when the stimuli are *removed* or *terminated.* Thus, the term *negative* in this context refers to the removal of a stimulus. But remember: Both positive and negative reinforcement cause behaviors to occur more often; both positive and negative punishment cause behaviors to occur less often.

Another dimension that applies to both reinforcers and punishers concerns whether the reinforcing or punishing power of the stimulus is intrinsic or learned. Food is a good example of a stimulus whose reinforcing power is intrinsic; animals require no special training for food to acquire the capacity to act as a positive reinforcer. Similarly, presenting electric shock is an intrinsic positive punisher, and terminating shock is an intrinsic negative reinforcer. Stimuli whose effectiveness as reinforcers or punishers requires no special training are said to be **primary reinforcers** or **primary punishers.** Other stimuli that lack intrinsic reinforcing or punishing power can acquire the capacity to act as reinforcers or punishers if they are paired with primary reinforcers or punishers. Money is a good example of a stimulus whose reinforcing power has been acquired in this way. There is nothing intrinsically reinforcing about money; it's just pieces of paper and metal disks. However, people learn to treat money as a powerful positive reinforcer because of its pairing with primary reinforcers such as food and drink. Stimuli that acquire reinforcing or punishing power as a result of pairing with primary reinforcers or punishers are called **secondary,** or **conditioned, reinforcers** or **punishers.**

In operant conditioning, organisms learn that particular behaviors produce particular consequences in particular situations. In more technical terms, many psychologists believe that operant conditioning involves learning a three-part association among a situation, a response, and a reinforcing or punishing consequence (Domjan, 1998; Mazur,

1998; Schwartz & Reisberg, 1991; Tarpy, 1997). The effect of reinforcement is to select for the reinforced behavior at the expense of other, unreinforced behaviors. In other words, the effect of reinforcement is to make the reinforced behavior occur more often; a side effect of reinforcement is that many unreinforced behaviors occur less often because the animal or person comes to perform the reinforced behavior so frequently that less time is available to do other things. The effect of punishment is just the opposite of that of reinforcement. Punishment selects against the punished behavior, thereby making it occur less often and, as a side effect, making other, unpunished behaviors occur somewhat more often. An animal's **behavioral repertoire** is a list of all the behaviors that the animal would ever produce. The effect of operant conditioning is always to modify the relative frequencies with which different behaviors in the behavioral repertoire occur.

Skinner argued that punishment, in either of its forms, is undesirable for several reasons. Apart from ethical considerations, perhaps the most important of these reasons is that punishment is a less effective training tool than reinforcement because punishment conveys less information. When you punish an animal or a child for doing something, you are in effect teaching the subject not to perform one particular item in its behavioral repertoire in the situation where the punishment occurred, but punishment provides no information about which other behaviors are appropriate. Reinforcement is a more powerful training tool because reinforcement specifically teaches the organism what to do.

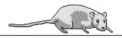

# 10

# Basic Operant Phenomena: Magazine Training, Shaping, Extinction, Spontaneous Recovery, and Secondary Reinforcement

## Operant Conditioning: Technique

Like a real rat, Sniffy will occasionally press the bar in the operant chamber even before you train him to do so. Thus, when you condition Sniffy to press the bar, you are not teaching him to do something that he was previously incapable of doing. Reinforcement simply increases the frequency with which bar pressing occurs. To train Sniffy to bar-press, you will administer a food pellet for each bar press. Thus, you will be using positive reinforcement to train Sniffy.

From what we've said so far, you might think that all you need to do to train Sniffy to bar-press is to set up the operant chamber so that the magazine releases a food pellet each time Sniffy presses the bar. In fact, if that's all you do, Sniffy will eventually learn to press the bar; but he will take rather a long time to do so. The reason for this slowness illustrates one of the most basic principles of operant conditioning: To be effective, reinforcement must occur *immediately* after the response. Delayed reinforcement is much less effective. The problem with food as a reinforcer in this situation is that even though a food pellet drops into the food hopper as soon as Sniffy presses the bar, the food can have no effect on Sniffy until he finds it; and Sniffy may not find the food immediately. When he does find it, the food will strengthen whatever behavior Sniffy was performing just before he found it, and that is much more likely to be sniffing around the hopper than bar pressing.

Food is a very effective reinforcer that can be used to train animals to do many kinds of things, but it is often hard to deliver food fast enough to reinforce effectively the response that the trainer wants to strengthen. To overcome this difficulty, animal trainers often transform a stimulus whose timing they can precisely control into a secondary reinforcer by associating that stimulus with food. Then the trainer uses the secondary reinforcer to increase the frequency of the response that the trainer wants the animal to learn. Fortunately, the magazine in an operant chamber produces a distinctive mechanical sound when it drops a food pellet into the hopper; and it is easy to transform this sound, which has no intrinsic power to act as a reinforcer, into a secondary reinforcer by pairing the sound with food delivery in a way that causes Sniffy to associate the sound with food presentation. The procedure that turns the magazine sound into a secondary reinforcer is called **magazine training.**

## The Operant Associations Mind Window

The Operant Associations mind window displays the strength of three associations that Sniffy will learn when you train him to press the bar. To display the Operant Associations mind window, click on the Windows menu and then select Operant Associations from the Mind Windows submenu. In an untrained Sniffy, the Operant Associations mind window looks like this:

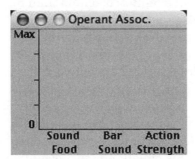

**The Sound-Food Association**

The **sound–food association** is the association between the sound of the food pellet-dispensing mechanism and the fact that a pellet of food is available in the hopper. You will teach Sniffy this association during the next exercise on magazine training. The **bar–sound association** is the association between the bar and the sound produced by the food-dispensing mechanism. When Sniffy is trained to press the bar, Sniffy learns that the bar is the device whose manipulation causes the sound that signals the presence of a food pellet in the hopper. **Action strength**

is Sniffy's association between a particular behavior pattern and obtaining food. A strong sound–food association is a prerequisite for training Sniffy to perform any operant behavior. Action strength will also develop whenever Sniffy is trained to perform any operantly conditioned behavior.[1] However, the bar–sound association develops only when Sniffy is trained to bar-press. The bar–sound association doesn't develop when Sniffy is trained to do something other than bar pressing because none of the other behaviors that Sniffy can be operantly conditioned to perform involves doing anything with the bar.

## Exercise 22: Magazine Training

Magazine training is a technique that involves using what amounts to a classical conditioning procedure to turn an originally neutral stimulus into a *secondary reinforcer*.[2] The training process involves an interaction between you and Sniffy. What you will do depends on what Sniffy does, and Sniffy's future responses to the magazine sound will depend on what you do. The idea is to operate the magazine to present pellets of food in such a way that Sniffy learns to associate the sound of the magazine with the availability of a food pellet in the hopper. One of the associations that the Operant Associations mind window displays is the sound–food association. By keeping an eye on the Operant Associations mind window, you can watch Sniffy develop an association between the magazine sound and food.

Here are the steps that you need to follow to magazine-train Sniffy:

- Start with a new Sniffy file.
- Use the Save As command in the File menu to save the file under an appropriate name (e.g., Ex22-MagTrain) in your Sniffy Files or Sniffy Pro for Windows folder.
- Display the Operant Associations mind window by selecting it from the Mind Windows section of the Windows menu.
- The message in the Lab Assistant window reads, "To set up an experiment, choose Design Classical Conditioning Experiment or Design Operant Conditioning Experiment from the Experiments menu. Sniffy is not being reinforced automatically. If you

---

[1] In Chapter 14, we will show you how to train Sniffy to perform several other behaviors.

[2] The concept of secondary reinforcement was defined and discussed in Chapter 9.

want to issue a reinforcement, press the space bar or click on the bar." The last sentence of the Lab Assistant message is the relevant instruction for this experiment.

- Wait until Sniffy closely approaches the food hopper. Then deliver a food pellet, either by *pressing the space bar on your computer keyboard* or by *pointing the cursor at the bar and clicking your (left) mouse button.*

- To save time at the start, you may want to give Sniffy several pellets in rapid succession before he wanders away from the hopper.

- After Sniffy has received several pellets, you can let him wander away a short distance before giving him the next pellet.

- Keep an eye on the Operant Associations mind window. When the height of the Sound–Food bar reaches about one-quarter of the way up the scale, the message in the Lab Assistant window will change to read, "Sniffy is developing an association between the sound of the hopper and the presentation of food. However, this association is not strong enough to properly train Sniffy. Continue to present food when Sniffy is near the hopper." Follow the Lab Assistant's advice. Continue to reinforce Sniffy when he is near the hopper.

- To be able to use this file as the basis for training Sniffy to perform several different behaviors, during magazine training do not consistently give Sniffy a food pellet after he performs any particular behavior or category of behavior.

- When the height of the Sound–Food bar in the Operant Associations mind window reaches about three-quarters of the way up the scale, the Lab Assistant will display the message, "Sniffy appears to have developed an association between the sound of the hopper and the food. You can now use the sound as a reinforcer to shape Sniffy's behavior."

- Sniffy's magazine training is now complete.

- Save the file.

## Exercise 23: Shaping Sniffy to Press the Bar

After magazine training, if the operant chamber is programmed to drop a pellet of food into the hopper every time Sniffy presses the bar, Sniffy's occasional spontaneous bar presses will be effectively rein-

forced, and Sniffy will learn to bar-press all by himself if you just leave him alone. Moreover, he will do so much more quickly than would have been the case without magazine training. However, if you are observant and have a good sense of timing, you can accelerate this learning process by using a technique called **shaping.**

Shaping is the technical name for a procedure used to train an animal to do something by reinforcing successive approximations of the desired **target behavior.** In this procedure, the trainer (teacher) leads the subject (learner) to progress by small steps. Reinforcement is delivered for progress and then withheld until more progress has been made.

To be a successful shaper, you have to be a careful and patient observer. Shaping works because behavior is variable. The idea is to pick a behavior that the animal performs fairly often and that is similar in some way to the target behavior you want the animal to perform eventually. Reinforcing this first approximation of the behavior will cause Sniffy to perform that behavior more frequently. Because Sniffy's behavior is composed of movements that occur with different probabilities, you will notice a number of different variations. Eventually, Sniffy will perform a variant of the behavior that more closely resembles the target behavior. That variant then becomes your second approximation, and you require him to repeat that variant to obtain reinforcement. As the second approximation is performed more frequently, Sniffy will eventually emit another variant that resembles the target even more closely, and so on.

Shaping an animal takes patience, careful observation, and good timing. It is a skill that you learn with practice. Sniffy is easier to shape than a real rat, partly because he never becomes satiated for food and partly because his behavioral repertoire is smaller than a real rat's. Nevertheless, shaping Sniffy is challenging enough for you to get some idea of both the frustration and the eventual feeling of triumph that shaping an animal engenders.

In the Sniffy Pro program, bar pressing is part of a **response class** (a group of similar movements) in which Sniffy lifts his front paws off the floor while facing the back wall of the chamber. We programmed Sniffy that way because, in order to press the bar, Sniffy must first go to the bar and then rear up in front of it. Thus, as your first approximation to bar pressing, try reinforcing Sniffy for rearing up anytime he is facing the back wall of the chamber on which the bar and food hopper are mounted. Once rearing up facing the back wall has become more frequent, require him to rear up with his feet against the back wall. If your patience, observational skills, and timing are good, you should have Sniffy bar pressing frequently in less than 30 minutes. If you are

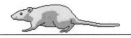

very skillful, you can shape Sniffy in less than 15 minutes. However, if you are inattentive or have bad timing, you might have been better off letting Sniffy learn to bar-press on his own after magazine training.[3]

Shaping is such an attention-demanding task that you should not pay attention to anything but Sniffy's behavior while you are shaping. However, once Sniffy has pressed the bar four or five times in a minute, you can stop shaping him and watch the progressive effect of reinforcement as Sniffy presses the bar more and more often. At that point, you should start keeping an eye on the Operant Associations mind window to observe the development of the bar–sound association and action strength. The bar–sound association tells Sniffy that the bar is the device he uses to produce the sound that signals the delivery of a food pellet. The action strength is the degree to which Sniffy has learned that pressing is what he does with the bar to get the sound that signals the delivery of a food pellet.

Here is a detailed description of the steps that you should follow to shape Sniffy to press the bar:

- Open the file from Exercise 22 that we suggested you call Ex22-MagTrain.
- Select the Save As command from the File menu to give the file an appropriate new name (e.g., Ex23-ShapeBP) and save it in the Sniffy Files folder on your computer's hard drive. *Saving the file with a new name before you start shaping Sniffy preserves your original magazine-training file for future use.* You will need it for a number of subsequent exercises.
- If the Operant Associations mind window is not already visible, display it by selecting it from the Mind Windows section of the Windows menu.
- If Cumulative Record 1 is not visible, make it visible by selecting it from the Cumulative Record section of the Windows menu.
- Select the Design Operant Conditioning Experiment command from the Experiment menu.
- In the dialog box that appears, select Bar Press from the Target Behavior section of the drop-down menu under Reinforcement

---

[3] Psychologists who study operant conditioning in live rats approach shaping in a variety of ways. Some people start the shaping process by reinforcing the rat whenever it approaches the bar. Others begin by reinforcing the rat whenever it turns toward the bar. Some of these alternative approaches also work well with Sniffy.

Action. After making the selection, click on the OK button to close the dialog box.

- Note that the terms CRF and Bar Pressing appear in the cumulative record. CRF stands for Continuous Reinforcement, which means that the program will automatically reinforce every bar press. The Bar Press notation indicates that the cumulative record is recording bar presses.
- As your first approximation to bar pressing, give Sniffy a pellet of food when he rears up facing the back wall anywhere in the operant chamber.
- Gradually require Sniffy to rear up closer and closer to the wall.
- Whenever Sniffy rears up directly in front of the bar, there is a chance that he may press it. If he does press the bar, he will hear the magazine sound, receive a food pellet, and the bar–sound association will start to develop. After several reinforced bar presses, a red column will appear above the words "Bar–Sound" and "Action Strength" in the Operant Associations mind window.
- When the column above Bar–Sound in the Operant Associations mind window reaches about one-quarter of the maximum height, the message in the Lab Assistant window will change to read, "Sniffy is developing an association between the bar and the sound. Continue and Sniffy should be trained soon."
- Each time Sniffy presses the bar, watch closely what he does after eating the food pellet. He may press the bar again a second time either immediately or after rearing up near the bar a time or two. If he does press the bar again, you know you're making progress. Allow him to continue pressing the bar as long as he will do so. However, if he rears up more than twice without pressing the bar again, continue to reinforce rearing up.
- If you are patient, the time will come when Sniffy will press the bar eight to ten times in rapid succession. At that point, you can stop shaping, sit back, and watch the progressive effect of reinforcement as Sniffy continues to press the bar more and more frequently.
- Watch the rising levels of the Bar–Sound and Action Strength columns in the Operant Associations mind window. Sniffy's training is complete when the message displayed by the Lab Assistant changes to read, "Sniffy appears to be trained properly. You may experiment with different schedule effects."

- When Sniffy is fully trained, select the Save command from the File menu to preserve your trained Sniffy for future use.

After 30 to 45 minutes of attempting to shape Sniffy according to the instructions given above, Sniffy should be pressing the bar *at least* 20 times during each 5-minute interval delineated by the alternating solid and dotted vertical lines in the cumulative record. If your attempt at shaping fails to obtain that minimum result, something is wrong.

One possibility is that Sniffy has not been properly magazine trained. Look at the Operant Associations mind window. The Sound–Food column level should be *more than* three-quarters of the way up the scale. If it isn't, either go back and repeat Exercise 22 to create a properly magazine-trained Sniffy or use the file titled MagTrain from the Sample Files folder.

A second possibility is that you may not be reinforcing instances of rearing up toward the back wall as outlined above or not reinforcing these behaviors quickly enough.

For users who encounter difficulty with shaping, we have provided a section of the Reinforcement Action menu in the Design Operant Conditioning Experiment dialog box called the **Shaping Tutor.** If you are having trouble reinforcing Sniffy's rearing behaviors:

- Choose the Design Operant Conditioning Experiment command from the Experiment menu.
- Under the Shaping Tutor subsection of the Reinforcement Action menu, choose Rear Up Facing Back.
- The Sniffy Pro program will now automatically reinforce all instances of rearing up facing the back wall, including all bar presses. Watch which actions the program automatically reinforces.
- When you believe that you are capable of effectively reinforcing these behaviors manually, reopen the Design Operant Conditioning Experiment dialog box and choose Bar Press from the Target Behavior section of the Reinforcement Action menu.
- If you are unable to reinforce Sniffy effectively by hand, watch what is going on as the program automatically reinforces rearing up facing the back wall. Once Sniffy presses the bar 8 to 10 times in a 1- or 2-minute period, reopen the Design Operant Conditioning Experiment dialog box and choose Bar Press from

> the Target Behavior section of the Reinforcement Action menu. The program will complete Sniffy's training automatically.
> - When Sniffy's training is complete, the Lab Assistant will display the statement "Sniffy appears to be trained properly. You may experiment with different schedule effects." Save the file.

## Exercise 24: Cumulative Records—Visualizing Sniffy's Responding

In this exercise, you will learn how to interpret **cumulative records,** the means of recording and displaying a rat's bar-pressing behavior that B. F. Skinner (1930) invented. Although there is nothing specific for you to do with Sniffy in this exercise, we suggest you read the following paragraphs while seated in front of your computer with the program running so that you can look at Sniffy's cumulative record from time to time to check out the various features that we are going to describe.

> - If the Sniffy Pro program is not running, start it.
> - Use the Open command from the File menu to open the file that we suggested you name Ex23-ShapeBP in Exercise 23.
> - If the latest cumulative record isn't visible, display it by selecting it from Cumulative Responses submenu of the Windows menu.
> - Note that as time passes, the visible part of the cumulative record automatically scrolls to the right to follow Sniffy's current behavior. If you want to look at something that happened earlier, you can use the scroll bar at the bottom of the window to scroll back to the left.

How do we know whether a rat has learned anything as a result of training in the operant chamber? With Sniffy, you can observe the learning process directly in the Operant Associations mind window. However, when dealing with real animals whose psychological processes are invisible, psychologists treat learning as a process whose operation they must infer solely on the basis of changes in behavior.

Because bar pressing becomes more frequent as a result of training, Skinner chose to measure learning in the operant chamber as an

increase in the frequency of bar pressing. To make the necessary measurements, he invented the **cumulative recorder.** Skinner's cumulative recorder was a mechanical device that pulled a long roll of paper at a constant speed under a pen that rested on the moving paper. At the start, the pen was positioned at the bottom of the record; if the rat did not press the bar, the pen would simply draw a long, straight horizontal line. However, every time the rat pressed the bar, the pen moved a notch upward toward the top of the paper. When the rat was pressing the bar, the resulting record was a sloping line that moved from the bottom edge toward the top of the record. The more rapidly the rat responded, the steeper the slope of line. In other words, Skinner's cumulative recorder drew a record in which the steepness of the line was directly proportional to the rate of bar pressing.

The roll of paper that Skinner used in his cumulative recorder was not very wide. After recording a certain number of responses, the slanted line would reach the top edge of the paper. When that happened, the pen very quickly reset to the bottom edge of the paper, causing a vertical line to be drawn down the paper from top to bottom. This pattern of a slanted line working its way to the top of the paper, followed by a sharp straight line to the bottom of the page, gives a cumulative record the appearance of mountain peaks or waves.

These days, mechanical cumulative recorders of the sort that Skinner invented are obsolete. Scientists who study operant conditioning use computers to draw cumulative records of bar pressing in a fashion similar to the way the Sniffy Pro program produces them. We have described the workings of Skinner's original mechanical device because we think its operation is easier to understand than that of a computer program that simulates the device.

There are several important things to remember about the cumulative records that the Sniffy Pro program produces, and about cumulative records in general:

- The slope of the rising lines on the graph represents the speed with which Sniffy is responding. The steeper the slope, the more rapidly Sniffy was pressing when the record was made. If Sniffy is pressing the bar slowly, the slanted line will take a long time to reach the top of the paper, where it resets to the bottom. This will result in a record that looks like gentle, undulating waves. If Sniffy is pressing fast, the slanted line will reach the top faster, the pen will have to reset more often, and the resulting record will look like more and steeper waves.
- Reinforced responses are marked by short, oblique lines drawn through the record.

- If you let it run long enough, the Sniffy Pro program will produce a series of 10 Cumulative Record windows. The Cumulative Record windows, which are called Cumulative Record 1, Cumulative Record 2, and so on, are accessible under the Cumulative Records section of the Windows menu.
- Each Cumulative Record window depicts Sniffy's bar-pressing performance during two hours of Sniffy Pro program time. *Program time and clock time are not the same thing.* The relationship between program time and clock time depends on both the speed of your computer and the animation speed setting. You can adjust the animation speed in the dialog box that appears when you execute the Preferences command under the File menu in Windows or under the Sniffy menu in Mac OS X. When the animation speed has been adjusted so that Sniffy is moving at a rate that looks realistic, program time and clock time should pass at approximately the same rates.
- The fact that there is a maximum of 10 Cumulative Record windows means that no Sniffy experiment can last more than about 20 hours in program time. After that program time limit has been reached, you can examine and save your results, but you cannot add any additional stages to that particular Sniffy Pro file.

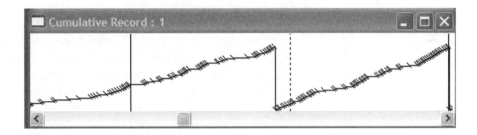

The cumulative record depicted here shows the acquisition of bar pressing as a consequence of shaping in a "typical" experiment. No two cumulative records are ever exactly alike, because Sniffy never behaves in exactly the same way in any two experiments. However, if you were a successful shaper, the part of your cumulative record from Exercise 23 that recorded Sniffy's acquisition of the bar-pressing response should resemble the one shown. Here are some characteristic things about the record shown above that you can expect to see in your own cumulative record:

- The flat, horizontal portions of the line show periods when Sniffy was not pressing the bar.

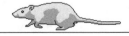

- Sniffy begins to press the bar slowly and intermittently at first, then more and more frequently and steadily.
- Note that the steepness of the cumulative record increases rather rapidly at first and then more slowly. A similar increase in the rate of bar pressing should be visible in your record. However, its relationship to pen resets is likely to be different.
- In addition to depicting Sniffy's response rate and showing which responses were reinforced, the cumulative records that the Sniffy Pro program produces denote the times at which a variety of other significant events occur during experiments. We will explain these additional features in connection with descriptions of experiments where they are important.

Here are a couple of important features that are specific to the cumulative records that the Sniffy Pro program produces:

- The "height" of Sniffy's cumulative record is always 75 responses. There are always 75 responses between any two consecutive pen resets. When the pen resets the first time, Sniffy has made 75 responses. When it resets the second time, he has made 150 responses, and so on. Knowing this will come in handy later on when you need to figure out how many responses Sniffy has made.
- In addition to the dark vertical lines that the cumulative record produces when the pen resets from the top of the record to the bottom, there are thinner, alternating solid and dotted vertical lines spaced at regular intervals. These thinner vertical lines are 5-minute time markers. The time between one thin vertical line and the next (between a solid line and the next dotted line or a dotted line and the next solid line) is 5 minutes in Sniffy Pro program time; the time between two successive solid or two successive dotted vertical lines is 10 minutes in program time.

## Exercise 25: Extinction

After training Sniffy to press the bar, you might wonder what would happen if you stopped reinforcing bar presses. This sounds like a simple question, but it reflects some of the complexity of life in a world where food sources come and go. Animals need to be flexible. They need to be able to learn what to do to obtain whatever food happens to be available at the moment, and they need to be able to stop doing things that no longer produce food. **Extinction** is the technical

name for the behavior changes that occur when a previously reinforced behavior no longer produces reinforcement.

Here is what you need to do to set up and run an extinction experiment:

- If the Sniffy Pro program is not running, start it.
- Use the Open command under the File menu to open the file containing your trained Sniffy from Exercise 23.
- Use the Save As command to save the file under an appropriate new name (e.g., Ex25-Ext, for "extinction") in the Sniffy Files folder on your computer's hard drive. *This step is important because it preserves your original trained Sniffy file for future use.* You will need your trained Sniffy file for the next and other exercises.
- Choose the Design Operant Conditioning Experiment command from the Experiment menu. Executing this command opens the following dialog box.

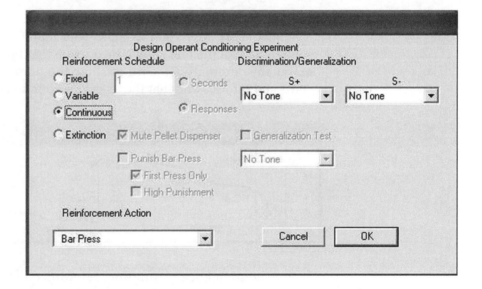

- When the dialog box opens, the button labeled Continuous and the reinforcement action Bar Press are selected because you have been reinforcing all of Sniffy's bar-press responses. Reinforcing every response is a procedure called **continuous reinforcement.**

- To select extinction, point the cursor at the button labeled Extinction and click your (left) mouse button.
- Be sure there is a check mark in the box next to Mute Pellet Dispenser. (If the check mark isn't there, place the cursor over the box and click your (left) mouse button to put a check mark in the box.) Setting up extinction with Mute Pellet Dispenser selected means that Sniffy's bar presses will no longer produce food pellets and that he will no longer hear the magazine sound as a consequence of bar pressing. In other words, both the primary reinforcer (food) and the secondary reinforcer (the magazine sound) are turned off. This is the standard extinction procedure. After checking to be sure that you have made the correct settings, click the OK command button.
- After you click OK, the dialog box will disappear, and the Sniffy Pro program will begin running again, but Sniffy's bar presses will no longer be reinforced.
- If you want to speed up the experiment, select the Isolate Sniffy (Accelerate Time) command from the Experiment menu.

Immediately after you click OK, your cumulative record will look something like the one shown next. Note that the Sniffy Pro program marks the cumulative record to show the point at which extinction starts and informs you that the magazine sound is muted.

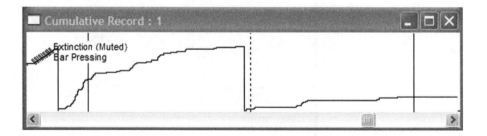

As a consequence of stopping reinforcement, Sniffy's rate of bar pressing will eventually decline until he presses the bar no more often than he did before he was trained. However, the first effect of extinction is to *increase* Sniffy's bar-pressing rate. This increase in response rate is called an **extinction burst,** and it commonly occurs when an animal is switched from continuous reinforcement to extinction.

Your extinction criterion is a 5-min period during which Sniffy presses the bar no more than twice. When that point is reached:

- Mark the cumulative record by executing the Mark Record command in Experiment menu.
- Save your extinction file by selecting the Save command from the File menu.

When the extinction criterion is reached, you should estimate the number of responses that Sniffy made between the onset of extinction and the time when the criterion was reached. You should also estimate the time required to reach the extinction criterion.

When estimating the number of responses and the time elapsed during extinction, remember that:

- The thin alternating dotted and solid vertical lines on the cumulative record mark off 5-min periods in program time.
- Sniffy always makes 75 responses between two successive pen resets.

Determining how many responses Sniffy has made during extinction and the time that extinction required will typically require you to estimate fractional parts of 75-response vertical pen excursions and fractional parts of 5-min time intervals. You can elect either to make precise measurements or to do "eyeball" estimates.

If you want to make precise measurements, you should print your cumulative record and make the appropriate measurements with a ruler. To print your cumulative record:

- Select the Cumulative Record window by pointing the cursor at it and clicking your (left) mouse button once.
- Select the Print Window command from the File menu.

To do an "eyeball" estimate, look at the cumulative record and estimate the appropriate horizontal (time) and vertical (response) movements as a proportion of 5-min intervals and 75-response vertical pen excursions. For example, have another look at the cumulative record shown on page 158 that displays the point at which the change from continuous reinforcement to extinction occurred. The change occurred partway through a 5-min interval between two vertical lines and partway up from the bottom of the cumulative record.

- With regard to time, the change occurred not very long before a vertical line marking the end of a 5-min interval. Let's say that it occurred about 4/5 or 80% of the way through the 5-min interval. Four-

fifths of 5 is 4, so our estimate is that the change occurred about 4 min into the 5-min interval, so that about 1 min remained before the cumulative record reached the time marker.

- With regard to the number of responses that Sniffy made after the previous time marker and before the switch to extinction, it looks as though the cumulative record had moved no more than 2 or 3 responses up from the bottom. We know that there are 75 responses between pen resets, which means that Sniffy had about 72 or 73 responses to go before the pen reset again.

A couple of things about the standard extinction experiment are worthy of some discussion. One of them is the *extinction burst*—the increase in response rate that occurs immediately after Sniffy (or a real rat) is switched from continuous reinforcement to extinction. With real animals, the concept of *frustration* is sometimes evoked as an explanation. An animal that has become accustomed to continuous reinforcement expects to be reinforced for every response. When the expected reinforcement fails to occur, frustration, a hypothetical emotional state, results. This emotion supposedly energizes the animal to make a burst of responses.

With Sniffy, the explanation is much simpler. Sniffy does not manifest frustration. We know this because we did not model frustration in the Sniffy Pro program. When Sniffy is being maintained on continuous reinforcement, he hears the magazine sound after each bar press and comes down off the bar to eat the pellet of food whose availability the magazine sound signals. When Sniffy is switched to standard extinction, the magazine sound no longer occurs. Without the magazine sound to "call" him from the bar, Sniffy can do several things. He *may* come down off the bar and sniff the food hopper. He *may* also come down off the bar and do something else such as grooming himself or walking around in the operant chamber. However, in the first stages of extinction, the bar-pressing response is still very strong. Thus, the thing that Sniffy is most likely to do is to remain mounted at the bar and continue to press it again and again. Because Sniffy can press the bar faster if he doesn't come down to examine the food hopper after each bar press, his response rate goes up.

A second thing to note about the standard extinction procedure is that the Operant Associations mind window shows that extinction results in the elimination of the bar–sound association and action strength. However, the sound–food association remains intact. The bar–sound association and action strength dissipate because bar presses no longer produce the sound. The sound–food association remains intact because Sniffy never hears the sound without receiving a food pellet.

# Exercise 26: Secondary Reinforcement

To get Sniffy to bar-press in the first place, you did two things. During magazine training, you turned the magazine sound into a secondary reinforcer by pairing it with food. Then during shaping, you strengthened an association between the bar and the sound. Finally, during standard extinction, you turned off both the sound and the food. In this exercise, you will demonstrate the reinforcing power of the magazine sound by leaving it turned on during extinction. In other words, you will set up an extinction experiment in which Sniffy no longer receives any food when he presses the bar. However, bar presses will continue to produce the magazine sound (as if the magazine continued to operate when it contained no food pellets). Presenting the magazine sound as a consequence of bar pressing during extinction will have two effects. First, presenting the sound after each bar press during extinction will for a while continue to reinforce bar presses, with the result that the extinction process will be slowed down. Second, because the sound occurs but no food pellets are delivered, the sound–food association will eventually dissipate.

To set up the experiment, you should follow these steps:

- If the Sniffy Pro program is not running, start it.
- Use the Open command under the File menu to open the file containing the Sniffy that you trained to bar-press for continuous reinforcement in Exercise 23. (This is the file called Ex23-ShapeBP if you followed our file-naming suggestion.)
- Use the Save As command to save the file under an appropriate new name (e.g., Ex26-SecRef) in the Sniffy Files folder on your computer's hard drive. *This step is important because it preserves your original trained Sniffy file for future use.* You will need your trained Sniffy for future exercises.
- Choose the Design Operant Conditioning Experiment command from the Experiment menu.
- When the dialog box opens, point the cursor at the button labeled Extinction and click your (left) mouse button to select that option.
- Then point the cursor at the box next to Mute Pellet Dispenser and click it to uncheck this option. Setting up extinction with Mute Pellet Dispenser turned off means that Sniffy's bar presses will no longer produce food pellets, but he will continue hear

> the magazine sound as a consequence of bar pressing. The primary reinforcer (food) is turned off, but the secondary reinforcer (the magazine sound) remains on.
> - After checking to be sure that you have made the correct settings, click the OK command button. After you click OK, the dialog box will disappear, and the Sniffy Pro program will begin running again.
> - If you want to speed up the experiment, select the Isolate Sniffy (Accelerate Time) command from the Experiment menu.

Immediately after clicking OK, your cumulative record will look something like that shown next. Note that the Sniffy Pro program marks the cumulative record to show the point at which extinction starts and informs you that the magazine is not muted.

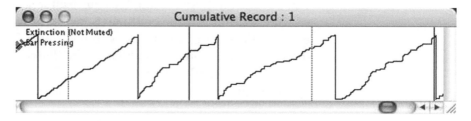

Because Sniffy hears the magazine sound after each bar press, we no longer see the *extinction burst*, the initial increase in the rate of bar pressing, that we saw during standard extinction without the magazine sound. Each time he hears the magazine sound, Sniffy comes down off the bar and sniffs at the food hopper.

Your extinction criterion is a 5-min period during which Sniffy presses the bar no more than twice. When that point is reached:

- Save your Secondary Reinforcement file.

When the extinction criterion is reached, you should estimate the number of responses that Sniffy made between the onset of extinction and the time when the criterion was reached and the time required to reach the extinction criterion.

Compare Sniffy's extinction with the magazine sound turned on with the extinction that you observed in the previous exercise. This comparison will reveal that Sniffy makes more responses and that the extinction process takes more time when the magazine sound remains

on than when it is muted. This difference is caused by the initial secondary reinforcing power of the magazine sound when it occurs during extinction.

Finally, note that after extinction with the magazine sound turned on, the sound–food association extinguished, but the bar–sound association did not. The sound–food association dissipates because the sound occurs but no food pellet is presented. The bar–sound association remains intact because Sniffy continues to hear the sound after each bar press.

## Exercise 27: Spontaneous Recovery

A single extinction session is not enough to permanently reduce the frequency of an operant response to its pre-training frequency. If an animal that has apparently been fully extinguished is removed from the operant chamber, allowed to rest in its home cage for 24 hours, and then returned to the operant chamber for a second extinction session, its response rate at the start of the second session will be greater than it was at the end of the first extinction session. This rest-produced reappearance of an extinguished operant response is called **spontaneous recovery.**

To simulate the phenomenon with Sniffy:

- Open a file in which Sniffy has been trained to press the bar and then extinguished. Either your Ex25-Ext or your Ex26-SecRef file will work for this purpose.
- Use the Save As command to save the file under a new appropriate name (e.g., Ex27-SponRec) in the Sniffy Files folder on your computer's hard drive.
- Choose Remove Sniffy for Time-Out from the Experiment menu. To simulate taking a rest, Sniffy will disappear momentarily and then reappear.
- If you want to speed up the experiment, select the Isolate Sniffy (Accelerate Time) command from the Experiment menu.

When Sniffy reappears, his bar-pressing rate will be higher than it was at the end of extinction, but lower than it was before extinction. Immediately after the timeout, your cumulative record should resemble that shown next:

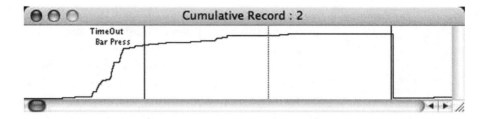

Check the Operant Associations mind window shortly after starting your spontaneous recovery experiment. You'll recall that standard extinction (with the magazine sound muted) produces extinction of the bar–sound association and action strength, whereas extinction with the magazine sound not muted causes extinction of the sound–food association. At the beginning of the spontaneous recovery experiment, the extinguished items are partly restored. This partial reappearance of the extinguished items is the "psychological" reason why Sniffy presses the bar more often at the beginning of the second extinction session than he did at the end of the first extinction session.

Let the Sniffy Pro program run until Sniffy meets the extinction criterion again. Compare the number of responses made and the time required to reach the extinction criterion during this second extinction session with the number of responses and time required during the first extinction session. This comparison will reveal that the second time around Sniffy makes fewer responses and takes less time to reach the criterion.

## Some Things to Do

### Behavioral Repertoire

Roughly speaking, the items in the behavioral repertoire of an untrained Sniffy can be categorized into eight major components:

- *Paw lifting:* Sniffy lifts his front paws off the floor anywhere in the operant chamber. Do not include bar pressing in this category.
- *Face touching:* Sniffy touches his face with one of his front paws.
- *Head lowering:* Sniffy lowers his head down between his back legs as if he were licking his genitals.
- *Sniffing:* Sniffy stands with all four paws on the floor and twitches his whiskers. You can see his whiskers twitch when he is facing ei-

ther toward you or toward the left or right wall of the operant chamber. When he is facing the back wall, you can't see his whiskers, but you can see him wiggling a bit.

- *Locomotion:* Sniffy walks around or turns his body.
- *Bar pressing:* Sniffy presses the bar.
- *Hopper sniffing and eating:* Sniffy sticks his head into the food hopper. If a food pellet is there, he eats it.
- *Drinking:* Sniffy places his mouth against the side or end of the drinking spout and makes licking movements (similar to sniffs).

Training Sniffy to press the bar modifies the frequencies with which he performs many of the behaviors in his behavior repertoire. To determine how the frequencies are changed, first watch a completely untrained Sniffy for 15 minutes and record how frequently he performs each kind of behavior. (To produce a completely untrained Sniffy, simply open a new file.) Then watch and record the behavior of the completely trained Sniffy that you produced in Exercise 23 for the same length of time.

- How much more often does the trained Sniffy press the bar, compared to the untrained Sniffy?
- Which categories of behavior occur less often in the trained Sniffy?
- Are the frequencies of any categories of behavior unchanged?
- Do any categories except bar pressing increase in frequency?

A major component of this exercise is figuring out how to set things up so that you can accurately and objectively record the frequencies with which Sniffy performs the various categories of behavior. It is a good idea to work with a partner, where one person watches Sniffy continuously and calls out the behaviors as they occur while the other person enters the data on paper.

## Another Effect of Magazine Training

If left entirely to his own devices in an operant chamber that has been programmed to a deliver food pellet each time the bar is pressed, Sniffy will train himself to press the bar. To find out how long it takes a completely naïve Sniffy to train himself to press the bar, open a new file, set up the program to deliver a food pellet for each bar press, hide Sniffy to accelerate time, and keep an eye on the Operant Associations mind window. When the Lab Assistant says that Sniffy is fully trained, mark the cumulative record (by choosing Mark Record from

the Experiment menu). Repeat the process with the magazine-trained Sniffy that you produced in Exercise 22. Compare the times that the completely naïve Sniffy and the magazine-trained Sniffy require to complete their self-training. The magazine-trained Sniffy should self-train faster. Why?

# 11

## The Effects of Punishment on Response Elimination

As noted in Chapter 10, the effect of punishment is the opposite that of reinforcement. Reinforcing a response makes the response more likely to occur under similar circumstances in the future or increases the rate at which a response occurs in a situation where the response is appropriate. In contrast, punishment makes a response less likely to occur or decreases the rate at which it occurs. In Exercises 25 and 26, you saw that discontinuing reinforcement of a previously reinforced response causes the response to occur less often until eventually the response occurs no more often than it did originally. As we noted, eliminating a previously reinforced response by no longer reinforcing it is called **extinction.** In the present chapter, you will examine the effect of mildly or severely punishing the first response that Sniffy makes at the start of an extinction session and of mildly punishing each response that Sniffy makes during extinction. If the effect of punishment is opposite to the effect of extinction, then punishing Sniffy for responding during extinction should lead to more rapid elimination of bar pressing.

### Exercise 28: The Effect of a Single Mild Punishment

In this experiment, you will examine the effect of administering a single mild electric shock after the first response that Sniffy makes during extinction.

> ■ Open your trained Sniffy file from Exercise 23. This is the file that we recommended you save under the name Ex23-ShapeBP. If you no longer have the file, you can use the file called ShapeBP from your Sample Files folder.

- Use the Save As command in the File menu to save the file under a new name (e.g., Ex28-1MildPun in the Sniffy Files folder. *This step preserves your original trained Sniffy for future use.* You will need this file in several further experiments.
- If the most recent cumulative record is not visible, make it visible by selecting it from the Windows menu.
- If Sniffy is hidden, make him visible by selecting Show Sniffy from the Experiment menu.
- Execute the Design Operant Conditioning Experiment command by selecting it from the Experiment menu.
- In the dialog box that appears:
  □ Select Extinction.
  □ Click on the box titled Punish Bar Press.
  □ Make sure that a check mark appears next to First Press Only.
  □ Make sure that a check mark also appears next to Mute Pellet Dispenser.
- Click OK.
- You will note that the first time Sniffy presses the bar, he leaps in the air, indicating that he has been shocked.
- If you want to speed up the experiment, you may do so by selecting Hide Sniffy (Accelerate Time) from the Experiment menu.

Shortly after you close the Design Operant Conditioning Experiment dialog box, the cumulative record will resemble that shown here:

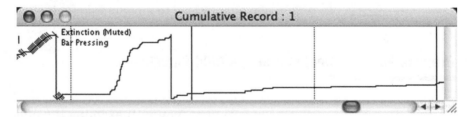

After receiving the single mild shock, Sniffy doesn't press the bar again for a couple of minutes, after which he begins to press it more or less as if he had not been shocked at all. Your extinction criterion is a 5-minute period in which Sniffy presses the bar no more than twice. When Sniffy meets the extinction criterion:

- Save the file.

Compare the number of bar presses that Sniffy makes prior to reaching the extinction criterion in this experiment with the results of Exercise 25, in which Sniffy's bar pressing was extinguished without shocking the first bar press. The number of bar presses prior to reaching the extinction criterion in the two experiments will not be very different.

This exercise shows that a single mild punishment administered at the beginning of extinction briefly suppresses bar pressing but has little effect on the total number of bar presses required to produce extinction.

## Exercise 29: The Effect of a Single Severe Punishment

If a single mild shock has little effect on extinction, you might wonder what the effect of a single severe shock would be.

- Open your trained Sniffy file from Exercise 23. This is the file that we recommended you save under the name Ex23-ShapeBP. If you no longer have the file, you can use the file called ShapeBP from your Sample Files folder.
- Use the Save As command in the File menu to save the file under a new name (e.g., Ex29-1SeverePun in the Sniffy Files folder. *This step preserves your original trained Sniffy for future use.* You will need this file in several further experiments.
- If the most recent cumulative record is not visible, make it visible by selecting it from the Windows menu.
- If Sniffy is hidden, make him visible by selecting Show Sniffy from the Experiment menu.
- Select the Design Operant Conditioning Experiment command from the Experiment menu.
- In the dialog box that appears:
  - Select Extinction.
  - Click on the box titled Punish Bar Press.
  - Make sure that a check mark appears next to First Press Only.
  - Click on the box next to High Punishment. This setting will cause Sniffy's first bar press to be followed by a severe shock.
  - Make sure that a check mark also appears next to Mute Pellet Dispenser.
- Click OK.

- You will note that the first time Sniffy presses the bar, he leaps in the air, indicating that he has been shocked.
- If you want to speed up the experiment, you may do so by selecting Hide Sniffy (Accelerate Time) from the Experiment menu.

Shortly after you close the Design Operant Conditioning Experiment dialog box, the cumulative record will resemble that shown next:

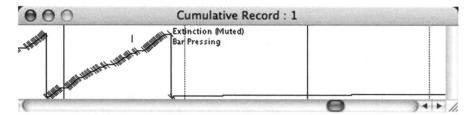

After receiving the single severe shock, Sniffy doesn't press the bar again for an extended period. And when he does press it, he doesn't press it again very quickly. Your extinction criterion is a 5-minute period in which Sniffy presses the bar no more than twice. When Sniffy meets the extinction criterion:

- Save the file.

Compare the number of bar presses that Sniffy makes prior to reaching the extinction criterion in this experiment with the results of Exercise 25, in which Sniffy's bar pressing was extinguished without shocking the first bar press. The number of bar presses prior to reaching the extinction criterion in the two experiments will be very different. A single severe shock is enough to produce very rapid, nearly complete elimination of the response.

## Exercise 30: The Effect of Repeated Mild Punishment

So far, we've seen that although a single mild punishment has little overall effect on extinction, a single severe punishment produces substantial long-term inhibition of the punished response. In this experiment, you will examine the effect of repeated mild punishment.

- Open your trained Sniffy file from Exercise 23. This is the file that we recommended you save under the name Ex23-ShapeBP. If you no longer have the file, you can use the file called ShapeBP from the Sample Files folder.
- Use the Save As command in the File menu to save the file under a new name (e.g., Ex30-RepeatMildPun in the Sniffy Files folder. *This step preserves your original trained Sniffy for future use.* You will need this file in several further experiments.
- If the most recent cumulative record is not visible, make it visible by selecting it from the Windows menu.
- If Sniffy is hidden, make him visible by selecting Show Sniffy from the Experiment menu.
- Select the Design Operant Conditioning Experiment command from the Experiment menu.
- In the dialog box that appears:
  □ Select Extinction.
  □ Click on the box titled Punish Bar Press.
  □ Click on the check mark that appears next to First Press Only to make it disappear. Without the check mark, each bar press will be followed by a shock.
  □ Make sure that High Punishment is *not* checked.
  □ Make sure that a check mark appears next to Mute Pellet Dispenser.
- Click OK.
- You will note that each time Sniffy presses the bar, he leaps in the air, indicating that he has been shocked.
- If you want to speed up the experiment, you may do so by selecting Hide Sniffy (Accelerate Time) from the Experiment menu.

Shortly after you close the Design Operant Conditioning Experiment dialog box, the cumulative record will resemble that shown next:

| ○ ○ ○ | Cumulative Record : 1 | |
|---|---|---|

Extinction (Muted)
Bar Pressing

Repeated mild shocks cause Sniffy not to press again for a couple of minutes after each bar press. Your extinction criterion is a 5-minute period in which Sniffy presses the bar no more than twice. When Sniffy meets the extinction criterion:

- Save the file.

Compare the number of bar presses that Sniffy makes prior to reaching the extinction criterion in this experiment with the results of Exercise 25, in which Sniffy's bar pressing was extinguished without shocking the first bar press. The result of the comparison will likely be that when Sniffy is shocked after each bar press, he will reach the extinction criterion after fewer bar presses. However, repeatedly shocking Sniffy may not reduce the amount of time before he meets the extinction criterion. In fact, the amount of time required to meet the criterion may be longer.

## Some Questions

- What is the difference between reinforcement and punishment?
- What is the difference between extinction and punishment?

# 12 Schedules of Reinforcement and the Partial-Reinforcement Effect

## Background and Examples

In extinction, reinforcement is completely cut off. This action simulates the situation in which a once available food source has ceased to exist. Another, even more common real-world scenario is one in which a response is sometimes reinforced and sometimes not reinforced. When a wild rat searches for food, there is no guarantee it will find food in the same place every time. The rat's searches are based on the probability of locating food. Going to a location where there once was food and finding none would not necessarily discourage the rat from trying there again at some other time when food might be available.

In a similar way, consider what your reaction might be if you turned on a light switch and the light failed to come on. How you would react would likely depend on your previous experience with that light switch. If the switch had worked reliably in the past, you would probably immediately go to look for a new light bulb. However, if the switch had sometimes required several flicks before the light came on, you would probably spend some time flicking it on and off before you decided that this time the problem was likely a burnt-out bulb.

With regard to Sniffy, so far we have discussed reinforcement as something that occurs either every time Sniffy presses the bar or not at all. However, you can also choose to reinforce only some of Sniffy's bar presses. The technical name for reinforcing every instance of a target behavior is **continuous reinforcement (CRF).** The technical term for reinforcing some, but not all, instances of a behavior is **partial reinforcement (PRF).** A rule that determines which instances of a response to reinforce is called a **schedule of reinforcement.** PRF schedules affect the temporal patterning of responses as viewed on a cumulative record.

In addition, PRF schedules enhance resistance to extinction. By enhanced resistance to extinction, we mean that if a response has been reinforced on a PRF schedule, the animal will make more responses during extinction than would be the case if the response had always been reinforced (continuous reinforcement).

The comparative effects of partial and continuous reinforcement on resistance to extinction can have real-life implications. Suppose that you are a parent of a young child. Many children who are about 2 years old develop a tendency to exhibit temper tantrums. In fact, this problem is so common that children in that age group are sometimes called the "terrible twos." How parents react to tantrums can have a profound influence on the duration of this phase of their child's development.

When a child has a tantrum, you can either reinforce the tantrum behavior by giving the child what he or she wants, or not reinforce the behavior by letting the child kick and scream until he or she gets tired and stops. (We assume you are not a person who would spank a child for tantrum behavior.) The best advice to parents of children who are just beginning to have tantrums is never to reinforce the behavior. If you never reinforce a tantrum, your child should pass through this phase quickly. However, many parents end up giving in to the child, especially if a tantrum occurs in public. The findings of operant conditioning suggest that if you are going to reinforce the behavior, it is better to do so consistently. That way, when the time comes to extinguish the behavior, the process should be faster than if you sometimes let the child scream and sometimes give the child what he or she wants.

Continuous reinforcement is the most efficient way to shape a new behavior quickly. But once the target behavior has been conditioned, continuous reinforcement is no longer necessary. Imagine the nursery school teacher's task with a new class of children. The children need to learn a great many new things—not only the prescribed lessons, but also social skills that will allow them to participate in the classroom. In the beginning, the teacher needs to reinforce the children's appropriate behaviors as often as possible. The teacher dispenses praise, stickers, and certificates and stamps stars on their hands. The nursery school teacher is a dispenser of reinforcers who at first must provide as close to a continuous-reinforcement schedule as is possible. However, this level of reinforcement is impossible to maintain, and children are soon exposed to a partial-reinforcement schedule. In first grade, children who know an answer to a question are expected to raise their hands and wait to be called on, and not every raised hand is recog-

nized. As long as each child gets occasional recognition, the skills that they have learned will not disappear because, with partial reinforcement, it is difficult to extinguish their learned behaviors.

As noted, a schedule of reinforcement is a rule for determining which responses to reinforce. In their book *Schedules of Reinforcement*, C. B. Ferster and B. F. Skinner (1957) describe many different possible schedules. However, all these schedules are made up of combinations of two basic "families" of schedules: **ratio schedules** and **interval schedules.**

**Ratio schedules** reinforce the subject for making some particular number of responses. On a **fixed-ratio (FR) schedule,** the number of responses required is always the same. On an FR-5 schedule, the subject must make five responses for each reinforcement. This is rather like being paid for piecework, where the amount of money earned depends on the amount of work accomplished according to a prearranged pay scale. Because the amount of money earned is directly proportional to the amount of work performed, piecework tends to produce high rates of output.

When we observe animals on an FR schedule in the operant chamber, the pattern of performance seen on the cumulative record depends on the size of the ratio. Small FR schedules, which require only a small number of responses for each reinforcement, produce fast, steady responding. However, the performance of an animal that is being maintained on a large FR schedule is characterized by a pause after the receipt of each reinforcement, followed by an abrupt transition to rapid, steady responding until the next reinforcement occurs. As the size of a large FR schedule is increased, the pause after each reinforcement becomes longer. We can see something that resembles this pattern of responding in the behavior of a student who finds it difficult to start the next task after finishing a major assignment. The student's behavior is affected by the fact that a lot more work is required before the next reinforcement is obtained.

On a **variable-ratio (VR) schedule,** the value of the schedule specifies an average number of responses required to obtain reinforcement, but the exact number of responses varies from reinforcement to reinforcement. On a VR-5 schedule, the subject must make 5 responses on average for each reinforcement. Sometimes the subject must make 8 or 10 responses before reinforcement occurs, but these large values are balanced by occasions when reinforcement occurs after only 1 or 2 responses. VR schedules typically produce high rates of responding with no long pauses.

VR schedules are common in everyday life. Las Vegas–style slot machines pay off on a VR schedule, as does trying to arrange a date for Saturday night, or selling something on a commission basis. In all these situations, there is some chance or probability of success associated with every "response" that you make. The more often you respond, the more often you will be reinforced.

**Interval schedules** reinforce the subject for the first response made after a specified time interval has elapsed since the last reinforcement was received. The time period during which reinforcement is unavailable begins when the subject receives a reinforcer. The interval thus specifies a minimum amount of time that must elapse between reinforced responses. On a **fixed-interval (FI) schedule,** the interval that must elapse before another response will be reinforced is always the same. On an FI–60 second schedule, exactly 60 seconds must always elapse after the receipt of one reinforcer before another response will be reinforced.

If your school is typical, every class period ends at a specified time. If you observe your fellow students, you will notice that their behavior changes as the time when the class is scheduled to end approaches. Early in the class period, everyone listens fairly attentively, and many students busily take notes. However, as the end of class approaches, students begin to put their notes away and prepare to leave.

On a **variable-interval (VI) schedule,** the time interval following reinforcement that must elapse before the next response is reinforced varies from reinforcement to reinforcement. On a VI–10 second schedule, the time interval would average 10 seconds. Few, if any, real-life situations are exactly equivalent to VI scheduling in the laboratory. However, trying to telephone someone whose line is frequently busy is similar to reinforcement on a VI schedule. Your call won't go through until the line is free, and the line is busy for varying periods. The difference is that on a pure VI schedule, once the time interval has elapsed, the reinforcer becomes available and remains available until the subject responds; but when you are trying to call an often busy telephone number, the line is busy and free intermittently. You can miss chances to complete the call by not trying often enough.

Each of these simple schedules produces a characteristic performance from subjects maintained on the schedule long enough for their behavior to stabilize. Depending on which schedule is involved, the animal may press the bar at a steady, predictable rate, or its response rate may vary in predictable ways. Prior to the appearance of the characteristic pattern of responding associated with the schedule, there is a period of acquisition during which the animal gradually adjusts to the schedule.

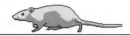

# Variable-Ratio (VR) and Variable-Interval (VI) Schedules

Both variable-ratio (VR) and variable-interval (VI) schedules produce steady responding, but at different rates. VR schedules produce fast, steady responding. VI schedules produce slow, steady responding.

The difference between the performances maintained by VR and VI schedules is nicely illustrated in an experiment described by Reynolds (1975). The experiment involved two pigeons pecking at disks for food reinforcement in separate operant chambers. The experiment involved a **yoked experimental design,** which means that the behavior of the first pigeon could affect the other bird's reinforcement schedule. In the first chamber, pigeon A's disk pecking was reinforced on a VR schedule that the experimenter had programmed. In the other, completely isolated chamber, pigeon B's disk pecking was reinforced on a VI schedule in which the values of the intervals were determined by pigeon A's behavior. Each time pigeon A received a reinforcer for completing a ratio, a reinforcer became available for pigeon B's next response.

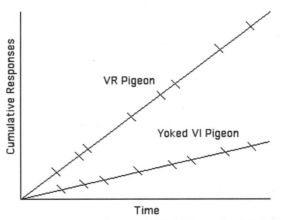

Idealized performances of two pigeons in yoked operant chambers. Both birds peck steadily. However, although both birds receive the same number of reinforcements almost simultaneously, the VR bird makes many more responses.

The graph shows hypothetical cumulative records generated by two birds in this kind of experiment. Note that both birds respond at a nearly constant rate, but the bird on the VR schedule responds faster than the bird on the VI schedule. Although both birds' pecking behaviors are reinforced at virtually the same instant and although both always receive the same amount of reinforcement, there is a distinct

difference in the rate at which they peck. This difference is caused by differences in the way in which the schedules interact with the birds' pecking behavior.

## Fixed-Ratio (FR) Schedules

As shown in the next graph, the typical FR performance depends on the size of the ratio—that is, on the fixed number of responses required for each reinforcement. What constitutes a small ratio depends on the organism and the effort required in making the response. For Sniffy and other rats pressing a bar, a small ratio is anything requiring up to about 20 bar presses. For a pigeon pecking an illuminated disk, a small ratio is anything up to about 50. With small ratios, the performance is quite steady with no pause after each reinforcement. With large ratios, there is a pause after each reinforcement, followed by an abrupt transition to a high, stable rate until the next reinforcer is received.

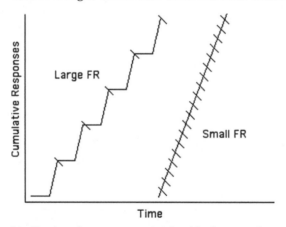

Idealized performances maintained by large and small FR schedules.

## Fixed-Interval (FI) Schedules

Overall, FI schedules maintain rather slow rates of responding, more or less comparable to those maintained by VI schedules. However, whereas the VI performance is steady, the typical FI performance involves a pause after the receipt of each reinforcement, followed by a gradually accelerating response rate until the subject is responding moderately fast just before the next reinforcement is due. This typical

FI response pattern, an idealized version of which is depicted in the next graph, is often called the **FI scallop.** As is the case with FR schedules, the pauses that occur after the receipt of a reinforcer are much more pronounced on large FI schedules than on small FI schedules.

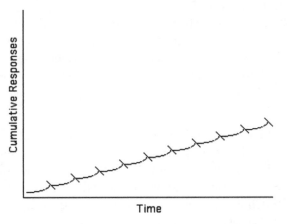

Idealized performance maintained by an FI schedule.

## Setting Up a Schedule in the Design Operant Conditioning Experiment Dialog Box

Let's consider how to set up schedule experiments in Sniffy Pro. You establish different reinforcement schedules by choosing the Design Operant Conditioning Experiment command from the Experiment menu. When you execute this command, the following dialog box appears:

When you are programming reinforcement schedules, you work with the upper left-hand part of the dialog box under Reinforcement Schedule. The right-hand part under Discrimination/Generalization is used to set up experiments on stimulus discrimination and stimulus generalization. Its operation will be explained in the next chapter. When you are setting up reinforcement schedules, you can ignore the right-hand part of the dialog box except for checking to be sure that the pull-down menus under S+ and S- are both set to None or No Tone and that there is no check mark in the box next to Generalization Test.

Here is how the Reinforcement Schedule section of the dialog box works:

- The Fixed and Variable alternatives at the far left determine whether the schedule requirements will be fixed or variable.
- The buttons labeled Responses and Seconds determine whether Sniffy is on a ratio or an interval schedule.
  □ Choosing Responses sets up a ratio schedule.
  □ Choosing Seconds sets up an interval schedule.
- You set the value of the schedule (the number of responses required or the number of seconds after a reinforcement before another response can be reinforced) by typing a number into the text box. For example, if you wanted to set up a VI–20 second schedule, you would select the Variable and Seconds alternatives and type 20 in the text box.
- Sniffy can be trained to bar press on schedules with very large values (for example, VR-250 or FI-120). However, you need to approach large schedule values gradually. In the following exercises, you will train Sniffy to bar press on VR, VI, FR, and FI schedules with values of 50. This task can be accomplished easily if you approach the value of 50 by first training Sniffy to respond on a schedule with a value of 5 and then go through the intermediate values of 10, 20, and 35.
- When you first place Sniffy on a reinforcement schedule and each time you increase the value of the schedule, the Bar-Sound association and Action Strength will start to go down. In other words, Sniffy will begin to extinguish. However, if he was fully enough trained before the change and if the increase in the schedule value isn't too large, the Bar-Sound association and Action Strength will bottom out well above their minimum values and start to increase again after a while. Wait until they reach or very closely approach their maximum levels before again increasing the value of the schedule.
- Selecting the button labeled Continuous sets up continuous reinforcement. All Sniffy's bar presses are reinforced. This setting is the

default in effect when you first select a target behavior for the program to reinforce automatically.

- As you saw in previous exercises, selecting the button labeled Extinction sets up an extinction condition. If there is a check mark in the box labeled Mute Pellet Dispenser, the magazine sound is turned off during extinction. This is the usual way in which extinction is studied. If there is no check mark in the box labeled Mute Pellet Dispenser, Sniffy continues to hear the magazine sound whenever he presses the bar even though he no longer receives a food pellet. As we saw in Chapter 10, this nonstandard extinction setting enables you to study the secondary reinforcing power of the magazine sound.

- When you click the OK button after setting up a reinforcement schedule, the dialog box disappears and the Sniffy Pro program starts reinforcing Sniffy according to the schedule you have established.

- If you click Cancel, the dialog box disappears and the program continues reinforcing Sniffy according to whatever schedule was in effect before you opened the dialog box. None of the settings that you made while the dialog box was open are implemented.

## Exercise 31: Placing Sniffy on a Small VR Schedule

Here are the steps that you should follow to place Sniffy on a small variable-ratio (VR) schedule of reinforcement. Except for the settings in the Design Operant Conditioning Experiment dialog box, you would follow the same steps to place Sniffy on any small-value schedule.

- Before Sniffy can be placed on a schedule, he must first be fully trained to press the bar for continuous reinforcement. If you still have the file that you created after first training Sniffy to press the bar in Exercise 23 (the file that we suggested you name Ex23-ShapeBP), use the Open command in the File menu to open the file. If you do not have your original trained Sniffy file, you can use the file named ShapeBP located in the Sample Files folder.

- Look at the Operant Associations mind window. (If necessary, make the Operant Associations window visible by selecting it from the Mind Windows section of the Windows menu.) Make sure that the sound–food association, bar–sound association,

and action strength are at their maximum levels. If you have opened your own file and discover that any of these measures is below its maximum level, you can let the program run until they reach their maximum levels before going on to the next step.

- Select the Save As command from the File menu to give the file an appropriate new name and save it in the Sniffy Files folder on your computer's hard drive. *This step is important because it preserves your original CRF-trained Sniffy for use in other experiments.* Because in this example we will be creating a file in which Sniffy is trained to respond on a VR-5 schedule, we suggest that you call the new file Ex31-VR5.

- Choose the Design Operant Conditioning Experiment command from the Experiment menu. Under Reinforcement Schedule, select the Variable and Responses alternatives. Type 5 in the text box. Click OK.

- If you want to speed up the experiment, select the Isolate Sniffy (Accelerate Time) command from the Experiment menu.

Shortly after the Design Operant Conditioning Experiment dialog box closes, your Cumulative Record window will look something like the following. Note that the Sniffy Pro program marks the point at which the VR-5 schedule was introduced.

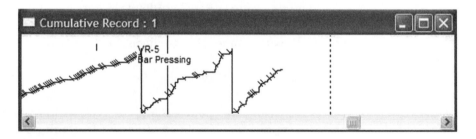

Immediately after being switched onto a schedule, when Sniffy encounters unreinforced responding for the first time, he will begin to extinguish. The Operant Associations mind window will display this process as a decrease in the strength of the bar–sound association and action strength. If Sniffy is fully trained on continuous reinforcement before you place him on a VR-5 schedule, he will not extinguish fully. However, if his continuous reinforcement training was incomplete, or if you tried to place him on a schedule with too large an initial value (such as VR-25), he would extinguish.

If Sniffy is going to adjust successfully to the schedule on which you have placed him, the bar–sound association and action strength will begin to increase again after Sniffy has received several reinforcements on the schedule. Sniffy is completely trained on the schedule when the bar–sound association and action strength approach their maximum values. At that point, Sniffy's cumulative record will be displaying the response pattern typical of the schedule on which Sniffy is being maintained. When you are satisfied that Sniffy's training is sufficient:

- Choose the Save command from the File menu to save your file.

## Exercise 32: Increasing the Value of Sniffy's VR Schedule

Sniffy can be trained to respond on schedules with quite high values (such as VR-100 or FI–60 sec) provided these high values are approached gradually through intermediate stages. Here are the steps to increase the value of a schedule. As an illustration, we will assume that you are going to increase the value of the VR-5 schedule from the previous exercise.

- If the Sniffy Pro program is not running, start it.
- Use the Open command under the File menu to open your VR-5 file from Exercise 31.
- Check the Operant Associations mind window to be sure that the bar–sound association and action strength are at or near their maximum levels. If not, let the program run longer.
- Select the Save As command from the File menu and save the file under an appropriate name in the Sniffy Files folder on your computer's hard drive. Because we are going to be increasing the value of Sniffy's VR-5 schedule to VR-10, we suggest that you call the new file Ex32-VR10. Saving the new file under a different name preserves your original VR-5 file for future use if the need arises.
- Select the Design Operant Conditioning Experiment command from the Experiment menu. Be sure that the Variable and Responses alternatives are selected, type the number 10 in the text box, and click OK.
- If you want to speed up the experiment, select the Isolate Sniffy (Accelerate Time) command from the Experiment menu.

Because Sniffy is now experiencing longer runs of unreinforced trials, the bar–sound association and action strength will weaken at first. However, after Sniffy has received several reinforcements on the new schedule, these values will start going back up. When they approach their maxima again:

- Choose the Save command from the File menu to preserve your VR-10 trained Sniffy.

Repeat relevant parts of the instructions given above to shape Sniffy up to a VR-50 schedule. Sniffy will easily and quickly reach the VR-50 endpoint if you use as your intermediate steps VR-20 and VR-35. If you like to "live dangerously," try stepping Sniffy up to a VR-50 after VR-10 or VR-20. He may or may not extinguish with larger steps.

The cumulative record that you obtain once Sniffy has fully adapted to the VR-50 schedule should resemble that shown below. Note the rapid, reasonably steady response pattern.

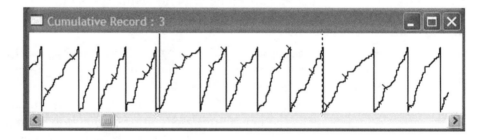

## Exercise 33: Variable-Interval Schedules

Follow the generalized instructions given in the section entitled Setting Up a Schedule in the Design Operant Conditioning Experiment dialog box to shape Sniffy up to a VI–50 second schedule. If you want to speed up the experiment, select the Isolate Sniffy (Accelerate Time) command from the Experiment menu.

The cumulative record that you obtain once Sniffy has fully adapted to the VI–50 second schedule should resemble that shown next. Note the slow, reasonably steady response pattern.

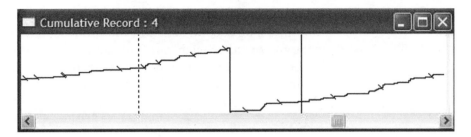

## Exercise 34: Fixed-Ratio Schedules

Follow the generalized instructions given in the section entitled Setting Up a Schedule in the Design Operant Conditioning Experiment dialog box to shape Sniffy up to an FR-50 schedule. If you want to speed up the experiment, select the Isolate Sniffy (Accelerate Time) command from the Experiment menu.

The cumulative record that you obtain once Sniffy has fully adapted to the FR-50 schedule should resemble that shown next. Note the pauses in responding that occur after each reinforcement is received and the abrupt transitions to rapid responding at the end of each pause.

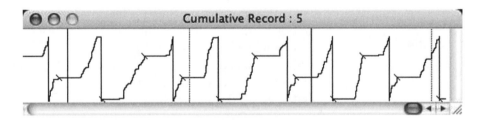

## Exercise 35: Fixed-Interval Schedules

Follow the generalized instructions given in the section entitled Setting Up a Schedule in the Design Operant Conditioning Experiment dialog box to shape Sniffy up to a FI–50 second schedule. If you want to speed up the experiment, select the Isolate Sniffy (Accelerate Time) command from the Experiment menu.

The cumulative record that you obtain once Sniffy has fully adapted to the FI–50 second schedule should resemble that shown next. Note the pauses after each reinforcement is received, followed by rather gradual transitions to moderate response rates shortly before the next reinforcement is due to occur.

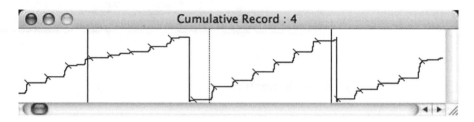

## How Realistic Are Sniffy's Schedule Performances?

The speed with which Sniffy adapts to reinforcement schedules is one of the places where we sacrificed realism for convenience. Real rats adapt to schedules and changes in schedules quite slowly. In many instances, a real rat requires several daily one-hour training sessions before its pattern of responding in the cumulative record begins to resemble the response pattern that a particular schedule "typically" produces. Sniffy adapts to schedules and schedule changes much faster. We speeded up Sniffy's learning process so that you will have the opportunity to look at the effects of many different schedules in a reasonable amount of time.

Sniffy's schedule performances are not perfect replicas of the idealized performances shown in the first part of this chapter and in many textbooks on the psychology of learning. Idealized performances are designed to communicate ideas about what psychologists think schedule performances would look like if all the "noise" could be averaged out. The actual performances that you obtain with Sniffy and the actual performances of real rats are rarely ideal, because the factors that tend to produce ideal performances are not the only things determining the animal's behavior. For example, VR schedules are supposed to produce rapid, steady responding, and they tend to do so. However, pressing the bar is not the only thing that rats do while being reinforced on a VR schedule. Sometimes they take drinks of water. Sometimes they groom or scratch themselves. Sometimes they wander around the operant chamber for a little while. All these interruptions

make actual VR performances less rapid and especially less steady than they would be if the only factors involved were those discussed in the first parts of this chapter.

Thus the fact that Sniffy's cumulative records are not perfect replicas of ideal schedule performances means that, to a degree, Sniffy is behaving like a real rat. If you look at reproductions of the actual performances of real rats in scientific journal articles and in specialized books on reinforcement schedules, you will discover that Sniffy's schedule performances fall within the range of performances that real rats sometimes produce.

## Exercise 36: The Effect of Partial Reinforcement on Extinction

Partial reinforcement dramatically increases a response's resistance to extinction. Animals whose responding has been maintained by a partial-reinforcement schedule make many more responses during extinction than do animals whose responding has been maintained on continuous reinforcement. In addition, ratio schedules tend to produce greater resistance to extinction than interval schedules; and variable schedules tend to produce greater resistance to extinction than fixed schedules. The Sniffy Pro program enables you to observe these differences in resistance to extinction. To measure Sniffy's resistance to extinction following partial reinforcement, you should follow these steps:

- Open a Sniffy Pro file in which Sniffy has been fully trained to respond on a moderate- or large-value schedule. We suggest you use a file in which you have trained Sniffy to respond on a schedule with a value of at least 25 (that is, VR-25, FR-25, VI–25 sec, or FI–25 sec).
- Look at the Operant Associations mind window to verify that bar–sound association is at or near its maximum level.
- Save the file under an appropriate new name (e.g., Ex36-VR25Ext) to preserve your original schedule file for future use.
- Choose the Design Operant Conditioning Experiment command from the Experiment menu.
- Click the Extinction option in the dialog box, make sure there is a check mark in the box next to Mute Pellet Dispenser, and click the OK command button.

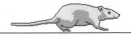

- If you want to speed up the experiment, select the Isolate Sniffy (Accelerate Time) command from the Experiment menu.
- Let the program run until Sniffy reaches the extinction criterion of no more than 2 responses during a 5-minute period.
- Save the file.

Print the cumulative record and determine how many responses Sniffy made and how much time elapsed before he reached the extinction criterion. Compare your partial-reinforcement extinction results with the extinction results that you obtained earlier when Sniffy's responding had been maintained by continuous reinforcement.

## Some Questions and Things to Do

The exercises in this chapter barely scratch the surface of the things that it is possible to do with schedules of reinforcement.

### Does Schedule Size Affect Overall Response Rate?

On an interval schedule, the schedule's "size" is the number of seconds after reinforcement before the next reinforcement becomes available. On a ratio schedule, the schedule's "size" is the number of responses required for a reinforcement. Exercises 32, 33, 34, and 35 ask you to set up, respectively, VR, VI, FR, and FI schedules of "size" 50.

Manipulating schedule size should have different effects for different schedule types. Pick a couple of different schedule types, such as VI and VR. Fully train Sniffy (so that the bar–sound association and action strength approach their maxima) to respond to values of 5, 10, 25, 50, and 100 for each of the two schedule types. Then determine the number of times he presses the bar during 30 minutes of program time and divide that number by 30 to obtain an average number of responses per minute.

- How does the response rate change as the value of the schedules increases?
- Does it change in the same way for the two kinds of schedules?

## Does Schedule Size Affect Resistance to Extinction?

Pick a schedule type (VR, VI, FR, or FI) and fully train Sniffy (so that the bar–sound association is at or very close to its maximum value) to respond at values of 5, 10, 25, 50, and 100. Then determine how many responses Sniffy will make and how much time passes before bar pressing extinguishes with schedules of different values.

- How does the value of the schedule affect resistance to extinction?

# 13  Stimulus Discrimination and Stimulus Generalization

## Background and Theory

Operant conditioning involves the formation of a three-part association among a situation, a behavior pattern (response), and a reinforcer (Domjan, 1998; Mazur, 1998; Schwartz & Reisberg, 1991; Tarpy, 1997). As a result, animals and people learn which behaviors produce which reinforcers in which situations. Because the situation (the stimulus environment) is part of this associative process, organisms can learn to behave in appropriately different ways in the presence of different stimuli. Learning to behave differently in the presence of different stimuli is called **stimulus discrimination learning.** The capacity to learn stimulus discriminations is the reason why a cat can learn to defecate in its litter box and not in the middle of the kitchen floor and why people learn to behave differently in a law courts and pubs.

However, the same stimulus situation is rarely duplicated exactly. People do not have to relearn appropriate pub behavior when they visit a new drinking establishment, and a cat's appropriate toilet habits will usually survive a switch from one kind of litter box to another. This capacity to respond in a similar way in the presence of similar, but not identical, stimuli is called **stimulus generalization.**

The Sniffy Pro program models auditory stimulus discrimination learning and stimulus generalization. In designing Sniffy's simulations of these processes, we have taken some liberties with reality in order to create a teaching tool that will help you understand some of the phenomena that textbooks on the psychology of learning commonly discuss. For one thing, we have endowed Sniffy with the ability to learn discriminations unrealistically fast. Real rats typically require many daily training sessions to master the kinds of discriminations that the

Sniffy program simulates, but Sniffy will usually learn them in an hour or less of program time. More significantly, we have modeled Sniffy's auditory discrimination learning and stimulus generalization to simulate phenomena that were for the most part discovered with pigeons trained on visual discriminations of colors and geometric figures (Hanson, 1959; Honig, Boneau, Burstein, & Pennypacker, 1963). Because real rats are colorblind and have generally very poor eyesight, we couldn't bring ourselves to endow Sniffy with excellent color vision. However, we designed Sniffy's auditory discrimination learning and stimulus generalization capacities to reproduce phenomena of visual discrimination learning and stimulus generalization in pigeons, even though data indicate that there are certain differences between pigeons and rats and between vision and audition (Jenkins & Harrison, 1960, 1962). We have taken these liberties in order to enable Sniffy to simulate *peak shift* and *behavioral contrast,* two phenomena that most textbooks on the psychology of learning discuss and that many students have a hard time understanding. We believe that doing the Sniffy Pro exercises described in this chapter will help you understand these phenomena. Just keep in mind that the same experiments performed with real rats would likely produce results that are different from Sniffy's.

In operant conditioning, a stimulus that is correlated with a change in a reinforcement schedule is called a **discriminative stimulus.** A stimulus in whose presence a response is reinforced is called a **positive discriminative stimulus.** The abbreviation for this term is **S+** (or **$S^D$**). A stimulus in whose presence a response is extinguished is called a **negative discriminative stimulus,** which is abbreviated **S–** (or **$S^\Delta$**).

The Sniffy program uses tones to simulate two forms of stimulus discrimination learning. In **simple discrimination learning,** a tone is either on or off. If the tone is a positive discriminative stimulus (S+), then Sniffy is reinforced when the tone is on and extinguished when it is off. If the tone is a negative discriminative stimulus (S–), then Sniffy is extinguished when the tone is on and reinforced when it is off. We call the second kind of discrimination learning that the Sniffy program simulates **S+/S– discrimination learning.** In this case, the S+ and S– are tones of different frequencies.

Once Sniffy has learned a simple discrimination using a tone as either the S+ or S–, you can measure stimulus generalization. Generalization tests are carried out under conditions of extinction. To see why this is so, imagine that you have trained Sniffy on a simple discrimination in which a 2 kHz tone was the S+ and the tone-off condition was the S–. To determine how the amount of generalization is related to the

degree of similarity between various possible test stimuli and the original training S+, you would test Sniffy by presenting tones of several different frequencies (for example, 1.0, 1.25, 1.5, 1.75, 2.0, 2.25, 2.5, 2.75, and 3.0 kHz). In addition, you would probably want to create a stimulus generalization gradient, a graph in which you plot on the vertical axis (as your dependent variable) the number of responses that Sniffy makes during test periods of standard duration and on the horizontal axis (as your independent variable) the frequency of the different test tones. You want Sniffy's performance during the presence of these test tones to reflect in an unbiased way his tendency to generalize as a result of the discrimination learning. Running the tests without reinforcing Sniffy in the presence of any of the test tones is the best procedure because reinforcing Sniffy in the presence of any of the stimuli would modify his original discrimination learning by causing him to start treating the test tones as additional S+'s. Testing under conditions of extinction also modifies the original discrimination learning. Tests in which Sniffy hears a tone but is not reinforced make him less likely to respond in the presence of any tone. However, this is a less serious problem because it is easier to deal with the effect of extinction than with the effect of starting to teach Sniffy that the test tones are S+'s.

To get an unbiased estimate of stimulus generalization (in order to construct a stimulus generalization gradient graph that is not affected either by the effects of reinforcing animals in the presence of test stimuli or by the effects of extinction), experimenters working with real organisms usually train several animals on the original discrimination problem and then test them by briefly presenting each of the test stimuli one after another. Each animal experiences the test stimuli in a different sequence. With this procedure, the results for any particular animal are determined both by the degree of similarity between each test stimulus and the original S+ and by the ongoing effects of extinction. Because of stimulus generalization, the animal has a tendency to respond faster in the presence of stimuli that are quite similar to the S+ than in the presence of less similar stimuli. Because of extinction, the animal has a tendency to respond more slowly in the presence of stimuli that come late in the sequence than in the presence of stimuli that come early in the sequence. However, because different animals receive the stimuli in different random orders, each stimulus comes early in the sequence for some animals, in the middle of the sequence for others, and late in the sequence for still others. Thus the effect of extinction can be averaged out by computing mean bar-pressing rates for the different test stimuli. When you consider that several animals

must be trained and tested and that real animals learn stimulus discriminations slowly, it's easy to see that studying stimulus generalization with real animals requires a lot of time and effort.

The fact that Sniffy is a simulation and not a real animal simplifies the study of stimulus generalization for you. You can save a single discrimination-learning file when the learning process is complete and then revert to the status the file was in at the end of training for each generalization test. In this way, you create a situation in which each test stimulus is the "first" stimulus that Sniffy receives immediately after the end of discrimination learning. Thus, you don't have to worry about presenting the test stimuli in different random orders and then averaging out the effect of extinction.

The procedure for measuring stimulus generalization is the same whether an animal has learned a simple discrimination or an S+/S– discrimination, but the results will be different. When an animal is reinforced in the presence of a tone and extinguished when the tone is turned off, a procedure that in the context of the Sniffy Pro program we call **tone-on S+ simple discrimination learning,** it develops a positive tendency to respond in the presence of the S+ and stimuli that resemble the S+. The potential for stimulus generalization that develops as a result of this procedure is depicted schematically in the following figure:

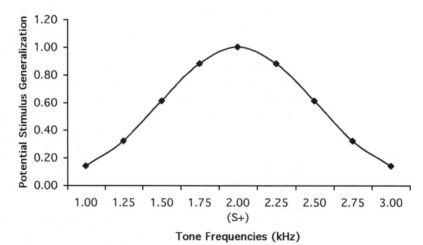

Potential stimulus generalization after tone-on S+ simple discrimination learning

In contrast, when an animal is extinguished in the presence of a tone and reinforced when the tone is turned off, a situation that we call

**tone-on S– simple discrimination learning,** it develops a negative tendency not to respond in the presence of the S– and stimuli resembling the S–. The potential for generalization of bar-press inhibition that develops as a result of this procedure is depicted in the next figure:

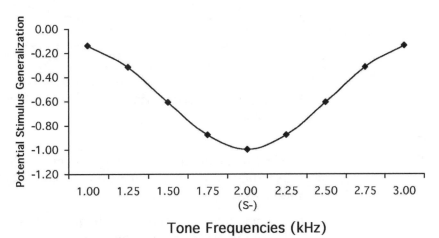

**Tone Frequencies (kHz)**

Potential stimulus generalization after tone-on S– simple discrimination learning

During S+/S– discrimination learning, when an animal is reinforced for responding in the presence of a tone of one frequency (the S+) and extinguished in the presence of a tone of another frequency (the S–), we might hypothesize that the animal would develop both a positive (excitatory) tendency to respond in the presence of the S+ and stimuli resembling the S+ and a negative (inhibitory) tendency not to respond to the S– and stimuli resembling the S– (Spence, 1937). If the S+ and S– are sufficiently similar, we might imagine that the excitatory and inhibitory generalization gradients would overlap and interact with each other. The next figure shows what might happen if the S+ were a 2 kHz tone and the S– a 1.75 kHz tone. The figure shows an excitatory generalization gradient that might develop as a result of reinforcing the animal in the presence of the 2 kHz tone and an inhibitory generalization gradient that might develop as a result of extinguishing the animal in the presence of the 1.75 kHz tone. In addition, the figure shows the net generalization gradient that would result from subtracting the inhibitory gradient from the excitatory gradient. The net generalization gradient is a prediction about what generalization test results might look like after an animal has received extensive S+/S– discrimination training with an S+ and an S– that are quite similar to each other.

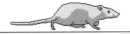

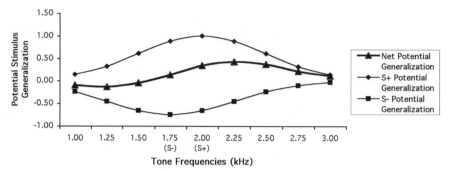

Potential stimulus generalization after S+/S– discrimination learning: showing peak shift only

The line depicting net potential generalization makes two interesting predictions about how the animal ought to behave during generalization tests:

- The net potential generalization gradient peaks not at the 2 kHz S+ but at the 2.25 kHz tone, the stimulus adjacent to the S+ on the side opposite the S–. This phenomenon is called **peak shift.** It results from the interaction of the excitatory and inhibitory generalization gradients. When the S+ and S– are close together, so much inhibition generalizes from the S– to the S+ that the animal's response rate in the presence of the S+ is reduced. When stimulus generalization is measured following S+/S– discrimination of colors in pigeons, the predicted peak shift effect is often seen (e.g., Hanson, 1959).

- In the simple model presented above, the predicted "height" of the peak following S+/S– discrimination learning is lower than it would be following simple tone-on S+ discrimination learning because the inhibitory generalization gradient reduces the positive tendency to respond to the S+ and stimuli similar to the S+. For this reason, the model predicts that, in general, animals should respond less in the presence of test stimuli following S+/S– discrimination learning than following simple tone-on S+ discrimination learning. Data from pigeons that have learned color discriminations contradict this prediction (e.g., Hanson, 1959). Following S+/S– discrimination learning, the peak rate of responding is higher than after simple S+ discrimination learning. This increased peak rate of responding is an example of a phenomenon called **behavioral contrast.**

The next figure depicts the excitatory and inhibitory generalization gradients that develop as a result of simple discrimination learning together with a net potential generalization curve that more accurately

reflects the way some animals actually respond during generalization tests following S+/S– discrimination learning. This curve, which is modeled after the behavior of pigeons that have learned color discriminations, was produced by subtracting the inhibitory curve from the excitatory curve and then multiplying the differences by a constant.

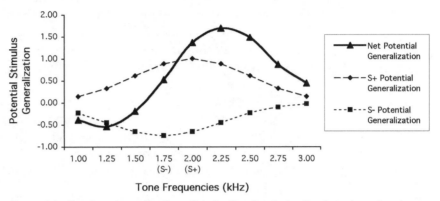

Tone Frequencies (kHz)

Potential stimulus generalization after S+/S– discrimination learning: showing both peak shift and behavioral contrast

## Setting Up Discrimination-Learning Experiments

When you choose the Design Operant Conditioning Experiment command under the Experiment menu, the following dialog box appears:

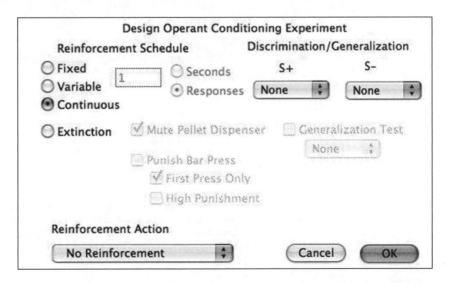

Here are the steps that you go through to set up a discrimination-learning experiment in the dialog box:

- Open a file in which Sniffy has been fully trained to respond with continuous reinforcement (either the file from Exercise 23 that we suggested you call Ex23-ShapeBP or the file named ShapeBP in the Sample Files folder).[1] Examine the associations in the Operant Associations mind window. The sound–food association, bar–sound association, and action strength should all be at their maximum levels before you begin a discrimination-learning experiment.
- Select the Save As command from the File menu to save the file under an appropriate new name on your hard drive. *This step is important because it preserves your original trained Sniffy file for use in future experiments.*
- Select Design Operant Conditioning Experiment under the Experiment menu.
- In the dialog box, select the stimuli that you want to use as the S+ (the stimulus in whose presence Sniffy's bar presses will be reinforced) and the S– (the stimulus in whose presence Sniffy's bar presses will not be reinforced).
  - ☐ To set up simple tone-on S+ discrimination learning, point the cursor at the pull-down menu under S+, click your (left) mouse button, and then drag down to select a tone of a particular frequency. During simple tone-on S+ discrimination learning, the S– is always None.
  - ☐ To set up simple tone-on S– discrimination learning, point the cursor at the pull-down menu under S–, click your (left) mouse button, and then drag down to select a tone of a particular frequency. During simple tone-on S– discrimination learning, the S+ is always None.

[1] As a variant of these exercises, you might try using a file in which Sniffy has been fully trained to respond on a PRF schedule. However, discrimination learning will take a lot longer if Sniffy is responding on a PRF schedule than if he is responding with continuous reinforcement. When Sniffy is reinforced for every response that he makes in the presence of the S+ and never reinforced in the presence of the S–, he can easily discriminate the reinforcement contingencies in effect under the two stimulus conditions. If Sniffy is being reinforced on a PRF schedule in the presence of the S+ and extinguished in the presence of the S–, the contrast between the two reinforcement contingencies is less apparent, and discrimination learning is slowed down. Because the S+ and S– occur during alternate 1-min periods, Sniffy can never learn a discrimination if the schedule in effect during the S+ reinforces him less often than once per minute.

> □ To set up S+/S− discrimination learning, select tones of different frequencies for the S+ and the S−.
>
> ■ After selecting the S+ and the S− for the particular discrimination-learning experiment that you want to perform, click the OK command button at the bottom of the dialog box to begin Sniffy's discrimination training.

During discrimination training, the S+ and the S− will be presented during alternating 1-minute intervals of program time. During the S+, Sniffy's bar presses are reinforced. During the S−, his bar presses are not reinforced.

During discrimination training, you can observe Sniffy's progress by examining the Cumulative Record window, the Operant Associations mind window, and the DS Response Strength mind window.

The cumulative record marks the occurrence of S+ and S− periods and shows how often Sniffy presses the bar during each period. The following figure shows the appearance of the cumulative record early in an S+/S− discrimination-learning experiment in which the S+ is the 2.0 kHz tone and the S− is the 2.25 kHz tone. Note how occurrences of these stimuli are denoted.

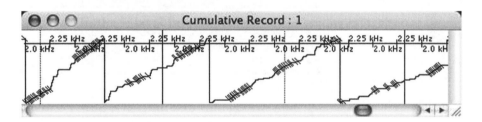

Very early in discrimination learning, Sniffy will press the bar equally often under the two stimulus conditions. As discrimination learning gets under way, he will begin pressing more often during the S+ than during the S−. When discrimination learning is complete, he will press the bar frequently during the S+ and very rarely, if ever, during the S−.

At the beginning of discrimination learning, the Operant Associations mind window will show that the bar–sound association and action strength are at high levels. Initially, when Sniffy's bar presses are not reinforced during the S−, the bar–sound association and action strength will weaken. As discrimination learning proceeds, the strength of the bar–sound association and action strength will stop

weakening and begin to increase. When discrimination learning is complete, the bar–sound association and action strength will be at or close to their maxima.

The DS Response Strength mind window shows Sniffy's tendency to press the bar in the presence of tones of different frequencies. This mind window thus predicts the results that you would obtain if you performed generalization tests. At the beginning of discrimination learning, this window shows an equal moderate tendency to respond in the presence of all the different tones. During discrimination training, the DS Response Strength window will show the development of excitatory (above zero) and/or inhibitory (below zero) response tendencies. The following illustration shows the DS Response Strength mind window as it appears at the end of an S+/S– discrimination experiment in which the S+ was the 2.0 kHz tone and the S– was the 2.25 kHz tone. In this case, both excitatory tendencies to respond and inhibitory tendencies not to respond are associated with most of the tones.

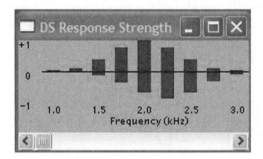

Your criteria for deciding that Sniffy's discrimination learning is complete should be based jointly on observations of the current Cumulative Record window and the Operant Associations and DS Response Strength mind windows. When discrimination learning is complete:

- The current Cumulative Record window will show that Sniffy is consistently (over several consecutive S+/S– cycles) responding frequently during the S+ and very rarely or not at all during the S–.
- In the Operant Associations mind window, the bar–sound association and action strength will approach their maxima.
- The appearance of the DS Response Strength mind window will have stabilized. The height of the bars will no longer be changing.

When Sniffy's training is complete, choose the Save command from the File menu to save your results for use in tests of stimulus generalization.

## Exporting DS Response Strength Data to a Spreadsheet or Statistical Analysis Program

The DS Response Strength mind window is drawn on the basis of numeric data that the Sniffy Pro program stores internally in the Sniffy Pro file. You can view these data by saving them in a exported data file and then opening that file with a spreadsheet or statistical analysis program. To create the exported data file:

- If the DS Response Strength mind window is hidden, make it visible by selecting it from the Mind Windows section of the Windows menu.
- Make sure that the DS Response Strength mind window is selected by pointing the cursor at any part of the window and clicking your (left) mouse button once.
- Select the Export Data command from the File menu.
- In the file-saving dialog box that appears, give the exported data file an appropriate name and save it in an appropriate place on your computer's hard drive.

The Sniffy Pro program creates a tab-delimited text file which most spreadsheet and statistical analysis programs are capable of reading. To view the file in a spreadsheet or statistical analysis program:

- Start the program in which you wish to view your exported Sniffy Pro data.
- Choose the Open command from that program's File menu.
- In the dialog box that appears, go to the location on your hard drive where you saved the Sniffy Pro data export file.
- If the Sniffy Pro data export file is not visible, choose the Show All Files option in the file-opening dialog box.
- If no Show All Files option is available or if the program does not open the file successfully when you select it, check to see whether the program has a special data import command. If necessary, read your spreadsheet or statistical analysis program's manual or search its online help files to determine how to import a tab-delimited text file.

The following figure depicts the appearance of the exported data when a file is opened with the Microsoft Office Version X of Microsoft

Excel for the Macintosh OS X. The data will have a similar appearance in most spreadsheet and statistical analysis programs.

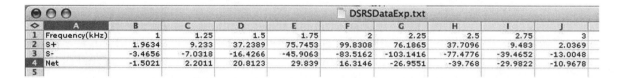

| | A | B | C | D | E | F | G | H | I | J |
|---|---|---|---|---|---|---|---|---|---|---|
| 1 | Frequency(kHz) | 1 | 1.25 | 1.5 | 1.75 | 2 | 2.25 | 2.5 | 2.75 | 3 |
| 2 | S+ | 1.9634 | 9.233 | 37.2389 | 75.7453 | 99.8308 | 76.1865 | 37.7096 | 9.483 | 2.0369 |
| 3 | S- | -3.4656 | -7.0318 | -16.4266 | -45.9063 | -83.5162 | -103.1416 | -77.4776 | -39.4652 | -13.0048 |
| 4 | Net | -1.5021 | 2.2011 | 20.8123 | 29.839 | 16.3146 | -26.9551 | -39.768 | -29.9822 | -10.9678 |
| 5 | | | | | | | | | | |

The data are displayed in Rows 1 through 4 and Columns B through J. The text entries in Column A describe the nature of the data in the other columns.

- In row 1, the values that appear after "Frequency(kHz)" are the frequencies of the nine possible test tones.
- In row 2, the values that appear after "S+" are Sniffy's excitatory tendencies to respond in the presence of each of the possible test tones.
- In row 3, the values that appear after "S−" are Sniffy's inhibitory tendencies not to respond in the presence of each of the possible test tones.
- In row 4, the values that appear after "Net" are derived by subtracting the inhibitory values from the excitatory values. These net values predict how Sniffy should respond during generalization tests. Sniffy should not bar-press in the presence of a tone with Net ≤ 0. For tones with Net > 0, Sniffy's response rate should be correlated with the magnitude of the value.

## Setting Up Stimulus Generalization Tests

Here are the steps that you need to follow to measure stimulus generalization:

- Open a file in which Sniffy has been fully trained on a discrimination-learning task.
- Select the Design Operant Conditioning Experiment command from the Experiment menu.
- In the Design Operant Conditioning Experiment dialog box:
  - Select Extinction.
  - Be sure that there is a check mark in the box next to Mute Pellet Dispenser.

- □ Place a check mark in the box next to Generalization Test by pointing the cursor at the box and clicking your (left) mouse button.
- □ Select the tone frequency that you want to test from the pull-down menu under Generalization Test.
- □ Click the OK command button.

The Sniffy Pro program will automatically perform a generalization test during which the selected tone is presented continuously for 2 minutes of program time. During the generalization test, the Lab Assistant will count the number of times Sniffy presses the bar. On a piece of paper, record the frequency of the test tone and the number of times that Sniffy pressed the bar during the test.

To perform your next generalization test, choose the Revert command from Sniffy Pro's File menu and repeat the steps above.

- **Warning 1:** *It is critically important to execute the Revert command to return the file to the state it was in at the end of discrimination training before performing the next test.*
- **Warning 2:** *It is also critically important not to save the file at the end of a generalization test. Saving the file at the end of a generalization test will leave you with a partially extinguished Sniffy and make it impossible to perform further unbiased generalization tests. If you save a partially extinguished Sniffy, your only option is to repeat the discrimination training before performing further generalization tests.*

## Exercise 37: Simple Tone-On S+ Discrimination Learning

In this exercise, you will teach Sniffy a simple discrimination using the 2.0 kHz tone as the S+ and tone-off (None) as the S–. Here are the steps that you should follow to set up the experiment:

- Open a file in which Sniffy has been fully trained to press the bar with continuous reinforcement. You can use either the file that we recommended you call Ex23-ShapeBP in Exercise 23 or the file called ShapeBP in the Sample Files folder.
- Use the Save As command to save the file under an appropriate new name (e.g., Ex37 S+2) in the Sniffy Files folder on your computer's hard drive.

- Select the Design Operant Conditioning Experiment command from the Experiment menu.
- Follow the generalized instructions given in the section of this chapter titled Setting Up Discrimination-Learning Experiments to set up an experiment in which the 2.0 kHz tone is the S+ and tone-off (None) is the S–.
- If you want to speed up the experiment, select the Isolate Sniffy (Accelerate Time) command from the Experiment menu.
- When Sniffy's discrimination learning is complete, save the file.

When discrimination learning is complete according to the criteria discussed in the section of this chapter titled Setting Up Discrimination-Learning Experiments, your Cumulative Record window and DS Response Strength mind window should resemble those shown next:

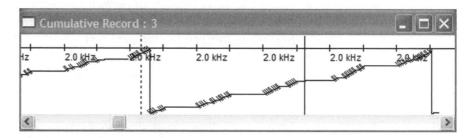

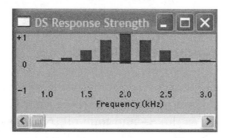

## Exercise 38: Stimulus Generalization After Simple Tone-On S+ Discrimination Learning

In this exercise, you will measure stimulus generalization following the simple tone-on S+ discrimination learning that Sniffy acquired in Exercise 37. To perform the exercise, follow these steps:

- Open the file from Exercise 37 that we suggested you call Ex37 S+2.
- Check the criteria given in the section of this chapter titled Setting Up Discrimination-Learning Experiments to make sure that discrimination learning is complete. If it isn't complete, run the file until it meets the completeness criteria.
- Follow the generalized instructions given in the section of this chapter titled Setting Up Generalization Tests to select the 1.0 kHz tone for a generalization test.
- When the test is complete, look at the Lab Assistant window to determine how many times Sniffy pressed the bar during the test. Record the number of bar presses on a piece of paper.
- Choose the Revert command from the File menu to return the file to the state it was in at the end of discrimination training.
- Repeat these steps to test Sniffy's generalization to the other eight tones.

Use a spreadsheet, statistical analysis, or drawing program to draw a generalization gradient in which you plot the number of times Sniffy pressed the bar on the vertical (*y*) axis and the tone frequencies on the horizontal (*x*) axis. Your finished generalization gradient should resemble this graph:

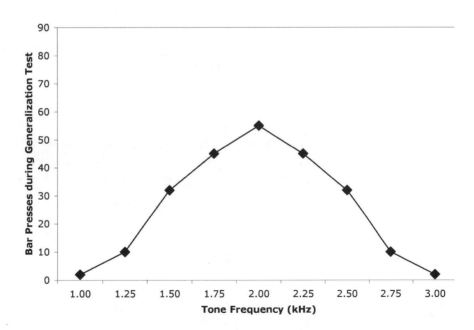

# Exercise 39: Simple Tone-On S– Discrimination Learning

In this exercise, you will teach Sniffy a simple discrimination using the 2.0 kHz tone as the S– and tone-off (None) as the S+. Here are the steps needed to set up the experiment:

- Open a file in which Sniffy has been fully trained to press the bar with continuous reinforcement. You can use either the file that we recommended you call Ex23-ShapeBP in Exercise 23 or the file called ShapeBP in the Sample Files folder.
- Use the Save As command to save the file under an appropriate new name (e.g., Ex39 S–2) on your computer's hard drive.
- Select the Design Operant Conditioning Experiment command from the Experiment menu.
- Follow the generalized instructions given earlier in this chapter in the section titled Setting Up Discrimination-Learning Experiments to set up a discrimination-learning experiment in which the 2.0 kHz tone is the S– and tone off (None) is the S+.
- If you want to speed up the experiment, select the Isolate Sniffy (Accelerate Time) command from the Experiment menu.
- When Sniffy's discrimination learning is complete, save the file.

When discrimination learning is complete, your Cumulative Record window and DS Response Strength mind window should resemble those shown next:

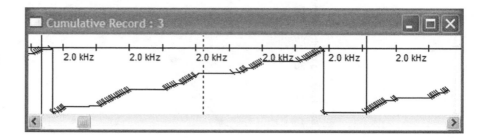

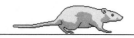

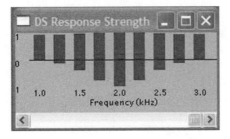

# Exercise 40: Stimulus Generalization After Simple Tone-On S– Discrimination Learning

In this exercise, you will measure stimulus generalization following the simple tone-on S– discrimination learning that Sniffy acquired in Exercise 39. To perform the exercise, follow these steps:

- Open the file from Exercise 39 that we suggested you call Ex39 S–2.
- Check the criteria given in the section of this chapter titled Setting Up Discrimination-Learning Experiments to make sure that discrimination learning is complete. If it isn't complete, run the file until it meets the completeness criteria.
- Follow the generalized instructions given in the section of this chapter titled Setting Up Generalization Tests to select the 1.0 kHz tone for a generalization test.
- When the test is complete, look at the Lab Assistant window to determine how many times Sniffy pressed the bar during the test. Record the number of bar presses on a piece of paper.
- Choose the Revert command from the File menu to return the file to the state it was in at the end of discrimination training.
- Repeat these steps to test Sniffy's generalization to the other eight tones.

Use a spreadsheet, statistical analysis, or drawing program to draw a generalization gradient in which you plot the number of times Sniffy pressed the bar on the vertical (y) axis and the tone frequencies on the

horizontal (x) axis. Your finished generalization gradient should resemble that shown next.

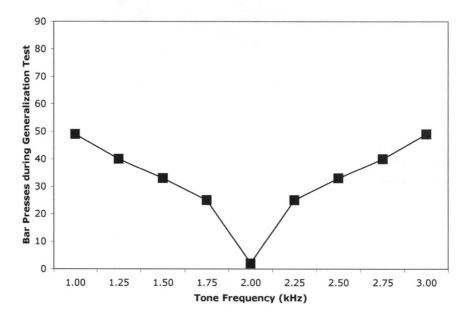

## Exercise 41: S+/S− Discrimination Learning

In this exercise, you will teach Sniffy an S+/S− discrimination using the 2.0 kHz tone as the S+ and the 2.25 kHz tone as the S−. Here are the steps that you should follow to set up the experiment:

- Open a file in which Sniffy has been fully trained to press the bar with continuous reinforcement. You can use either the file that we recommended you call Ex23-ShapeBP in Exercise 23 or the file called ShapeBP in the Sample Files folder.
- Use the Save As command to save the file under an appropriate new name (e.g., Ex41 S+2 S−2.25) in the Sniffy Files folder on your hard drive.
- Select the Design Operant Conditioning Experiment command from the Experiment menu.
- Follow the generalized instructions given in the section of this chapter titled Setting Up Discrimination-Learning Experiments

to set up an experiment in which the 2.0 kHz tone is the S+ and the 2.25 kHz tone is the S–.

- If you want to speed up the experiment, select the Isolate Sniffy (Accelerate Time) command from the Experiment menu.
- When Sniffy's discrimination learning is complete, save the file.

When discrimination learning is complete, your Cumulative Record window and DS Response Strength mind window should resemble those shown below:

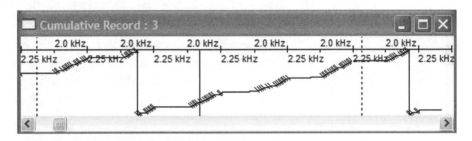

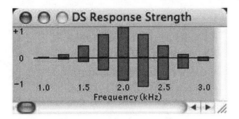

## Exercise 42: Stimulus Generalization After S+/S– Discrimination Learning

In this exercise, you will measure stimulus generalization following the S+/S– discrimination learning that Sniffy acquired in Exercise 41. To perform the exercise, follow these steps:

- Open the file from Exercise 41 that we suggested you call Ex41 S+2 S–2.25.
- Check the criteria given in the section of this chapter titled Setting Up Discrimination-Learning Experiments to make sure that

discrimination learning is complete. If it isn't complete, run the file until it meets the completeness criteria.

- Follow the generalized instructions given in the section of this chapter titled Setting Up Generalization Tests to select the 1.0 kHz tone for a generalization test.
- When the test is complete, look at the Lab Assistant window to determine how many times Sniffy pressed the bar during the test. Record the number of bar presses on a piece of paper.
- Choose the Revert command from the File menu to return the file to the state it was in at the end of discrimination training.
- Repeat these steps to test Sniffy's generalization to the other eight tones.

Use a spreadsheet, statistical analysis, or drawing program to draw a generalization gradient in which you plot the number of times Sniffy pressed the bar on the vertical ($y$) axis and the tone frequencies on the horizontal ($x$) axis. Your finished generalization gradient should resemble that shown next:

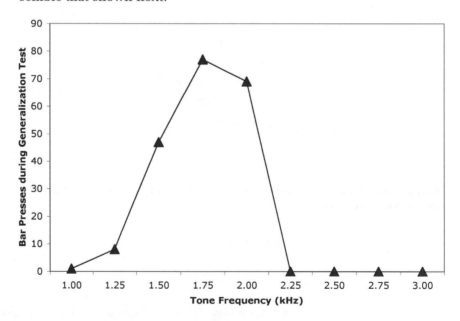

## Comparing the Three Generalization Gradients

The following line graph depicts Sniffy's generalization gradients from Exercises 38, 40, and 42 together.

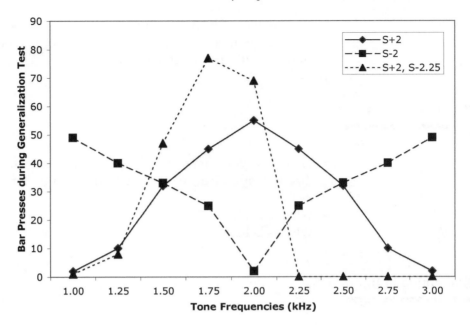

Note the following comparative characteristics:

- The peak rate of responding after S+/S– discrimination learning is higher than the peak rate of responding after simple S+ discrimination learning. The comparatively higher peak response rate after S+/S– discrimination learning exemplifies the phenomenon called *behavioral contrast.* This phenomenon is commonly seen in pigeons that have learned to discriminate lights of different wavelengths (colors) (e.g., Hanson, 1959), but not in real rats trained to discriminate tones of different frequencies (Jenkins & Harrison, 1960, 1962).

- In the S+/S– discrimination-learning task, the S+ was the 2.0 kHz tone and the S– was the 2.25 kHz tone. Yet Sniffy's peak rate of responding was to the 1.75 kHz tone. The fact that Sniffy responded more in the presence of the 1.75 kHz tone than in the presence of the 2.0 kHz S+ exemplifies the phenomena called *peak shift.* Real rats trained on auditory S+/S– discriminations show peak shift (Jenkins & Harrison, 1960, 1962). However, Sniffy's generalization gradient is probably not an accurate quantitative reproduction of the generalization gradient that real rats would produce.

- Sniffy's generalization gradient after simple S– discrimination learning demonstrates that he responds least to the 2.0 kHz S– tone and that his rates of responding to the most dissimilar 1.0 and 3.0 kHz tones are lower than his peak rate of responding after either simple S+ or S+/S– discrimination learning. In this instance, we don't know

how realistic Sniffy's performance is, but real animals sometimes produce generalization gradients with these characteristics after simple S– discrimination learning.

## Some Questions

- Why do you need to revert to the saved version of the discrimination-learning file each time you perform a generalization test?
- What is peak shift?
- What is behavioral contrast?

## Something to Do

The exercises in this chapter are a tiny subset of the discrimination and generalization experiments that it is possible to run with Sniffy. Here are a couple of the many possible additional exercises:

- Examine a number of different S+/S– discrimination-learning tasks. For example, with the 2 kHz tone as the S+, vary the frequency of the S–. Does the amount of time required to fully learn the discrimination depend on the difference between the frequency of the S+ and the S–?
- Does the phenomenon of peak shift occur if the S+ and S– frequencies are not "adjacent" to each other? Explain your results on the basis of the values in the DS Response Strength mind windows.

# 14

## Shaping Behaviors Other Than Bar Pressing

If you have ever watched circus animals performing, you will likely have seen the animals do a variety of "amazing" things that untrained animals of the same species do not do—things like bears riding bicycles or dogs walking tight ropes. Or you may have visited a roadside attraction such as the I.Q. Zoo in Hot Springs, Arkansas, where chickens jump through hoops and play baseball and a duck plays the piano. One of the most important techniques that animal trainers employ to get animals to do these unusual things is shaping. To give you additional experience with shaping and to provide a bit of fun, we have enabled you to shape Sniffy to perform some interesting behaviors.

Shaping a live animal involves a number of steps. The first step is to establish a secondary reinforcer through a procedure resembling magazine training. The secondary reinforcer must be a stimulus whose timing you can precisely control. A common procedure used with dogs and many other kinds of animals is called "clicker training." You get a little noisemaker and teach the animal that whenever it hears the clicker sound, you will give it a small treat.

Before beginning to shape an animal, many trainers set up a **shaping hierarchy**—a sequence of behaviors that progressively resemble the target behavior more and more closely. At the bottom of the hierarchy is a behavior that (the trainer hopes) the animal will perform spontaneously and that resembles the target behavior in some way. When the animal performs this first behavior, the trainer starts out by reinforcing that behavior whenever it occurs. As a consequence, the animal will begin to perform the first-step behavior more frequently.

Animals do not always do things in exactly the same way. Their behavior is variable. Eventually, the animal will do something that resembles the target behavior more closely than was the case with the first item in the hierarchy. At that point, the trainer reinforces the second-step behavior and requires the animal to repeat that behavior to obtain further reinforcements.

If the trainer is skillful and persistent enough, the process of reinforcing behaviors that resemble the target behavior more and more closely will eventually lead the animal to perform a target behavior that an untrained member of its species would never perform spontaneously and that looks spectacular enough to be impressive.

The exercises in this chapter will not make you into an expert animal trainer. However, they will provide you with practice taking Sniffy through short shaping hierarchies that culminate in behaviors that are fun to watch. The target behaviors that you can train Sniffy to perform are:

- Beg
- Roll (that is, turn a somersault)
- Face wipe

To ensure that you succeed in shaping Sniffy to perform these behaviors if you try, we have provided lots of unrealistic help. The Sniffy Pro program will automatically record and reinforce target behaviors even though the behaviors do not involve interacting with a device in a way that would permit automatic recording with a live animal. And if you have trouble figuring out what to do, you can get help from the Shaping Tutor, which can be set to record and reinforce precursor behaviors for each of the target behaviors.

---

**Disclaimer:** *The exercises in this chapter do not provide a realistic preview of what you can expect if you ever try to shape a live animal.*

---

- To train Sniffy to roll or face-wipe, you begin by reinforcing grooming movements with a sound associated with food. Yet research with several kinds of mammals has shown that presenting food or secondary reinforcers associated with food is not an effective way of increasing the frequency of grooming movements (e.g., Shettleworth, 1975).
- Reinforcing a precursor behavior will cause Sniffy to start doing something else that is qualitatively different from (and we think more interesting than) the precursor behavior. In contrast, shaping a real animal ordinarily involves leading the animal through a large number of small quantitative changes that add up to a major change in behavior only after a protracted program of training.

Nevertheless, we believe that practicing with these simple examples will help you learn the *principles* of shaping. Just don't expect a real animal to be as "cooperative" as Sniffy.

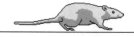

## Exercise 43: Shaping Sniffy to Beg

To see what the behavior that we call begging looks like, open the file named BegDemo in the Sample Files folder. Once you've seen what the target behavior looks like, follow the steps below to train Sniffy to beg:

- Open the file from Exercise 22 that we suggested you call Ex22-MagTrain.
- Select the Save As command from the File menu to give the file an appropriate new name (such as Ex43-ShapeBeg) and save it in the Sniffy Files folder on your computer's hard drive. *Saving the file with a new name before you start shaping Sniffy preserves your original magazine-training file for future use.* If your first attempt at shaping is unsuccessful, you can go back and try again without having to magazine-train Sniffy again.
- If Cumulative Record 1 is not visible, make it visible by selecting it from the Cumulative Record section of the Windows menu.
- Select the Design Operant Conditioning Experiment command from the Experiment menu.
- In the dialog box that appears, select Beg from the Target Behavior section of the drop-down menu under Reinforcement Action. After making the selection, click on the OK button to close the dialog box.
- Note that the terms CRF and Beg appear in the Cumulative Record window. This notation means that the program will automatically reinforce every instance of begging and that the cumulative record will record begging movements.
- As your first approximation to begging, give Sniffy a pellet of food whenever he rears up facing forward (that is, facing you) anywhere in the operant chamber.
- After you have reinforced rearing up facing forward a number of times, you will begin to see instances of begging; and the program will automatically reinforce these.
- If you are patient, the time will come when Sniffy will beg 10 or more times during a 5-minute interval. At that point, you can stop shaping, sit back, and watch the progressive effect of reinforcement as Sniffy continues to beg more and more frequently.
- Sniffy is fully trained when the Action Strength column in the Operant Associations mind window approaches its maximum

with Beg as the automatically reinforced behavior. At that point, select the Save command from the File menu to preserve your trained Sniffy for future use.

After 45 to 60 minutes of attempting to shape Sniffy according to the instructions given above, Sniffy should be begging *at least* 10 times during each 5-minute interval delineated by the alternating solid and dotted vertical lines in the cumulative record. If your attempt at shaping fails to obtain that minimum result, something is wrong with what you're doing.

One possibility is that Sniffy has not been properly magazine trained. Look at the Operant Associations mind window. The sound–food association should be at its maximum level on the scale. If it isn't, either go back and repeat Exercise 22 to create a properly magazine-trained Sniffy or use the file named MagTrain from the Sample Files folder.

A second possibility is that you may not be reinforcing instances of rearing up toward the front wall as outlined above, or not reinforcing these behaviors quickly enough.

For users who encounter difficulty with shaping, we have provided a section of the Reinforcement Action menu in the Design Operant Experiment dialog box called the Shaping Tutor. If you are having trouble reinforcing Sniffy's rearing behaviors:

- Choose the Design Operant Conditioning Experiment command from the Experiment menu.
- Under the Shaping Tutor subsection of the Reinforcement Action menu, choose Rear Up Facing Front.
- The Sniffy Pro program will now automatically reinforce all instances of rearing up facing the front of the cage, including all begs. Watch which actions the program automatically reinforces.
- Once you've figured out what you were doing wrong, reopen the Design Operant Conditioning Experiment dialog box and choose Beg from the Target Behavior section of the Reinforcement Action menu.
- Alternatively, if you are still unable to reinforce Sniffy effectively by hand, watch what is going on as the program reinforces front-facing rears automatically. Once Sniffy begs 10 or more times in a 5-minute period, reopen the Design Operant

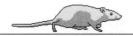

Conditioning Experiment dialog box and choose Beg from the Target Behavior section of the Reinforcement Action menu. The program will complete Sniffy's training automatically.
- When Sniffy is fully trained, save the file.

## Exercise 44: Shaping Sniffy to Wipe His Face

To see what face wiping looks like, open the file named FaceWipeDemo in the Sample Files folder of your Sniffy Pro CD. Face Wipe involves Sniffy touching his face with his paw and moving his paw up and down across his eye three times in rapid succession. The precursor behavior for Face Wipe is Face Touch, in which Sniffy touches his face with a paw but does not move his paw up and down across his eye repeatedly. Once you've seen what face wiping looks like, follow the steps below to shape the behavior:

- Open the file from Exercise 22 that we suggested you call Ex22-MagTrain.
- Select the Save As command from the File menu to give the file an appropriate new name (e.g., Ex44-ShapeFaceWipe) and save it in the Sniffy Files folder on your computer's hard drive. *Saving the file with a new name before you start shaping Sniffy preserves your original magazine-training file for future use.*
- If Cumulative Record 1 is not visible, make it visible by selecting it from the Cumulative Record section of the Windows menu.
- If the Operant Associations mind window is not visible, make it visible by selecting it from the Mind Windows section of the Windows menu.
- Select the Design Operant Conditioning Experiment command from the Experiment menu.
- In the dialog box that appears, select Face Wipe from the Target Behavior section of the drop-down menu under Reinforcement Action. After making the selection, click on the OK button to close the dialog box.
- Note that the terms CRF and Face Wipe appear in the cumulative record. These notations mean that the program will auto-

matically reinforce every face wipe and that the cumulative record will record instances of face wiping.

- As your first approximation to face wiping, give Sniffy a pellet of food whenever he touches his face with one of his paws.
- When Sniffy has been reinforced often enough for touching his face, he will sometimes repeatedly wipe his paw across his eye instead of merely touching his face. This is the behavior we call Face Wipe, and the program will reinforce it automatically whenever it occurs.
- Each time Sniffy performs a face wipe, watch closely what he does after eating the food pellet. He may face-wipe again quickly after eating. If he does so, you know you're making progress. Allow him to continue face wiping as long as he will do so. However, if he does something else or touches his face without wiping, continue to reinforce face touching whenever it occurs.
- If you are patient, the time will come when Sniffy will perform a face wipe 8 to 10 times in rapid succession. At that point, you can stop shaping, sit back, and allow the program to automatically reinforce face wiping.
- Sniffy is fully trained when the Action Strength column in the Operant Associations mind window approaches its maximum. At that point, select the Save command from the File menu to preserve your trained Sniffy for future use.

After 30 minutes or so of attempting to shape Sniffy according to the instructions given above, Sniffy should be face wiping *at least* 10 times during each 5-minute interval delineated by the alternating solid and dotted vertical lines in the cumulative record. If your attempt at shaping fails to obtain that minimum result, something is wrong with what you are doing.

One possibility is that Sniffy has not been properly magazine trained. Look at the Operant Associations mind window. The sound–food association level should be at least three-quarters of the way up the scale. If it isn't, either go back and repeat Exercise 22 to created a properly magazine-trained Sniffy or use the file named MagTrain from the Sample Files folder.

A second possibility is that you may not be reinforcing instances of face touching as outlined above, or not reinforcing these behaviors quickly enough.

For users who encounter difficulty with shaping, we have provided a section of the Reinforcement Action menu in the Design Operant Conditioning Experiment dialog box called the Shaping Tutor. If you are having trouble reinforcing Sniffy's face touching behavior:

- Choose the Design Operant Conditioning Experiment command from the Experiment menu.
- Under the Shaping Tutor subsection of the Reinforcement Action menu, choose Face Touch.
- The Sniffy Pro program will now automatically reinforce all instances of face touching, including all face wipes. Watch which actions the program automatically reinforces.
- When you believe that you are capable of effectively reinforcing these behaviors manually, reopen the Design Operant Conditioning Experiment dialog box and choose Face Wipe from the Target Behavior section of the Reinforcement Action menu.
- If you still are unable to reinforce Sniffy effectively by hand, watch what is going on as the program reinforces face touching and wiping automatically. Once Sniffy face-wipes 8 to 10 times in a 1- or 2-minute period, reopen the Design Operant Conditioning Experiment dialog box and choose Face Wipe from the Target Behavior section of the Reinforcement Action menu. The program will complete Sniffy's training automatically.
- When Sniffy is fully trained, save the file.

## Exercise 45: Shaping Sniffy to Roll

The behavior that we call Roll involves Sniffy turning a somersault as he moves from left to right or right to left across the operant chamber. To see what the behavior looks like, open the file called RollDemo in the Sample Files folder.

Shaping Sniffy to roll involves a shaping hierarchy with two precursor behaviors: head lowering and head tucking. You start out reinforcing instances of head lowering. When the head-lowering movement has been reinforced often enough, head tucking will begin to occur. Head tucking is thus the second item in your shaping hierarchy. Once head tucking is occurring fairly often, you should stop reinforcing head lowering and reinforce head tucking only. Eventually, reinforcing

head tucking will begin to produce rolls. Finally, when rolls are occurring reasonably often, you stop reinforcing head tucking and reinforce rolls only. Eventually, Sniffy will have a high probability of rolling whenever he is in a position where he can do so without hitting a wall.

To shape rolling, follow these steps:

- Open the file from Exercise 22 that we suggested you call Ex22-MagTrain.
- Select the Save As command from the File menu to give the file an appropriate new name (such as Ex45-ShapeRoll) and save it in the Sniffy Files folder on your computer's hard drive. *Saving the file with a new name before you start shaping Sniffy preserves your original magazine-training file for future use.*
- If Cumulative Record 1 is not visible, make it visible by selecting it from the Cumulative Record section of the Windows menu.
- Select the Design Operant Conditioning Experiment command from the Experiment menu.
- In the dialog box that appears, select Roll from the Target Behavior section of the drop-down menu under Reinforcement Action. After making the selection, click on the OK button to close the dialog box.
- Note that the terms CRF and Roll appear in the cumulative record. These notations mean that the program will automatically reinforce every roll and that the cumulative record will record rolls.
- As your first approximation to rolling, give Sniffy a pellet of food whenever he lowers his head down between his hind legs (as if he were licking his genitals).
- When Sniffy has been reinforced often enough for lowering his head, he will sometimes begin to rock back and forth with his head tucked between his hind legs. This is the behavior we call Head Tuck.
- Reinforce all head tucks. At first, also continue to reinforce instances of head lowering. However, when head tucking has become fairly common, stop reinforcing instances of head lowering and reinforce head tucks only.
- When you have reinforced head tucking often enough, you will begin to see the first instances of rolling, and the program will reinforce rolls automatically. At first, continue to reinforce instances of head tucking manually. However, once you have

seen a total of about 50 rolls, you can stop reinforcing head tucking. At that point, sit back and allow the program to reinforce rolling automatically.

- When the Action Strength column has approached its maximum value with Roll as the automatically reinforced behavior, Sniffy is fully trained. At that point, select the Save command from the File menu to preserve your trained Sniffy for future use.

You can expect that shaping Sniffy to roll, starting with a file in which Sniffy has only been magazine trained, should take anywhere from half an hour to an hour. So be patient and don't give up easily.

After an hour or so of attempting to shape Sniffy according to the instructions given above, Sniffy should be rolling *at least* 2 or 3 times during each 5-minute interval delineated by the alternating solid and dotted vertical lines in the cumulative record. If your attempt at shaping fails to obtain that minimum result after an hour, something is wrong with what you are doing.

One possibility is that Sniffy has not been properly magazine trained. Look at the Operant Associations mind window. The sound–food association level should be at least three-quarters of the way up the scale. If it isn't, either go back and repeat Exercise 22 to created a properly magazine-trained Sniffy or use the file named MagTrain from the Sample Files folder.

A second possibility is that you may not be reinforcing instances of head lowering and head tucking as outlined above, or not reinforcing these behaviors quickly enough.

For users who encounter difficulty with shaping, we have provided a section of the Reinforcement Action menu in the Design Operant Conditioning Experiment dialog box called the Shaping Tutor. If you are having trouble reinforcing Sniffy's head-lowering and head-tucking behaviors:

- Choose the Design Operant Conditioning Experiment command from the Experiment menu.
- Under the Shaping Tutor subsection of the Reinforcement Action menu, choose Head Lower.
- The Sniffy Pro program will now automatically reinforce all instances of head lowering, including all head tucks and rolls. Watch which actions the program automatically reinforces.

- When you believe that you are capable of effectively reinforcing these behaviors manually, reopen the Design Operant Conditioning Experiment dialog box and choose Roll from the Target Behavior section of the Reinforcement Action menu.
- If you are still unable to reinforce Sniffy effectively by hand, allow the program to train rolling automatically.
- When Sniffy is fully trained, save the file.

## Exercise 46: Shaping Sniffy to Perform Other Behaviors

Manually reinforcing any behavior that Sniffy performs spontaneously will have the effect of making that behavior and other similar behaviors occur more frequently. Thus, if you are patient and have good timing, it is possible to train Sniffy to perform a variety of "tricks" other than those that we have documented in this chapter. One family of behaviors is something that we call sniffing. Sniffy sits with his head down near the metal bars that form the floor of the operant chamber and twitches his whiskers. Four basic examples of this behavior form a family: sniff to front (Sniffy sniffs while facing you), sniff left and sniff right (Sniffy sniffs with his head pointed toward the left or right side of the chamber), and sniff rear (Sniffy's back is to you and he wiggles a bit, but his nose is invisible). Reinforcing any one of these behaviors will make the reinforced behavior and the other behaviors in the "sniffing family" occur more often. If you consistently reinforce any one of these behaviors and do not reinforce the others, the one that you reinforce will eventually occur much more often than the others. We invite you to explore and discover Sniffy's full repertoire of trainable "tricks."

## Exercise 47: Shaping a Cat to Beg or Walk on Its Hind Legs

Limitations in the Sniffy simulation mean there are limits to the variety of things Sniffy can be trained to do. However, animal trainers routinely use shaping to teach real animals to do an enormous variety of things that are physically possible but that an untrained animal would never do. As a simple example, training a physically fit cat to sit up

and beg for food and to stand or walk on its hind legs without support is a fairly straightforward process even though untrained cats rarely, if ever, do these things.

Pet food manufacturers produce bite-size cat treats in several flavors, and it is often possible to find a flavor that your cat likes so much that the animal will work to obtain them. In fact, the cat may like them so much that you'll have to keep the treats container locked away to prevent theft. Once you've found your cat's favorite, the treats will constitute a primary reinforcer that you can use to teach the animal to sit up and beg, to stand and walk on its hind legs, or to do other tricks.

As with Sniffy, the first step in training your cat will be magazine training. You need to find a stimulus that can be delivered with split-second timing when your cat does something right and that can be easily transformed into a secondary reinforcer by pairing it with treat presentation. Stores that sell party supplies often stock a variety of noisemakers, and many pet supply stores sell "clickers" that are designed to provide a sound that can be established as a secondary reinforcer.

You magazine-train a cat in much the same way that you magazine-trained Sniffy. To begin, wait until the cat is near you. Then operate the noisemaker and give the cat a treat. After you have sounded the clicker and given the cat a treat a couple of times with the cat very close by, walk a short distance away before sounding the clicker and giving the cat the next treat. You will know your cat is well magazine trained when you can call it from anywhere in the house (or neighborhood!) just by sounding the clicker.

Training a cat to sit up and beg or to stand and walk on its hind legs involves requiring the animal to raise its head progressively higher and higher off the ground before you reinforce it by sounding the noisemaker and giving it a treat. Start by watching the cat until it lifts its head somewhat higher than usual. (Standing with its front paws up on something doesn't count.) Then sound the clicker and give the cat a treat. After several reinforcements, the cat will begin walking around with its head held high more often. Because the cat's behavior is variable, sooner or later it will raise its head higher than your first criterion level, and that new higher level then becomes your second approximation that the cat must match to get additional treats. By the time you have reached the third or fourth approximation, the cat will probably be sitting on its hind legs with its front paws off the ground. Once the cat starts to lift its front paws off the ground, it will rather quickly reach a training plateau in which it sits up and "begs" for treats. Depending on your patience, you can either decide that sitting up is good

enough or elect to embark on the somewhat more challenging task of shaping the cat to stand on its hind legs and walk.

Once the cat is sitting up, it may or may not spontaneously start to stand on its hind legs. Some cats do, but many don't. If the cat just sits there without starting to rise up on its hind legs, try to elicit standing by holding a treat above the cat's head. Then, as soon as the cat starts to rise, sound the clicker and give it the treat. On the next trial, wait a bit before again eliciting a stand by holding out a treat. If you are patient enough, the animal will eventually start to stand on its hind legs spontaneously. Finally, if you want the animal to walk on its hind legs, you will have to wait for or elicit behavioral variants in which the animal not only stands up on its hind legs but walks increasingly long distances before you sound the clicker and give it a treat.

If you decide to train your cat, you will discover that training a real animal is harder than training Sniffy. One reason for the difference is that your cat has a larger behavior repertoire than Sniffy; another is that the cat is free to move about and approach you in a way that Sniffy cannot. One difficulty will almost certainly arise: During magazine training, when you start to move away from the cat, it will follow you. If you sit down with the treats and clicker in hand, the cat will jump into your lap. If you are standing up and walking, the cat may jump on your shoulder. When these problems arise, don't punish the cat. You will significantly retard the learning process if you do anything to frighten the animal. However, if you never give the cat a treat unless you have first sounded the clicker, and if you never sound the clicker unless the cat is on the floor, the cat will eventually learn to stay off you and "cooperate."

"Clicker training" is also a technique that has become popular with many dog trainers. However, because dogs form stronger social bonds with people than cats do, enthusiastic verbal praise and physical affection are often the only reinforcers that dogs require. For a dog, the verbal praise probably comes to act as a secondary reinforcer that predicts the availability of physical affection. Whether treats should ever be used in addition to physical affection is a somewhat controversial issue among dog trainers, but many dogs train faster when treats are used.

Another variant of operant conditioning that professional animal trainers use to teach animals to perform sequences of behaviors is called *backward chaining*. For example, suppose that you wanted to train a rat to climb a ladder, walk across an elevated plank to a door, and open the door to obtain food. You would first train the rat to go through the open door to the food, then you would shape it to open the door to get access to the food. The next step would be to place the rat

on the elevated platform at the top of the ladder so that it has to "walk the plank" to get to the door. Finally, you would shape ladder climbing to get to the platform. In other words, the idea of backward chaining is first to train the animal to do the last thing in the sequence just before receiving the food. Then you make the opportunity to perform the last behavior in the sequence contingent on performing the next-to-last behavior, and so on. Most of the complex trained animal performances that you see in a circus or zoo are achieved through a combination of shaping and backward chaining.

## Some Questions and Things to Do

- To get additional information about how the principles of operant conditioning can be applied in the real world, search the World Wide Web for pages dealing with "clicker training." You'll find numerous articles on how to train dogs, cats, horses, fish, and many other kinds of animals. Many people have a lot of fun training their animals to do an astonishing variety of interesting and useful things. You will also discover how operant conditioning is used to modify human behavior. For example, some coaches use clicker training to improve the performances of athletes.
- You can set up experiments on extinction, spontaneous recovery, secondary reinforcement, reinforcement scheduling, stimulus discrimination, and stimulus generalization using files in which Sniffy has been trained to beg, face-wipe, or roll. The results of these explorations will be variable. In some instances, you will obtain results that parallel those obtained with bar pressing. In other cases, you will get quite different results.

Because the Sniffy program always uses the same neural network model of operant conditioning, you can be sure that the differences you observe are not due to differences in the underlying mechanisms of learning.[1] Instead, differences in things like scheduling effects and stimulus generalization must be the result of differences in the place the behaviors are performed and in the way the movements cause Sniffy to interact with his environment in the operant chamber. Think about differences between bar pressing and the other behaviors that might account for any differences you observe.

[1] We know that Sniffy always uses the same learning mechanism because we didn't give him any others. Psychologists often assume that animals always use the same learning mechanisms, but that assumption may not always be correct with live animals.

- Bar pressing is the only behavior in Sniffy's repertoire that involves interaction with a device (the bar). What is the importance of that?
- Bar pressing is the only behavior that must be performed in close proximity to the hopper into which the magazine drops food pellets. Is that important?
- Bar pressing can be repeated rapidly. For which other behaviors is that true? What factors limit the frequency with which other behaviors can be performed?

# APPENDIX

## How to Manage Your Sniffy Pro Files

### Floppy Disks and Hard Disks

**Floppy disks** are small, portable devices that can hold small amounts of data. Each floppy disk is capable of storing about 1400 kilobytes (KB) of data. Here is a picture of a floppy disk of the kind used in many contemporary Windows computers and in older Macintosh computers.

In addition, your computer contains one or more hard disks. A **hard disk** is a device located inside your computer. The hard disks in contemporary computers usually have storage capacities ranging from as little as 800 megabytes (MB) up to 100 gigabytes (GB) of data. The fact that 1 MB = 1024 KB, and 1 GB = 1024 MB means that your computer's hard disk can store from several hundred to many thousands of times as much data as a floppy disk.

Sniffy Pro data files range in size from as little as 240 KB for the shortest, least complex exercises up to about 900 KB for the longest, most complex exercises. The point of all this arithmetic is to point out that although you cannot store very many Sniffy files on a floppy disk, you can store a very large number of Sniffy files on your computer's hard disk. It is for this reason that *we strongly urge you to save your Sniffy files on your computer's hard disk.*

In addition, Sniffy data files grow during experiments. A Sniffy file that occupies 250 KB of disk space when you save it immediately after setting up an experiment might require 900 KB of disk space when you save it again after the experiment has been completed. Sniffy files grow as experiments progress because the Sniffy Pro program records a lot of information about Sniffy's behavior and psychological processes during experiments. For this reason, if you saved a Sniffy file on a floppy disk, the floppy disk might have enough room to save the file at the beginning of the experiment but not at the end. In that event, you would get an error message when you tried to save the file on the floppy disk at the end of the experiment, and you might end up having to do the exercise over again. This is another reason why *we implore you to save your Sniffy files on your hard disk, not on a floppy disk.*

Here are some tips that will save time and minimize frustration:

- *Always save your Sniffy files on the hard disk of the computer you're using.*
- *If your professor wants you to hand in your Sniffy files on a floppy disk:*
  - Save the files on the hard disk of the computer that you're using when you create the files.
  - Then copy the files from the computer's hard disk onto one or more floppy disks and give them to your professor when the time comes to hand in the files. We explain in detail how to copy files onto floppy disks in a later section of this appendix.
  - A second advantage of this approach is that if you or your professor loses the floppy disk containing your files, you will still have a copy of the files on your computer's hard disk.
- *If you don't have your own computer and must store your Sniffy files on floppy disks:*
  - Save your Sniffy files on the hard disk of the computer that you're using when you create the files.
  - Copy your files from the hard disk onto one or more floppy disks when the experiment is completed.
  - Copy your files from your floppy disks back onto the hard disk of the computer that you're using before you use the files again.
  - Because floppy disks are fragile and easily damaged, always keep at least two copies of your files on different floppy disks.

Here are some tips to reduce the chance of losing data stored on floppy disks:

- Keep your floppy disks in a sturdy container designed for storing floppy disks.
- Never carry an unprotected floppy disk in your pocket or purse.
- Keep your floppy disks away from heat sources such as radiators or direct sunlight.
- Keep your floppy disks away from anything that contains a magnet. For example, don't set a floppy disk on top of a stereo speaker, which contains a magnet that could erase the data. Telephone handsets also contain magnets that might be a hazard to floppy disks.

## Deciding Where to Save Your Files

In Windows, the Sniffy Pro installer places your files in a folder called
Sniffy Pro for Windows, which is located inside a folder called Program Files on your C drive. The following picture shows a typical Windows XP installation. The open Sniffy Pro for Windows folder is displayed in front of the open Program Files folder.

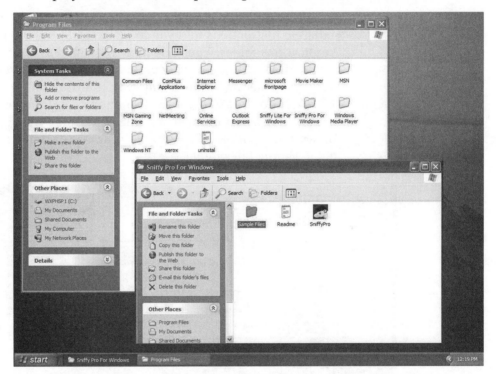

To display the windows this way, you would do the following.

- To show the Program Files window:
  - Click with your left mouse button while pointing at the Start icon
    in the task bar at the bottom of your screen. In the pop-up menu
    that appears above the Start icon, select My Computer.
  - In the My Computer window, double-click with your left mouse
    button on the icon that appears under Hard Disk Drives.
  - In the Hard Disk window that appears, left double-click on the
    Program Files icon.
  - If all you wanted to see were the contents of the Sniffy Pro for
    Windows folder by itself, you could now simply left double-click
    on that folder's icon.

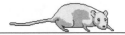

- To show both the Sniffy Pro for Windows window and the Program Files window simultaneously (as in the illustration):
  - ☐ Repeat the steps given above to show a second copy of the Program Files window.
  - ☐ Left double-click on the Sniffy Pro for Windows icon to display the Sniffy Pro for Windows window.
  - ☐ Rearrange and resize the windows to produce the display shown on the previous page.

The next picture shows a typical installation in Mac OS X. The installation instructions told you to place the Sniffy Pro program in your Applications folder. You were also instructed to create a folder called Sniffy Files inside your Documents folder and to place the Sample Files and other material inside it. In the illustration, we see parts of three windows: a portion of the "home" folder for a user named "adhb," a portion of a Documents folder containing a Sniffy Files folder, and a portion of a Sniffy Files folder showing several exercises and a Sample Files folder.

To display the windows in this fashion:

- Double-click the mouse button while pointing the cursor at the icon of the start-up disk. Unless you have moved it, the start-up disk

icon will be always located in the upper right-hand corner of your desktop.

- With the Finder active, either choose the New Window command from the Window menu or press the N key while holding down the command key.
- In the new window that appears, click on the Documents icon in the panel on the left side of the window.
- Scroll through the Documents window to display the Sniffy Files folder.
- Repeat the previous two steps to display another copy of the Documents window and double-click on the Sniffy Files folder icon.
- Rearrange and resize the windows to display them as shown.

**To create a new folder in Windows:**

- Point the cursor at the File menu located at the top of the folder's window and click your left mouse button.
- In the drop-down menu that appears, drag down to New, then drag across to Folder, and release the mouse button. A new folder appears.
- Immediately type the name that you want to give the new folder.

**To create a new folder on a Macintosh:**

- Click your mouse button once while pointing at the open folder window. (This operation ensures that the new folder will be created in the correct window.)
- Choose the New Folder command from the Finder's File menu. A new untitled folder appears.
- Immediately type the name you want to give the folder.

## Getting Easy Access to the Sniffy Program and Files From Your Computer Desktop

### Creating a Windows Shortcut

In Windows XP, the "ordinary" way of reaching your Sniffy Pro for Windows folder involves the following steps.

- Left click on the Start icon at the bottom of your screen.
- Select My Computer from the pop-up menu that appears above the Start icon.

- Open your hard drive root directory by left double-clicking on the icon below the words "Hard Disks."
- Left double-click on the Program Files icon.

What a process! Fortunately, there is a simple way to reduce the number of steps involved: Create a shortcut to your Sniffy Pro for Windows folder and place the shortcut on your Windows desktop. Here is what you need to do to set up the shortcut.

- Go through the four steps listed above to open your Program Files window.
- While pointing the cursor at the Sniffy Pro for Windows folder icon, click and hold down your right mouse button.
- A drop-down menu appears with a number of commands listed.
- Release the mouse button, drag the cursor down to the Create Shortcut command, and click on it with your left mouse button.
- A folder icon with an arrow on it titled Shortcut to Sniffy Pro for Windows appears inside your Program Files folder.
- Click on the shortcut icon with your left mouse button, hold the mouse button down, and drag the icon onto your Windows desktop.

Once the shortcut icon is on the desktop, you can drag it around and place it wherever you want it. In the future, all you have to do to open your Sniffy Pro for Windows folder is to left double-click the shortcut icon.

If you want, you can follow an analogous procedure to create and place on your desktop a shortcut to the Sniffy Pro program. A shortcut to the program can be left doubled-clicked to launch the program. Dragging the icon of a Sniffy Pro file onto the program shortcut will launch the program and open the file.

## Placing Aliases in the Mac OS X Dock

For Mac OS X users, the easiest way of quickly launching the Sniffy Pro program and getting to your Sniffy Files folder is to place aliases of the program and the folder in the Mac OS X dock.

To place an alias of the program in the dock:

- Locate the Sniffy Pro for Macintosh program in your Applications folder.
- Click once on the program icon and, while holding the mouse button down, drag the program icon into the dock.

- If your dock is displayed horizontally at the bottom of your screen, drag the program icon to any convenient place left of the vertical line that separates program icons from folder icons.
- If your dock is displayed vertically on the left- or right-hand side of your screen, drag the program icon to any convenient place above the line that separates program icons from folder icons.

When the program icon is in the dock, you can launch the program by clicking once on the dock icon.

To place an alias of your Sniffy Files folder in the dock:

- Locate your Sniffy Files folder inside your Documents folder.
- Click once on the folder icon and, while holding the mouse button down, drag the folder icon into the dock.
- If your dock is displayed horizontally at the bottom of your screen, drag the folder icon to any convenient place to the right of the vertical line that separates program icons from folder icons.
- If your dock is displayed vertically on the left-hand or right-hand side of your screen, drag the folder icon to any convenient place below the line that separates program icons from folder icons.

When the Sniffy Files folder is in the dock, you can open the folder by clicking once on the folder icon in the dock. You can also launch the Sniffy Pro program and simultaneously open a particular file by dragging a Sniffy program file icon onto the program icon in the dock.

## Saving Files

Let's imagine you have come to the point in the instructions for an exercise where we tell you to execute the Save As command and save the exercise with some specified name in an appropriate place on your computer's hard disk. Here is specific information about what Windows and Macintosh users need to do at that point in order to save the file in the place where we suggest that you keep your Sniffy Pro files.

### Saving Files in Windows XP

We assume that you want to save a file in a folder called My Sniffy Files that is located inside the Sniffy Pro for Windows folder on your hard disk.

- Select the Save As command from the File menu in the Sniffy Pro program. A dialog box resembling the following will appear.

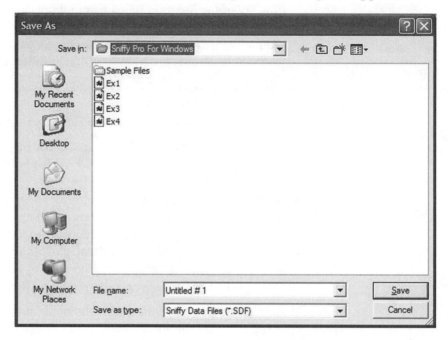

Look carefully at the dialog box. At the top after the words "Save in:" is a space containing an icon and the name of the place where the file will be saved unless you do something to change the location. In this case, the icon is a picture of an open folder, which tells you the current place is a folder. Different icons would appear for different kinds of places (for example, the desktop, a floppy disk, or the root level of a hard disk[1]).

In the large white space below the place name is a closed folder icon with the name Sample Files and several file icons with their associated file names. This part of the dialog box always displays the contents of the place named in the area to the right of "Save in:". Depending on what's in the currently displayed location, you may see names and icons representing files, folders, hard disks, or a floppy disk.

If the name after "Save in:" is the place where you want to save your file, all you have to do is:

- Type the name that you want to give the file in the text box located to the right of "File name:".
- Point the cursor at the command button labeled Save and click once with your left mouse button.

[1] The root level of a hard disk is the contents you see when you open a hard-disk icon by double-clicking on it.

If the name to the right of "Save in:" is not the place where you want to save the file (for instance, if it's not your Sniffy Pro for Windows folder), clicking on the small triangle at the right side of the box where the current location is displayed will change the dialog box so that it resembles the following illustration.

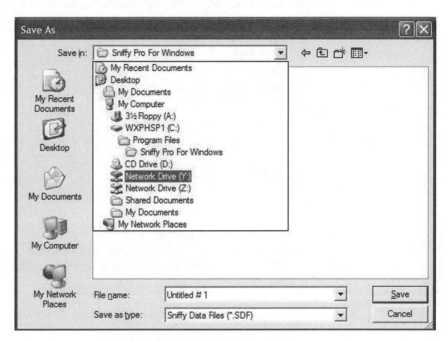

The area inside the box below "Save in:" now shows a diagram of the relationships between your current location and other places where your computer might be able to save files. Remember that your Sniffy Pro for Windows folder is inside the Program Files folder which is inside the hard drive (C: drive). By left double-clicking on icons in the location diagram, you can navigate from wherever you happen to be until you find your Sniffy Pro for Windows folder. Once you reach the Sniffy Pro for Windows folder:

- Point the cursor at the text box to the right of "File name:" and click the left mouse button once.
- Type the name that you want to give the file.
- Point the cursor at the Save command button and click once with your left mouse button.

If you are using a version of Windows other than Windows XP, the dialog boxes may look somewhat different, but the principles involved in saving a file in a particular place will be very similar.

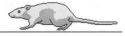

## Saving Files in Mac OS X

We assume that you want to save a file in a folder called Sniffy Files that is located inside the Documents folder on your hard disk.

- Select the Save As command from the File menu in the Sniffy Pro program. Either an abbreviated or a detailed version of the Save dialog box may appear. The abbreviated version of the dialog box is shown below.

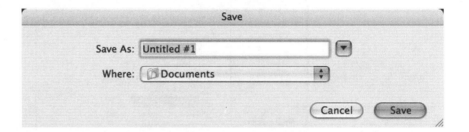

- If the abbreviated dialog box appears, click on the button with a triangle in it that is located on the right end of the text box next to "Save As:". Clicking on the triangle will cause the detailed version of the dialog box, shown below, to appear.

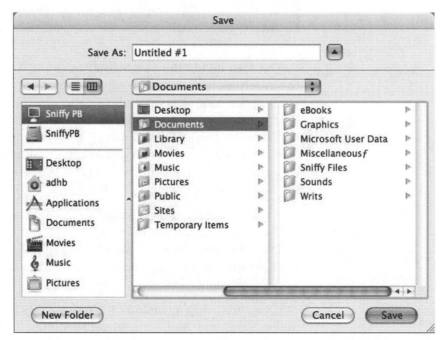

Look carefully at the detailed dialog box. At the top to the right of the words "Save As:" is a text box into which you will type the name that you want to give the file. Because in this instance the file has not yet been named, the name Untitled #1 appears.

Below the text box is a button showing a folder icon and the name of the location where the file will be saved unless you do something to change the location. In the example shown, the word Documents indicates that the file will be saved in your Documents folder unless you change the location.

The main part of the dialog box consists of two large white spaces separated by a vertical column. The area directly below the button containing the name of the current location contains a list of places in your user area of the computer. Note that the word "Documents" and the icon to its left are highlighted. The highlighting is another indication that the Documents folder is your current location.

The large white area to the right of the vertical bar displays the contents of the highlighted item in the left panel. In this instance, because the Documents folder is highlighted, the right panel displays the contents of the Documents folder.

We assume that you want to save the file in your Sniffy Files folder. To do so,

- Click once on the Sniffy Files folder in the right-hand panel. Then the items that had been displayed in the right-hand panel move into the left-hand panel and the contents of the Sniffy Files folder is displayed in the right-hand panel.
- Once you're in the place where you want to save your file:
  - Type the name that you want to give the file in the text box under "Save As:".
  - Point the cursor at the Save command button and click your mouse button once.

## Opening Files

### Opening Files in Windows XP

There are several ways to open files in Windows, but we will describe only the most basic approaches. In the first example, we assume that you have already started the Sniffy Pro program and that you have just executed the Open command found under the File menu. When you

execute the Open command, the Sniffy Pro program will always put up a dialog box asking whether you want to save the file that is currently open. If you want to save the file, click on the Yes command button and go through the file-saving process. If you do not want to save the file (for example, because you've just started the Sniffy Pro program and there is no point in saving an Untitled file that contains no data), click the No command button. In either case, a dialog box resembling the following will appear.

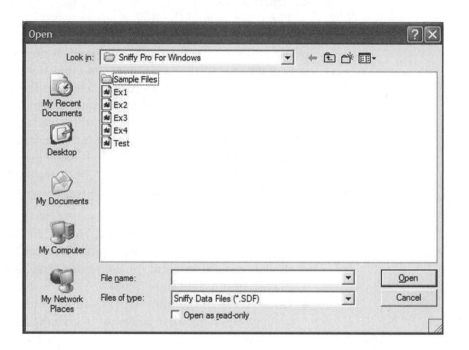

In many ways, the Open dialog box resembles the Save dialog box. Here are the main things to note about it:

- At the top in the space to the right of "Look in:" is the name of the place (the folder or disk) whose contents are currently being shown.
- The icon just to the left of the place name tells you what kind of place it is. In the example, the open folder icon tells us that we are examining the contents of a folder.
- At the right-hand side of the place name is a button with a triangle on it. Clicking on this button will produce a box inside the dialog box showing the location of the current place in the hierarchy of folders and drives where there might be files that you could open. If you need to, you can scroll around to find the file you want.

- In the large area in the middle of the dialog box is a listing of the contents of the place named at the top. You will see the names of the various items with icons that identify what kinds of items they are.
- When you see the name of the file that you want to open, point the cursor at its icon and click your left mouse button once. The name of the file will appear in the text box located to the right of "File name:" at the bottom of the dialog box.
- When you've identified the right item, point the cursor at the Open command button and click your left mouse button once to open the file.

A second way to open a file in Windows is to open your Sniffy Pro for Windows and left double-click on the file icon.

- If the program is not running, it will start up automatically with the file you selected open.
- If the program is running, you will be asked whether you want to save the file that was already open before the file on which you just left double-clicked is opened.

A third way to open a file is to drag the file icon onto the icon of the program or onto the icon of a shortcut to the program.

- If the program is not running, it will start up automatically with the file you selected open.
- If the program is running, you will be asked whether you want to save the file that was already open before the file whose icon you just dragged is opened.

## Opening Files in Mac OS X

There are several ways to open files on a Macintosh, but we will describe only the most basic approaches. In the first example, we assume that you have already started the Sniffy Pro program and that you have just executed the Open command found under the File menu. When you execute the Open command, the Sniffy Pro program will always put up a dialog box asking whether you want to save the file that is currently open. If you want to save the file, click on the Save command button and go through the file-saving process. If you do not want to save the file (for example, because you've just started the Sniffy Pro program and there is no point in saving an Untitled file that contains no data), click the Don't Save command button. In either case, a dialog box resembling the following will appear.

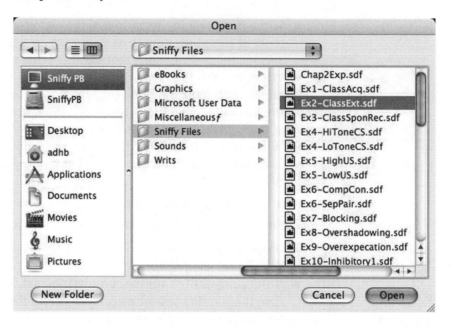

In many ways, this Open dialog box resembles the Save dialog box. Here are the main things to note about it:

- At the top is a button containing the name of the place (the folder or disk) whose contents are currently being shown.
- The icon just to the left of the place name tells you what kind of place it is. In the example, the folder icon tells us that we are examining the contents of a folder.
- Clicking on the place name button will produce a drop-down menu showing the location of the current place in the hierarchy of folders and disks where there might be files that you could open and a list of folders in which you have recently opened or saved files. If you are not in your Sniffy Files folder, you may see it in the list of recent places. If it's there, you can select it from the list.
- In the large area below the place name button are two panels separated by a vertical bar. The panel on the left contains the place named at the top of the dialog box. In the panel on the right is a list of the contents of that place. When you are inside the Sniffy Files folder, you will see a list of files and other items.
- Select the file that you want to open by clicking on it once.
- Then click on the Open command button at the bottom right of the dialog box.

A second way to open a file in Mac OS X is to open your Sniffy Files folder and double-click on a file icon.

- If the program is not running, it will start up automatically with the file you selected open.
- If the program is running, you will be asked whether you want to save the file that was already open before the file on which you just double-clicked is opened.

A third way to open a file is to drag the file icon onto the icon of the program or onto the icon of an alias to the program. This is an especially handy way of opening a file if you have aliases of the program and your Sniffy Files folder in the dock. Just click on the folder icon to open the folder. Then drag the icon of the file that you want to open onto the program icon in the dock.

- If the program is not running, it will start up automatically with the file you selected open.
- If the program is running, you will be asked whether you want to save the file that was already open before the file whose icon you just dragged is opened.

## Copying Files From a Hard Disk to a Floppy Disk

### Instructions for Windows XP Users

Many contemporary Windows computers have floppy disk drives. Add-on internal and external drives can also be purchased relatively inexpensively for computers that did not come with one already installed. To copy one or more files from your hard drive onto a floppy disk:

- Open your Sniffy Pro for Windows folder. If you made a shortcut to the folder and placed it on your desktop, left double-click on the shortcut icon. Otherwise:
  - □ Left click on the Start icon at the bottom of your screen.
  - □ In the pop-up menu that appears, select My Computer.
  - □ In the My Computer window, left double-click on the hard drive icon.
  - □ In the window that appears, left double-click on the Program Files folder.
  - □ In the Program Files window, left double-click on the Sniffy Pro for Windows folder.
- In the Sniffy Pro for Windows window, select the files that you want to copy to the floppy disk.

- Left click once on the Edit menu at the top of the Sniffy Pro for Windows folder.
- In the drop-down menu that appears, select Copy to Folder.
- In the dialog box that appears, select 3 1/2 Floppy (A:).
- Left click once on the Copy button at the bottom of the dialog box.
- Windows will present an animation telling you that it is copying the files.
- If there is not enough room on the floppy disk to hold all the files that you want to copy, Windows will put up a dialog box saying that the destination disk is full. If that happens:
  □ Remove the full floppy disk from the floppy drive by pressing the button on the front of the drive.
  □ Insert a new floppy.
  □ Click on the Retry command button in the full-disk dialog box to continue copying on the new floppy disk.

## Instructions for Mac OS X Users

Because Apple Computer, Inc., considers floppy disks to be an obsolete storage medium, new Macintosh computers have not contained floppy drives for the past several years. However, external add-on drives are available on the market; and Mac OS X handles the copying of files to and from floppy disks adequately.

- Plug your external floppy drive into a USB port on your computer.
- Insert a floppy disk in the drive.
- The floppy disk icon will appear on the right-hand side of your desktop in the first available space under the icon for your startup disk.
- Open the folder in which you have stored your Sniffy files on your hard disk.
- Place the folder window in a position so that both the names of the files that you want to copy and the floppy disk icon are visible.
- Select one or more files that you want to copy.
- Point the cursor at one of the files, hold down the mouse button, and drag the files onto the floppy disk icon. When the icon darkens, release the mouse button. (As an alternative, you could open the floppy disk window and drag the files that you want to copy into the window.)
- The Macintosh operating system will present an animation telling you that it is copying the files.
- If there is not enough room on the floppy disk to hold all the files that you have selected, the operating system will tell you so. If that happens, select fewer files and try again.

- Dismount the floppy disk by dragging the disk icon into the trash.
- When the disk icon disappears, eject the floppy disk from the drive by pressing the button on the front of the drive.

## Copying Files From a Floppy Disk to a Hard Disk

### Instructions for Windows XP Users

This procedure is basically the mirror image of the procedure for copying files from your hard disk to a floppy disk.

- Place the floppy disk containing the files that you want to copy in your floppy disk drive.
- Click on the Start icon at the bottom of your screen.
- Select My Computer from the pop-up menu.
- Open the 3 1/2 Floppy [A:] window by left double-clicking on its icon.
- Open your Sniffy Pro for Windows window.
- Arrange the 3 1/2 Floppy [A:] window and Sniffy Pro for Windows window so that the names of the files you want to copy are visible. (If your desktop is crowded, only a small part of your Sniffy Pro for Windows window needs to be visible.)
- Use your left mouse button to select one or more files in the floppy disk window. You know when you have selected a file because it darkens.
- Point the cursor at one of the files, hold down the left mouse button, and drag the files into the Sniffy Pro for Windows folder window.
- Windows will present an animation telling you that it is copying the files.
- When the copying process is completed, remove the floppy disk from the floppy drive by pressing the button on the front of the drive.

### Instructions for Mac OS X Users

This procedure is basically the mirror image of the procedure for copying files from your hard disk to a floppy disk.

- Connect your external floppy drive to a USB port on your computer.
- Place the floppy disk containing the files that you want to copy in your floppy disk drive.

- The floppy disk icon will appear on the right-hand side of your desktop in the first available space under the icon for your startup disk.
- Open the folder into which you want to copy the files.
- Open the floppy disk window.
- Arrange the floppy disk window and the Sniffy Files window so that the names of the files you want to copy are visible. (If your desktop is crowded, only a small part of the Sniffy Files window needs to be visible.)
- Use your mouse button to select the files that you want to copy.
- Point the cursor at one of the files you want to copy, hold down the mouse button, drag the files into the destination window, and release the mouse button.
- The Macintosh operating system will present an animation telling you that it is copying the files.
- To dismount and eject a floppy disk from your floppy drive:
  - □ Select the floppy disk icon by clicking on it once. The icon will darken.
  - □ Wait a moment.
  - □ With the cursor pointed at the floppy disk icon, depress and hold down the mouse button, and drag the floppy disk icon to the trash can.
  - □ After the disk icon has disappeared, eject the disk from the drive by pressing the button on the front of the drive.

## Using Sniffy Pro Macintosh Files on a Windows PC and Vice Versa

Sniffy Pro for Macintosh files are fully compatible with Sniffy Pro for Windows files, and vice versa. You can create a file on one kind of computer and look at the file on the other kind of computer. You can even set up an experiment on one kind of computer, save the file while the experiment is in progress, and then complete the experiment on the other kind of computer.

To transfer files from a Windows PC to a Macintosh:

- Copy the Sniffy Pro for Windows files onto a floppy disk.
- Insert the floppy disk into a Macintosh floppy disk drive. (Your Macintosh is capable of reading and writing 1.4 MB floppy disks that have been formatted on a PC.)
- When you open the floppy disk window, you will notice that all the Sniffy Pro for Windows file names end with the ".sdf" suffix. This

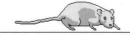

will be true even though the suffix is ordinarily invisible in Windows.

- Copy the Sniffy Pro for Windows files onto your Macintosh hard drive.
- Start your Sniffy Pro for Macintosh program.
- Use the Open command in the File menu to open the Sniffy Pro for Windows files.
- If you plan to use the files in Windows again, be sure to save each file with the ".sdf" suffix appended to each file name.

To transfer files from a Macintosh to a Windows PC:

- Save the files you want to transfer on the Macintosh hard disk with the ".sdf" suffix appended to each file name. To recognize them as Sniffy files, Sniffy Pro for Windows needs the suffix.
- Copy the Sniffy Pro for Macintosh files onto your PC-formatted floppy disk.[2]
- Copy the files from the floppy disk onto your Windows hard disk.
- Start your Sniffy Pro for Windows program.
- Use the Open command under the File menu to open the Macintosh files.

## Storing Files on a CD

Virtually all contemporary computers contain a drive that is capable of reading CDs. In many computers, the CD drive is also capable of burning[3] files onto a blank CD. Windows XP, Mac OS X, and Mac OS 9 have rudimentary software for burning CDs as part of the operating system. In addition, many programs are available for both Macintosh and Windows computers for burning CDs. Many of these programs enable you to format the CD and control the burning process in more sophisticated ways than is possible if you use the CD-burning software built into the operating system.

Most CDs have a capacity of 670 MB of data, which is approximately 490 times as much data as a floppy disk can hold. For this reason, you can store many more Sniffy files on a CD than on a floppy disk. However, CDs have a major drawback. Unless you have special software

---

[2] Virtually all floppy disks on the market today have been preformatted for use in a PC.

[3] The verb "burn" is typically used to describe the action of writing files onto a blank CD.

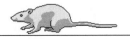

that permits burning multiple sessions and a CD drive capable of writing to multiple-session CDs, burning files onto a CD is a one-time-only event. No new files can be added to a CD once a first batch of files have been burned onto it. Nevertheless, blank CDs have become so inexpensive that this problem isn't as serious as it sounds. Once data have been transferred from a CD to a computer's hard drive, you can probably afford to throw the CD away and use a fresh one when you want to store another batch of files.

Using CDs to transfer data from one computer to another offers a viable alternative to floppy disks, especially if you have a newer computer that did not come with a floppy disk drive. At some schools, students currently use CDs to hand in various kinds of files to professors. For example, if your professor asks you to perform several Sniffy experiments and use them as the basis for a paper, s/he might be willing to let you hand in everything (Sniffy files, data analysis files, and your paper) on a CD.

Because of the great variety of CD-burning software on the market, explaining the process of burning CDs is beyond the scope of this manual. You should consult the manual or Help files that came with your operating system or with the CD-burning software that you have installed on your computer to learn what you need to do.

## E-mailing Files

Another good way to transfer files from one computer to another or to hand in files to your instructor is to include the files as e-mail attachments. Many students use e-mail to send pictures and other kinds of computer files to their friends. You can use the same process to transfer Sniffy files from one computer to another or to hand in files to your instructor. To transfer a file from your computer at home to a computer at school, either use your existing home and school e-mail accounts or get a free e-mail account with Microsoft Hotmail, Yahoo, or any of the other providers who offer e-mail accounts that can be accessed from any computer connected to the Internet.

- To transfer a file from your home computer to a computer at school, send the file as an enclosure (or attachment) in an e-mail to yourself, using an e-mail address that can be accessed from the school computer or any Web browser. Then open the e-mail and download the file using the computer at school.

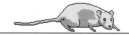

- To hand in a file to your instructor, just send the file as an enclosure (or attachment) in an e-mail to the professor's e-mail address.
- Here are a couple of things to keep in mind:
  - Many e-mail servers limit the amount of data that can be transferred in an enclosure in any one e-mail message. A typical limit is about 1 or 2 MB. This means that you may need to send two or more different e-mail messages to transfer all of your data if you need to send more than one large Sniffy file.
  - The free e-mail accounts available from Hotmail, Yahoo, and similar sources provide only a limited amount of storage space. When you have downloaded files at the destination computer, you may want to delete the e-mail messages from your account.

Because there is a wide variety of e-mail programs that people use, detailed instructions for sending and receiving e-mail and sending files as enclosures are beyond the scope of this manual. Fortunately, so many students (and instructors) use e-mail on a daily basis that you very likely already know how to do it. If you need more help, ask your classmates or your instructor.

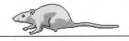

# Glossary

**Acquisition**  In classical conditioning, the development of a conditioned response as the consequence of pairing the conditioned and unconditioned stimuli. In operant conditioning, the increase in the frequency of an emitted behavior as the result of reinforcing occurrences of the behavior.

**Action strength**  The part of Sniffy's operant conditioning algorithm, displayed in the Operant Associations mind window, that increases as a consequence of repeatedly reinforcing a particular movement.

**Backward chaining**  An operant training procedure used to teach an animal to perform an improbable series of behaviors. The animal is first trained to perform the last behavior in the chain that would occur just before reinforcement at the end of the series. Then the next-to-last behavior in the chain is trained by making the opportunity to perform the last behavior contingent on the performance of the next-to-last behavior, and so on.

**Bar–sound association**  The part of Sniffy's operant conditioning algorithm, displayed in the Operant Associations mind window, that develops when manipulation of the bar is repeatedly followed by reinforcement.

**Begging**  An operantly shapeable behavior in which Sniffy faces the observer, lifts up his front paws, and moves his head up and down.

**Behavioral repertoire**  A list and description of all the behavior patterns that an animal emits.

**Blocking**  A phenomenon of classical conditioning in which a previous series of trials during which one conditioned stimulus ($CS_1$) has been paired with the unconditioned stimulus prevents a second conditioned stimulus ($CS_2$) from acquiring the ability to elicit a conditioned stimulus response strength when the two stimuli ($CS_1$ and $CS_2$) are subsequently presented as a compound conditioned stimulus paired with the unconditioned stimulus.

**Classical conditioning**  The form of learning that occurs when two stimuli are repeatedly presented in a temporal series so that occurrences of the first stimulus predict occurrences of the second stimulus.

**Clock time**  Time as measured in the real world.

**Compound conditioning**  A variant of classical conditioning in which two conditioned stimuli ($CS_1$ and $CS_2$) come on and go off simultaneously.

**Conditioned emotional response**  A form of classical conditioning in which a conditioned stimulus acquires the capacity to elicit freezing and other fear-related behaviors as the result of being paired with an aversive unconditioned stimulus.

**Conditioned response (CR)**  In classical conditioning, the learned response to a conditioned stimulus that develops as the result of repeatedly presenting the conditioned stimulus shortly before presenting the unconditioned stimulus. In operant conditioning, an emitted behavior whose frequency has been increased as the result of repeatedly reinforcing the behavior.

**Conditioned stimulus (CS)**  In classical conditioning, a stimulus that has the ability to acquire the capacity to elicit a conditioned response as the result of presenting the stimulus just before presentations of an unconditioned stimulus in a series of trials.

**Conditioned suppression** An alternative name for the conditioned emotional response.

**CS pre-exposure effect** A phenomenon of classical conditioning in which repeated presentations of a conditioned stimulus slow down subsequent conditioning when the conditioned stimulus is paired with an unconditioned stimulus in a series of trials.

**CS response strength** The part of Sniffy's classical conditioning algorithm, displayed in the CS Response Strength mind window, that predicts the strength of Sniffy's response to the conditioned stimulus the next time it is presented.

**Discriminative stimulus** In operant conditioning, a stimulus that signals that a particular response either will or will not be reinforced.

**DS response strength** The part of Sniffy's operant conditioning algorithm, displayed in the DS Response Strength mind window, that predicts how often Sniffy will make an operantly conditioned response in the presence of a tone of a particular frequency during generalization tests.

**Elicited behavior** A particular behavior that occurs as the direct result of presenting a particular stimulus.

**Emitted behavior** A behavior pattern that an animal performs "spontaneously" and for which no eliciting stimulus exists.

**Excitatory conditioning** Classical conditioning in which a conditioned stimulus acquires the capacity to elicit a conditioned response as the result of being paired with an unconditioned stimulus.

**Extinction** In classical conditioning, the diminution and eventual elimination of a previously conditioned response that occurs as the result of repeatedly presenting the conditioned stimulus without the unconditioned stimulus. In operant conditioning, the reduction in frequency of a previously conditioned response that occurs when the response is no longer reinforced.

**Face wiping** An operantly shapeable behavior in which Sniffy wipes one of his front paws repeatedly across an eye.

**Fear** The part of Sniffy's classical conditioning algorithm, exhibited in the Sensitivity & Fear mind window, that predicts the likelihood that Sniffy will exhibit freezing and other "fear-related" behaviors.

**Fixed interval (FI) schedule** A reinforcement schedule in which reinforcement of an operantly conditioned behavior is available only after a time period of a consistent duration has elapsed since the previous reinforcement.

**Fixed ratio (FR) schedule** A reinforcement schedule in which an operantly conditioned behavior is reinforced only after a specified number of unreinforced responses, which is always the same for each reinforcement, have been performed.

**Generalization gradient** A graph depicting response rate during generalization tests as a function of similarity to a discriminative stimulus used during discrimination learning.

**Habituation** The diminution or elimination of the response elicited by a stimulus that occurs as a consequence of repeated presentations of the stimulus.

**Higher-order conditioning** A form of classical conditioning in which a conditioned stimulus ($CS_1$) that has previously been paired with an unconditioned stimulus is used to condition a response to a second conditioned stimulus ($CS_2$) in a series of trials during which presentations of $CS_2$ briefly precede presentations of $CS_1$.

**Inhibitory conditioning** Classical conditioning in which a conditioned stimulus comes to act as a "signal" that a US that might otherwise be expected is *not* going occur. When presented by itself, an inhibitory conditioned stimulus elicits no conditioned response. When an inhibitory conditioned stimulus occurs in a compound with an excitatory conditioned stimulus, the inhibitory conditioned stimulus prevents or reduces the magnitude of the conditioned response that the excitatory conditioned stimulus would otherwise elicit.

**Interval schedule** In operant conditioning, a schedule of reinforcement in which a response can be reinforced only after a period of time has elapsed since the previous reinforcement.

**Latent inhibition** Another name for the CS Pre-Exposure Effect.

**Magazine training** The procedure by which the sound of the food dispenser in an operant chamber is turned into a secondary reinforcer

by pairing the sound with the delivery of food pellets.

**Mind window**   A feature of the Sniffy program that displays certain parameters of Sniffy's algorithms for classical and operant conditioning. The parameters displayed correspond to psychological processes that psychologists have proposed as explanations for aspects of classical and operant conditioning. The mind windows show how changes in Sniffy's "psychological processes" are related to changes in Sniffy's behavior.

**Movement ratio**   The proportion of time during the presentation of a conditioned stimulus that Sniffy is displaying freezing and other fear-related behaviors.

**Negative punisher**   A stimulus whose removal as the consequence of a behavior makes that behavior *less* likely to occur under similar circumstances in the future.

**Negative reinforcer**   A stimulus whose removal as the consequence of a behavior makes that behavior *more* likely to occur under similar circumstances in the future.

**Operant conditioning**   A learned change in the likelihood that an emitted behavior will occur again under similar circumstances in the future that occurs as the result of the events that follow occurrences of the behavior.

**Orienting response (OR)**   The initial, unlearned response to a conditioned stimulus.

**Overexpectation effect**   A phenomenon of classical conditioning in which two conditioned stimuli that have been separately paired with an unconditioned stimulus are subsequently presented together as a compound conditioned stimulus in an additional series of pairings with the unconditioned stimulus. At the end of the series of compound-conditioning trials, the magnitude of the conditioned response that the conditioned stimuli are separately capable of eliciting is less than the magnitude of the conditioned response that they separately elicited at the end of the separate-pairing trials.

**Overshadowing**   When a high-salience conditioned stimulus and a low-salience conditioned stimulus are presented together as a compound conditioned stimulus in a series of pairings with an unconditioned stimulus, the high-

salience conditioned stimulus acquires the capacity to elicit a larger conditioned response than the low-salience conditioned stimulus.

**Pain sensitivity**   The parameter of Sniffy's classical conditioning algorithm, displayed in the Sensitivity & Fear mind window, that predicts the duration of Sniffy's unconditioned response to the shock US the next time the shock occurs.

**Pavlovian conditioning**   Another name for classical conditioning.

**Positive punisher**   A stimulus whose presentation as a consequence of a behavior makes that behavior *less* likely to occur under similar circumstances in the future.

**Positive reinforcer**   A stimulus whose presentation as a consequence of a behavior makes that behavior *more* likely to occur under similar circumstances in the future.

**Primary punisher**   A stimulus whose capacity to function as a punisher is not dependent on previous experience.

**Primary reinforcer**   A stimulus whose capacity to function as a reinforcer is not dependent on previous experience.

**Program time**   Time as measured internally by the Sniffy program. When Sniffy is visible, the relationship between program time and clock time depends on animation speed. When Sniffy is hidden to "accelerate time," program time runs much faster than clock time.

**Punishment**   The operation of presenting a positive punisher or removing a negative punisher as a consequence of a behavior pattern, with the result that the punished behavior pattern becomes less likely to occur under similar circumstances in the future.

**RAM**   Random access memory, one of the electronic components of a computer that in part determines whether or how well the computer can run a program.

**Ratio schedule**   A reinforcement schedule in which reinforcement for a response becomes available only after a number of unreinforced responses have been completed.

**Reinforcement**   In operant conditioning, the operation of presenting a positive reinforcer or removing a negative reinforcer as the consequence of a behavior pattern, with the result that the reinforced behavior pattern becomes more likely to occur under similar circumstances in the future. In classical conditioning, the presentation of the unconditioned stimulus after an occurrence of the conditioned stimulus.

**Reinforcement schedule** A rule that determines which instances of a response to reinforce.

**Respondent conditioning** Another name for classical conditioning.

**Response measure** Any measurement of the duration, frequency, magnitude, or probability of a behavior.

**Rolling** An operantly shapeable behavior in which Sniffy turns somersaults.

**S+/S– discrimination learning** A discrimination learning procedure in which responding is reinforced in the presence of one explicit discriminative stimulus and extinguished in the presence of another explicit discriminative stimulus.

**Salience** A stimulus's ability to command an animal's attention.

**Secondary punisher** A stimulus whose capacity to act as a punisher depends upon its prior association with a primary punisher.

**Secondary reinforcer** A stimulus whose capacity to act as a reinforcer depends upon its prior association with a primary reinforcer.

**Sensitization** An increase in the magnitude of the response elicited by a stimulus that occurs as the result of repeatedly presenting the stimulus.

**Sensory preconditioning** A phenomenon of classical conditioning that demonstrates learning of an association between two conditioned stimuli. During the first stage of the experiment, two conditioned stimuli ($CS_1$ and $CS_2$) are sequentially paired with presentations of $CS_1$ briefly preceding presentations of $CS_2$. In the second stage of the experiment, $CS_2$ is repeatedly paired with an unconditioned stimulus. Finally, in the third stage of the experiment, $CS_1$ is presented by itself. The phenomenon is demonstrated if $CS_1$ elicits a conditioned response during Stage 3

**Shaping** An operant training procedure in which the animal is trained to perform an improbable target behavior as the consequence of reinforcing a series of behaviors that resemble the target more and more closely.

**Simple tone-on S– discrimination learning** A discrimination learning procedure in which re-

sponding is reinforced when a tone is absent and extinguished when the same tone is present.

**Simple tone-on S+ discrimination learning** A discrimination learning procedure in which responding is reinforced when a tone is present and extinguished when the same tone is absent.

**Sound–food association** The part of Sniffy's operant conditioning algorithm, displayed in the Operant Associations mind window, that develops when the delivery of a food pellet follows his hearing the sound of the food dispenser mechanism.

**Spontaneous recovery** The reappearance of a previously extinguished classically or operantly conditioned response that occurs when the animal is returned to the testing situation after spending time in another environment, such as its home cage.

**Stage (of a classical conditioning experiment)** A group of trials that must be completed before the next stage can begin.

**Stimulus generalization** Responding in the presence of a stimulus that resembles, but is not identical to, the discriminative stimulus used in discrimination learning.

**Suppression ratio** A response measure used to measure the conditioned emotional response. The suppression ratio is equal to the response rate during a CS presentation divided by the sum of the response rate during the CS plus the response rate during the period immediately preceding the CS.

**Target behavior** The behavior that a trainer seeks to get an animal to perform at the end of shaping.

**Trial type** The particular stimulus events that occur during a certain kind of classical conditioning trial. A stage of a classical conditioning experiment must contain trials of at least one trial type and may contain trials of more than one trial type.

**Unconditioned response (UR)** In classical conditioning, the response elicited by an unconditioned stimulus.

**Unconditioned stimulus (US)** In classical conditioning, a stimulus that has the intrinsic capacity to elicit an obvious and easy-to-measure response. In a standard classical conditioning training trials, the US is presented after the CS.

**Variable interval (VI) schedule**  A reinforcement schedule in which the period of time after reinforcement during which further responding is not reinforced varies from reinforcement to reinforcement.

**Variable ratio (VR) schedule**  A reinforcement schedule in which the number of unreinforced responses required before another response is reinforced varies from reinforcement to reinforcement.

**Yoked experimental design**  An experimental setup in which one animal's responding determines a second animal's schedule of reinforcement.

# References

Annau, Z., & Kamin, L. J. (1961). The conditioned emotional response as a function of intensity of the US. *Journal of Comparative and Physiological Psychology, 54,* 428–432.

Domjan, M. (1998). *The principles of learning and behavior* (4th ed.). Pacific Grove, CA: Brooks/Cole.

Domjan, M. (2003). *The principles of learning and behavior* (5th ed.). Belmont, CA: Wadsworth.

Estes, W. K., & Skinner, B. F. (1941). Some quantitative properties of anxiety. *Journal of Experimental Psychology, 29,* 390–400.

Ferster, C. B., & Skinner, B. F. (1957). *Schedules of reinforcement.* New York: Appleton-Century-Crofts.

Guthrie, E. R. (1960). *The psychology of learning* (rev. ed.). Gloucester, MA: Smith.

Hanson, H. M. (1959). Effects of discrimination training on stimulus generalization. *Journal of Experimental Psychology, 58,* 321–333.

Honig, W. K., Boneau, C. A., Burstein, K. R., & Pennypacker, H. S. (1963). Positive and negative generalization gradients obtained under equivalent training conditions. *Journal of Comparative and Physiological Psychology, 56,* 111–116.

Hull, C. L. (1943). *Principles of behavior.* New York: Appleton-Century-Crofts.

Hull, C. L. (1952). *A behavior system.* New Haven, CT: Yale University Press.

Imada, H., Yamazaki, A., & Morishita, M. (1981). The effects of signal intensity upon conditioned suppression: Effects upon responding during signals and intersignal intervals. *Animal Learning and Behavior, 9,* 269–274.

James, W. (1890). *Principles of psychology.* New York: Holt.

Jenkins, H. M., & Harrison, R. G. (1960). Effects of discrimination training on auditory generalization. *Journal of Experimental Psychology, 59,* 246–253.

Jenkins, H. M., & Harrison, R. G. (1962). Generalization of inhibition following auditory discrimination learning. *Journal of the Experimental Analysis of Behavior, 5,* 435–441.

Kamin, L. J. (1968). Attention-like processes in classical conditioning. In M. R. Jones (Ed.), *Miami Symposium on the Prediction of Behavior: Aversive stimulation.* Miami, FL: University of Miami Press.

Keller, F. S., & Schoenfeld, W. N. (1950). *Principles of psychology.* New York: Appleton-Century-Crofts.

Kimble, G. A. (1961). *Hilgard & Marquis' Conditioning and Learning* (2nd ed). New York: Appleton-Century-Crofts.

Mazur, J. E. (1998). *Learning and behavior* (4th ed). Upper Saddle River, NJ: Prentice Hall.

Pavlov, I. P. (1927). *Conditioned reflexes* (G. V. Anrep, Trans.). London: Oxford University Press.

Polenchar, B. E., Romano, A. G., Steinmetz, J. E., & Patterson, M. M. (1984). Effects of US parameters on classical conditioning of cat hindlimb flexion. *Animal Learning and Behavior, 12,* 69–72.

Rescorla, R. A. (1973). Second order conditioning: Implications for theories of learning. In E. J. McGuigan & D. B. Lumsden (Eds.), *Contemporary approaches to conditioning and learning.* New York: Wiley.

Rescorla, R. A., & Wagner, A. R. (1972). A theory of Pavlovian conditioning: Variations in the effectiveness of reinforcement and nonreinforcement. In A. H. Black & W. F. Prokasy (Eds.), *Classical conditioning II: Current research and theory* (pp. 64–99). New York: Appleton-Century-Crofts.

Reynolds, G. S. (1975). *A primer of operant conditioning*. Glenview, IL: Scott, Foresman.

Rizley, R. C., & Rescorla, R. A. (1972). Associations in second-order conditioning and sensory preconditioning. *Journal of Comparative and Physiological Psychology, 81,* 1–11.

Schwartz, B., & Reisberg, D. (1991). *Learning and memory*. New York: W. W. Norton.

Seligman, M. E. P. (1968). Chronic fear produced by unpredictable electric shock. *Journal of Comparative and Physiological Psychology, 66,* 402–411.

Seligman, M. E. P., Maier, S. F., & Solomon, R. L. (1971). Unpredictable and uncontrollable aversive events. In F. R. Bruch (Ed.), *Aversive conditioning and learning* (pp. 347–400). New York: Academic Press.

Shettleworth, S. J. (1975). Reinforcement and the organization of behavior in the golden hamster: Hunger, environment, and food reinforcement. *Journal of Experimental Psychology: Animal Behavior Processes, 1,* 56–87.

Skinner, B. F. (1930). On the conditions of elicitation of certain eating reflexes. *Proceedings of the National Academy of Science (Washington), 15,* 433–438.

Skinner, B. F. (1935). Two types of conditioned reflexes and a pseudo type. *Journal of General Psychology, 12,* 66–77.

Skinner, B. F. (1938). *The behavior of organisms.* New York: Appleton-Century-Crofts.

Skinner, B. F. (1953). *Science and human behavior.* New York: Macmillan.

Skinner, B. F. (1971). *Beyond freedom and dignity.* New York: Knopf.

Spence, K. W. (1937). The differential response in animals to stimuli varying within a single dimension. *Psychological Review, 44,* 430–444.

Tarpy, R. M. (1997). *Contemporary learning theory and research.* New York: McGraw-Hill.

Thorndike, E. L. (1898). Animal intelligence. An experimental study of associative processes in animals. *Psychological Monographs, 2*(8).

Tolman, E. C. (1932). *Purposive behavior in animals and men.* New York: Appleton-Century-Crofts.

# Index